D0095064

AMERICAN Survivors

AMERICAN Survivors

Cities & Other Scenes

Karen Gerard

HARCOURT BRACE JOVANOVICH, PUBLISHERS

San Diego   New York   London

Library of Congress Cataloging in Publication Data

Gerard, Karen.
    American survivors.

    1. City and town life—United States.   2. Municipal
government—United States.   3. Urban economics.
4. United States—Social conditions.   I. Title.
HT151.G42   1984   307.7′6′0973   84-6634
ISBN 0-15-106304-4

Designed by Joy Taylor

Printed in the United States of America
First edition

A B C D E

Contents

Contents

Introduction

I met William Jovanovich, chairman of Harcourt Brace Jovanovich, in the course of my duties as Deputy Mayor for Economic Policy and Development for the City of New York. HBJ was about to announce that it was moving its headquarters out of New York. Could city government do anything to alter the decision? I had a long session with Mr. Jovanovich—we talked about the publishing business; we talked about literature; we talked about the difficulties of functioning in New York; we even talked a little about my personal background. I did not succeed in changing Mr. Jovanovich's mind, but in the course of our conversation he said, "Are you writing? You really should be writing." I shook my head no and left his office with a copy of HBJ's 100th anniversary edition of Virginia Woolf's writings, Mr. Jovanovich's gift to me in compensation for moving his company out of New York.

When I left New York City government at the end of

1982, I decided it was time to take a "sabbatical" from the world of formal work after twenty-five years as an economist at Chase Manhattan Bank and two years as Deputy Mayor, and put down on paper some of my thoughts. I remembered my conversation with Mr. Jovanovich and telephoned for an appointment. The result—this book. Mr. Jovanovich set the challenge: Could I pose provocative questions about the environment I knew as an economist, as a participant in the political scene, and as a married woman living and working and bringing up children in the City of New York?

That is what I set out to do. The task turned out to be more difficult than I had anticipated. I had spent almost my entire career perfecting the art of writing the executive memorandum: ten pages maximum length, with a one-page cover sheet summarizing the conclusions in four paragraphs, each preceded with a bullet mark. The chairman or president did not need to read past the summary page of a skillfully written memorandum. The word "I" never appeared in the hundreds of memoranda I wrote over twenty-five years. Now, the guidelines were "Make it personal, but keep it to no more than 100,000 words."

What did I have to say that anyone besides me would want to read? My friends suggested a title for a bestseller, "Sex at City Hall"—for better or worse, I hadn't seen, or even heard about, much sex at City Hall. But living and working in New York City for more than twenty-five years, I had been a witness to and participant in an extraordinary case of American survival. New York City had teetered on the edge of bankruptcy; then the City confounded those who were ready to sign its death warrant and survived—in a different form, with continuing problems, but with a strong determination and ability to survive with vibrancy. New

York City's experience is not destined to be repeated in cities and towns across the nation; but New York City, as the nation's largest and most diverse conglomerate, provides insights into economic, social, and political issues faced by "survivors" all over the United States. This book is not a New York City book; it is, however, a book built upon the perspectives and experiences of a New Yorker.

Certain themes run through the twenty chapters. As an economist, I am convinced that the national economic environment exerts a pervasive influence over regions, cities, and neighborhoods. But beneath the large-scale national superstructure lies an intricate webbing of places, politics, and people, which in turn shapes the national economic and political scene. The combination of high inflation and low economic growth of the late 1970s and early 1980s produced a change in attitudes—more conservative, more hard-nosed, more realistic, more self-centered, more questioning—that will not disappear for years, even if we are successful in sustaining strong economic growth. The new technology of the 1980s will enable the nation to attain greater economic growth, but advanced technology also raises the possibility of greater mobility of resources and increased obsolescence of older plants, older skills, older places. Not all will be survivors. As a social observer, I am convinced that the aging of the postwar baby boom and the changing role of women are two of the most significant events altering social attitudes and feeding back into the overall economic structure.

I had hoped, when I took this long look back over my New York experiences and extended the view forward, that I could give a one-two-three prescription for the how-tos of survival. However, I find as I look at the complex interplay between the macroeconomy (the larger economic scene) and the microeconomy (its many smaller parts) that I am unable to embrace the doctrinaire philosophy of either extreme conservatives or of die-hard liberals. That makes it hard to preach with the passion of an ideologue, but not impossible—I hope—to display the passion of common sense.

Moving from the hectic pace of Deputy Mayor to the solitude of writing a book in my home, I found the transition difficult. I missed appointments, failed to return phone calls, and discovered that without the backup of a good secretary and research assistants my memory sometimes failed me. I learned to appreciate one of New York City's great resources, the New York Public Library, with its catalogues, books, and newspapers, and its dedicated staff. I rediscovered not only the huge main library, at 42nd Street and Fifth Avenue, but also our neighborhood St. Agnes branch, a microcosm of the city with its clientele of German-Jewish refugees, Central Park West matrons, schoolchildren, and the new generation of "gentrified" New Yorkers. Friends and colleagues were most helpful in refreshing my memory and discussing frankly with me issues as well as events.

My new persona as a writer tested the patience of my husband, Egon, whose judgment and literary standards I respect. The transition upset the entire household: my daughter, Deborah, whose room I took over as an office after she moved out on her own; and my son, Daniel, forced to share the typewriter when he was home from law school; and my housekeeper, Ann Rhymer, whose daytime dominion I invaded.

My editors simultaneously encouraged me to "keep on with it; you've got something to say," and to "be tough if you want anybody to read your book." I hope I have succeeded.

PART ONE

Places

Places

We are a young nation—a nation of movers and a nation of builders. We move from cities to suburbs and to small towns beyond. We move from the northeastern quadrant of the United States to the South and the West. But as the churning of our people and our economic resources continues, we ask: Are cities obsolete? Will the war between the North and the South ever end? People and businesses are more mobile than ever before—their choices, about where to live and where to establish their companies, combine hard cost comparisons and subjective value judgments. When the quality of their environment deteriorates—graffiti are one example—they can pick up their belongings and move. Conflicts erupt between those who want to maintain the status quo and those who seek to alter the environment. Mayors and governors try to stem the outflow of resources from their regions; architectural buffs attempt to protect older buildings from the demolition crews of developers;

longtime residents strive to limit the neighborhood changes brought by "gentrification." The object cannot be to freeze the clock, but to enable places—large and small—to adapt to a changing world—to be survivors!

1

Will Cities Survive?

Many things are happening. Citicorp moves its credit operations from New York City to Sioux Falls, South Dakota. A
struggling author writes her manuscript on a word processor
in a cabin in the Rockies. An investment consultant keeps
up to the minute on the state of the stock market with his
personal computer and advises his clients by telephone from
his office in Connecticut. Are cities obsolete when people
can instantly communicate with each other no matter where
they work or live?

Raw statistics suggest that cities are on their way out.
The population of more than one-half of our larger cities
declined in the 1970s, and, in the early 1980s, increasing
numbers of Americans moved beyond the suburban fringe.
But a picture of 17,000 runners crossing the Verrazano
Bridge during New York City's marathon race sends out a
different message: Even though population has dispersed,
cities are *not* obsolete. Cities continue to perform economic

and social functions: bringing people together to transact business, to plan political strategies, to undergo surgery, to teach and to be taught, and, not least of all, to have fun!

Many U.S. cities of the 1990s will contain fewer people than they do today. The process of shrinkage will inflict pain, and the problems of urban poverty will not disappear. But cities can adapt to changing conditions and survive with vigor even if their population fails to return to earlier peaks. I watched the process occur in the City of New York —decline, near-collapse, and then a recovery based on the City's unique economic and social advantages. I don't claim objectivity in my views—I may be one of the few New Yorkers who could be mugged twice and still sing "I Love New York." But, as an economist and former Deputy Mayor *and* as a person who lives in New York, I am convinced that cities are not obsolete.

It's easy to conclude that computers are one more nail in the coffin of the big city. After all, many cities have been losing population for years. The automobile and government policies encouraged millions of Americans to fulfill their dream of owning a single-family house in the suburbs within driving distance of work. Social change accelerated the outflow of the middle class as poor blacks and other minorities, mostly poor, migrated to the inner city. Regional expansion of the South and the West tipped the balance farther away from older urban cores during the 1970s. Now, in the 1980s, computers permit people and businesses to locate anywhere. Finally, when push comes to shove, Americans don't *like* cities—at least that's the way it's been for most of our history. Given an opportunity, they move on—uptown, out to the suburbs, off to the West. Some say a deep-seated distrust of cities springs from our Jeffersonian heritage—an agrarian society is good; an urban environment is associated with evil. You visit the city as a voyeur, but you don't want to live there. *The Daily News* captured the attitude of millions of Americans in its banner headline: "Ford to City: Drop Dead!" It was the autumn of 1975, and President Ford had just rejected New York's appeals for federal aid as the City teetered on the edge of bankruptcy. Later, of course, Washington and the public realized that the futures of New York and the nation were intertwined, and help was provided.

The mid-1970s marked the economic and fiscal nadir for New York City. But the forces bringing the city to the verge of bankruptcy did not develop overnight. As an economist and as a person living in New York, I could see the growing dangers in the City's fiscal situation as its economic base weakened and the number of jobs started to decline. High costs of business (labor, office rents, taxes); deteriorating infrastructure (a city's streets and bridges, mass transit, water and sewer systems); social unrest; the many forces pulling population and jobs to the suburbs and the Sunbelt —all of these were undermining the City's economy in the late 1960s and early 1970s as government continued to expand unchecked, falling deeper and deeper into debt. During this time, Mayor Abraham Beame would point the finger of blame at the "greedy bankers" for the City's escalating difficulties in marketing its debt. Bankers, in turn, up to the eleventh hour, ignored links between the City's sagging economy and the mounting fiscal crisis, placing their faith in the fine print on City bonds guaranteeing repayment through a first lien on real estate taxes. "There are some things we'd rather not know," one banker tersely said to me when this problem was discussed. The municipal unions also looked the other way, denying that their wage and benefit demands were part of the City's problem.

When the house of cards finally collapsed during the

dark days of 1975, many people believed that not only was the City on the brink of bankruptcy, but that it was also on the verge of economic and social death. Pronouncements about the City's impending death, however, turned out to be premature! The upturn, which started in late 1977, turned out to be vigorous. Sound state and local government policies restored confidence that the City was not about to go broke. Leaders who had never sat around a table before cooperated to work out solutions to the City's tangled fiscal problems: union presidents Victor Gotbaum, of District Council 37, and Albert Shanker, of the United Federation of Teachers, with their peppery adviser, Jack Bigel; bank chairmen David Rockefeller, of Chase Manhattan Bank, and Walter Wriston, of Citicorp; businessmen Felix Rohatyn, partner at Lazard Frères, and Richard Shinn, chairman of Metropolitan Life Insurance. Wages and office rents dropped relative to costs in other areas. Good luck favored the City when the dollar weakened—tourists flocked to New York and retailers staked their foreign outposts on Madison Avenue. The number of foreign banks located in New York doubled in the span of five years. The Los Angeles–based Bank of America built its eastern international headquarters in the most congested core of the City, next to Grand Central Terminal. Entrepreneurs (many of them representing foreign interests seeking a politically stable haven) dared to invest in new office buildings at a time when vacancy rates hovered at 15 percent. And, not least important, attitudes changed, and many young men and women decided that the City is where the action is for pursuing a career in business, the arts, and education. Between 1977 and 1982, a period during which the United States suffered two severe economic recessions, New York City regained 160,000 of the 600,000 jobs it had lost in the preceding eight years. Mayor Edward Koch and city boosters call the turnaround a "renaissance." That's a bit of hyperbole, but there is no doubt that the City economy proved to be far more vigorous than any of the naysayers thought possible.

I was a Cassandra in the early 1970s, warning about the City's economic weaknesses, and I was pretty accurate several years later, projecting that the employment decline would bottom out. But I was way off the mark in foreseeing both the severity of the decline and the strength of the subsequent recovery. Now I'm asked whether employment growth will continue or whether the upturn will prove to be a temporary blip on a long-term downward spiral. My conclusion: The new New York City will be far more international, finance-, and tourist-centered than the old New York City. However, dispersal of support activities will take place, given advanced technology, lower costs elsewhere, and personal preferences to live and do business in other locations. The net result is that New York City will not return to its earlier employment peaks. Rather, the City will function with economic vitality at employment levels perhaps slightly higher than in recent years. Can a city function in stasis, with only marginal overall change? I think the chances are fairly good that it can. But that does not mean New York will be a city without problems—poverty and its attendant costs will *not* disperse, and the struggle to improve the infrastructure and municipal services will be difficult.

Does New York City provide the model for survival for other cities? Not exactly—because New York is *one* of a kind. What New York City illustrates is not that the economic future of a city is an inevitable path downward but that the key to vitality is the ability to change. But in reaching a conclusion that cities are not obsolete, we have to come to terms with the reality that there is no perfect population size, no optimum population density, and no magic prescription for growth.

You'd think by now after all of the studies and millions of words written we would know how big the optimum city is and what it looks like. There is, however, no such thing as optimum size. The population of Tokyo is more than 8 million; Paris's, 2 million; Boston's, 500,000; Venice's, 335,000. For each of these cities, size is an accident of geography, history, politics, and economics. In my view, a population of 2 million seems to be a minimum for a truly international city; a city needs about that many people to provide a full range of business, financial, and personal services for the international community. There are about forty cities of this size in the world today. Devotees of planned new towns contend that a population of much more than 150,000 is too large. In their view, the advantages of the economies of scale in larger cities are more than offset by the undesirable stresses of urban life. I think that a city much smaller than 150,000 lacks the diversity of economic activities to be a full-service city where people can live and work in the same place if they choose. Cities work well not because they reach a predetermined scale, but because their economic base can support an infrastructure and services consistent with their specialized functions.

Part of the problem in talking about city size is that a city is whatever it is defined to be by its legal corporate boundaries. Boundaries may stay fixed for all time or they may expand as municipal governments follow the outward expansion of population and jobs. Five separate counties

consolidated to form New York City in 1898. New York
City's boundaries never changed afterward. Between 1960
and 1973, Jacksonville expanded its boundaries by 2,448
percent; San Jose, by 105 percent; Houston, by 55 percent.
A city does not necessarily solve all of its problems by
extending its boundaries, but when a city can't draw on its
migrating population for taxes, it can be left with a residue
of costs for maintaining services and a diminishing base of
taxpayers to pay for them. New York City mayors periodically try to capture part of that footloose income by
increasing the income tax on commuters working in New
York. But the state legislature makes that decision, and
the City doesn't have the necessary votes. The owners of the
Knicks and the Rangers threatened in 1981 to transfer the
teams from Madison Square Garden to the Meadowlands,
in New Jersey, so close that one can see the arena from
Manhattan. The Mayor told his staff, "Do what it takes to
keep the teams at Madison Square Garden." What it took
was special state legislation to exempt the Garden from real
estate taxes and to provide electricity at reduced rates. I
was a loner in the administration who thought the ransom
price negotiated to keep the teams was too high. No one
would have cared about a move across the Hudson River
if the New York–New Jersey region operated under a common municipal structure.

In the real world, city boundaries—though they define
tax jurisdictions and service responsibilities—rarely reflect
economic functions with accuracy. Today's urban economies, linked by transportation and communications, spread
far from their central core. This picture is true not only for
the United States; the pattern is repeated in urban concentrations all over the world. Eight million people live in

Tokyo; 25 million people live within the Tokyo metropolitan area. Nine million people live within the municipal boundaries of Mexico City; more than 14 million people live within its larger urban area. Los Angeles is the epitome of what we call "urban sprawl." But even Los Angeles has a center city that forms the core of its urban region. Within this vast area, 11 million people are spread out over 34,000 square miles. Contrasts in development are vivid. Los Angeles, a city of 3 million, is no longer growing. Anaheim increased its population by one-third in the 1970–1980 decade; Huntington Beach, a tiny resort town in 1950, mushroomed to become a small city of 170,000 within a span of thirty years. What we see in today's world of urban development is growth spilling from the older cores and new concentrations—minicities, if you will—arising in far from systematic configurations. The notion of the city as a tight urban core with development fanning out in neat concentric circles is indeed obsolete. On the other hand, the notion of far-flung population dispersal without urban concentrations is equally unreal.

Do we ever reach a point when we know that a city or its larger metropolitan area has become too large? Again, we are in a world without absolutes. A medieval town, picturesquely punctuating the landscape with its walled castle perched atop a hill, could be too large with a population of 200. Poor sanitation and inadequate food supplies produced "overcrowding" in these tiny settlements. Disease and high infant mortality were painful, self-correcting devices.

Later, Dickens's nineteenth-century London teemed with humanity, although only 2.5 million people lived in the London of 1850 compared with 7 million today. The difference lay in the density of population and in the quality of the support services. With crowded flats, no indoor plumbing, no underground subway, people spilled out onto the narrow winding streets, easy prey for the pickpockets sent out by the Fagans of the time. Smog, caused by the burning of bituminous coal and peat in fireplaces, enshrouded London. Smog produced a romantic atmosphere for Sherlock Holmes stories, but smog also threatened human life. When the burning of coal was banned in 1956, the smog lifted. Admirers of Sherlock Holmes may be disappointed with London's antiseptic appearance, but as an economic entity, London functions better than before.

Jacob Riis captured New York City's "overcrowding" in his photographs of the Lower East Side at the close of the nineteenth century. They show a city that has outgrown its capacity to function on a human scale. Tenements with inadequate light and sanitation housed sixteen people per 1,000 square feet. Today, some of those same tenements, approaching 100 years of age, provide "chic" living quarters for the middle class. Two people, one cat, one stereo, and one waterbed may be all that occupy 1,000 square feet. In 1870, about 1.5 million people lived in what is now called New York City; two out of three of them were "crowded" into the lower portion of Manhattan. Today, nearly 7 million people live in New York City, but only one out of seven is a resident of Manhattan. In other words, though more people live in New York than in earlier times, they are more spread out; population *density* is lower.

Of course, there are those who say that New York, in spite of its spreading out (or perhaps because of it), has reached an unmanageable size, and this is one of the reasons for its economic and social difficulties. What these people really mean is that the support services are not functioning properly. Take one example—the subway. In 1982, the New York City subway system carried 3.5 million passengers a day, only one-half the number of passengers using the subways in the early 1950s. Yet, ask a New Yorker whether the subways are crowded, and he'll reply yes, and he will be correct. The subways are crowded at rush hours! As ridership declines, trains are shortened and the waiting time between arrivals is lengthened. The result, naturally, is crowding. Discomfort leads to further ridership declines, and so the downward spiral continues. The problem is not too many riders; the problem is too few!

Low population density does not in and of itself guarantee sound economic and social functioning. You can see this in many of the newer cities that experienced their growth spurt in the age of the automobile. Cities that grew up with their economies shaped by the automobile tend to be spread out compared with older cities that rely heavily on mass transit. About 6,400 people per square mile live in Los Angeles. Barely 3,000 people per square mile reside in Houston, compared with New York City's 23,000 people per square mile. While New Yorkers endure their subway crises, Los Angelenos sit in their cars on crowded freeways, surrounded by smog. Houstonites, living in a "sparsely" settled city, suffer from legendary rush-hour traffic jams. Houston looks too large by this measure—its population has outstripped its transportation support system. As I read the evidence, these examples show that there is no law of physics that preordains that once a city reaches a certain size, diseconomies of scale take over and a city becomes unmanageable. Rather, it is a matter of how effectively available resources are organized.

Now that we've concluded that cities can come in many

sizes and many shapes and still function as economic enti-
ties, we're left with the question of whether a city must
grow to remain economically viable. In the 1960s, the
answer would have been an unqualified yes. Growth was a
"motherhood" phrase equated with higher incomes and
more goods and services. The chamber of commerce of
every town touted its success in terms of its growth record.
Decline was un-American; it was symptomatic of failure.
Then, in the 1970s, small became beautiful. Environmental-
ists questioned whether our natural resources could support exponential growth. Sociologists, bemoaning crime in
large cities, denounced public housing projects for being
too big (not recognizing that rich tenants willingly pay
$2,000 and more per month to live stacked on top of each
other in forty-story apartment houses). Local governments
discovered that added population and even new industry
can place greater demands on government for services than
the additional tax revenues can pay for. Jeno's, Inc., located
its pizza-manufacturing plant in Wellston, Ohio. This town
of 6,000 residents was bursting with pride. Only later did
they discover that Jeno's brought not only 1,000 new employees to Wellston, but also the need for a costly new town
sewer system—all that dough and mozzarella cheese down
the drain produced an intractable sludge.

For most older cities, the debate between "growth for
growth's sake" and "small is beautiful" does not present
real options. Rather, older cities face the question of
whether shrinkage is inevitable—a sign of economic obsolescence. Nearly a decade ago, Roger Starr, a New York
City housing official, looked at the City's falling population
and employment figures and concluded that decline was
inevitable. He advocated a policy of "planned shrinkage"

and was soundly denounced by almost everyone—for proposing what was called a plot to destroy blacks, New York's version of Hitler's Holocaust or, as some put it, of "triage." Even those who believed that the City would shrink further feared that planning for a smaller future would create a self-fulfilling prophecy. Roger Starr left city government shortly afterward to express his views in later years behind the anonymity of the editorial page of *The New York Times.* Planned shrinkage, the issue he had raised, is rarely discussed openly in the same terms today, but the problem has not gone away.

Neat theories of surging growth, maturity, and decline have been applied to family fortunes, to individual industries, to cities, and to nations. But history provides few reliable guides as to whether shrinkage of cities is either inevitable or whether it is necessarily a bad thing. Many European cities experienced forced shrinkage under the ravages of World War II, and they rose again, fertilized by large infusions of U.S. aid. However, their path of redevelopment has been far from uniform. Population in several European cities—Milan and Munich, for example—surpasses prewar levels. The forces of national and regional growth pushed their urban economies onto new high ground. Population in other European cities declined, but most of these cities continue to function as vital urban centers.

Both Paris and London are considerably smaller than they were forty years ago. I don't think anyone would seriously dispute that they remain great international cities. In part, their lack of growth reflects a low rate of economic expansion in their nations compared with that in other parts of Europe. But the development pattern also stems from government policies that consciously sought to encourage the movement of both population and jobs to areas outside city borders while retaining the historic core. These cities are part of a larger metropolitan government structure. It is the norm to prohibit or sharply limit high-rise construction in the historic core of many European cities, while encouraging office towers and multistory, subsidized housing to be built outside the cities' borders. It is something of a jolt to approach Toledo, Spain, by car with visions of El Greco's *View of Toledo* in your mind. The first thing you encounter in the distance is the specter of apartment buildings rising from the plateau on the outskirts of the city. Once you reach your destination, you breathe a sigh of relief. The view has been preserved, and Toledo's historic core remains untouched.

Metropolitan or regionwide government is not really a part of the American tradition. There has been much talk among urbanologists about the desirability of such governmental structures, but there is little political support. We have specialized regional agencies such as the Port Authority of New York and New Jersey and the Metropolitan Transportation Authority (responsible for mass transit in the New York metropolitan area). And we have a few cases of areawide units with quite broad governmental responsibilities—in Jacksonville, Nashville, and Indianapolis, for example. But these are exceptions rather than the rule. Most sections of the United States feel neither the nostalgia of a long history nor the push of population against scarce land, both of which have been such integral parts of the European experience. So we don't come under pressure to treat our urban areas as economic conglomerates. Rather, we jealously protect our prerogatives as discrete municipalities to compete for people and jobs or, at the other extreme, to bar the gate and keep newcomers out. Even if we should move in the direction of regional government (and I believe the chances are that we will for limited specific functions rather than for full areawide government), I don't think that additional layers will fundamentally alter the technological and social forces that are shaping urban development.

Further decline for many cities appears to be almost certain when we look at the postwar record. More than one-half of the seventy-two cities with populations of 200,000 and more lost population between 1970 and 1980. Several of these cities—Philadelphia, Baltimore, St. Louis, San Francisco—have been losing population for at least thirty years. Others, such as Denver, Tampa, and Norfolk, Virginia, are newcomers to the "losers" list. The outstanding feature of the 1970s is that the population decline spread to metropolitan areas and was not confined to center cities. Eight out of twenty-five of the largest metropolitan areas lost population between 1970 and 1980. During those years, growth in nonmetropolitan areas was faster than in metropolitan areas for the first time in a century, as populations spilled over metropolitan boundaries and settled even farther beyond in small towns and villages.

Is there any evidence that the process is about to stop? Certainly not on a major scale. So far, only a few older cities that lost residents in the 1970s are showing signs that population decline may be bottoming out. According to census "guesstimates" based on such measures as local birth and death records and federal tax returns, population in New York City, San Francisco, and Indianapolis, after dropping in the 1970s, rose slightly between 1980 and 1982. But there is little evidence to conclude that a long-term population growth surge is beginning.

If decline in older cities is so widespread, and expansion

beyond metropolitan borders is the new wave of population movement, how can I conclude that cities are not obsolete? The answer lies in the ability of cities to adapt to their changing circumstances and to build on their strengths, even though they serve as the home or the workplace for fewer people. And there is a short, evolving record that suggests this process can take place. New York City suffered a near-hemorrhaging of employment and then subsequently reversed the decline. Boston, with its Quincy Market, developed a new tourist industry that draws millions of visitors a year. Boston faces serious fiscal problems and sharp contrasts between its sectors where growth is occurring and the population left behind in poverty, but there is little dispute that a turnaround has taken place. White Plains, New York, symbolizes the remolding of an urban economy on a smaller scale. To many people, White Plains is only a stop on the commuter trains to New York City, but the downtown area lay gutted by urban renewal for years. Now this small "satellite" city is a bustling center of retail and business services. But other cities are not as fortunate. Detroit, for example, buffeted by the double thrust of long-term decline and the severe 1981–82 recession, appears to be fighting a losing battle in the struggle to recast its economy. Symbolic gestures of renewal, like Renaissance Center in downtown Detroit, have not been enough to overcome the difficulties manufacturing-dominated cities face finding substitute uses for their central areas where manufacturing can no longer operate efficiently. And in a city like Newark, New Jersey, where three out of five residents are black, the drag of poverty weighs more heavily on the city's structure than does the presence of financial-service industries that theoretically carry the potential for expansion.

The future of American cities thus appears mixed—some

will be winners, some will be losers. Cities will survive out of inertia; businesses and individuals have too large an investment to fully abandon cities. And cities will survive because urban concentrations still have functions to perform. Though computer technology permits the dispersal of activities, it also facilitates efficient clustering of key "nerve center" activities at the core. The concentration and diversity of goods and services centered in a city, and the personal communication that takes place, are key elements in the incubation of new activities as well as in the day-to-day conduct of a city's business. Investment bankers and lawyers meet with their clients in New York or Chicago or Los Angeles to negotiate a complex corporate merger. Doctors perform intricate surgery in the hospitals of Boston and Dallas. Grand opera is staged at the Metropolitan Opera House in New York. People will often ask, "But how often do you actually *go* to the opera (or the ballet, or the theater, or to see the Knicks or the Mets)?" My answer is, "Not often, but I feel good just knowing I can!"

What about attitudes toward cities? Will attitudes change? We're not about to give up the widespread preference for noncity living, particularly now that so much employment is locating nearby. Mayor Koch learned a painful lesson about the strength of these preferences when he lost the New York State gubernatorial primary in 1982, in large part because of his remarks disparaging the gingham dresses and Sears suits allegedly worn by upstate New Yorkers. Nor will the attractions of living in warm climates suddenly disappear. But some of the forces that shape attitudes toward cities are shifting. Cities no longer (if they ever did) hold a monopoly on sin. Crime, drugs, and illicit sex can be found anywhere. Reported crime rose 8.4 percent between 1976 and 1980 in cities with fewer than 10,000 people compared with an increase of only 4.5 percent in New York City. Our suburban friends spend thousands of dollars on elaborate security systems linked to the local police. A city-dweller's outlay of a few hundred dollars for strong apartment door locks looks like peanuts in comparison. Moreover, problems of population density—traffic, pollution, insufficient water supplies—are arriving in the newly developed cities of the United States. In many growth areas, housing is as expensive as, or even more costly than, it is in older, inner cities. Travel on Route 7, the north–south artery in exurban Connecticut, and you'll find cars and trucks moving at a crawl at almost any hour of the day. The quality of life that attracted many families and businesses to these areas is in danger of deteriorating.

On the positive side, cities, with their variety of life-styles, are drawing the two-career couple who can afford the costs of city life as long as they have only one or two children. Finally, we are developing a sense of history about our cities. Whether the explanation is sentiment or economics (the high costs of new construction and liberal tax benefits for rehabilitation), investment in the renovation of existing structures is taking place in many older areas. The scale of what's labeled "gentrification" is small in the context of larger cities, but the potential for positive multiplier effects is, I believe, substantial.

Why should we bother ourselves about the prospect of shrinkage if cities can function with vitality at lower population levels? The answer lies in both social and economic considerations. When a city declines precipitously, it is left with an infrastructure that was designed for a different-sized population and that no longer works efficiently. Firehouses are in the wrong place, subways go where no one lives, housing abandonment occurs in uneven patterns. Adjustments to smaller size are neither costless nor painless. Poverty, with its economic and social costs, remains concentrated in the inner city. More than half of all black teenagers in New York City are unemployed. The costs of educating and training them for jobs run into the millions of dollars. But the costs of not successfully preparing them for the world of work are even higher—more crime, increased numbers of homeless people, more unmarried mothers dependent on public assistance. And, contrary to its media image, New York City is not a center of the super rich with the wealth to pay for the costs! According to the 1980 census, only 5 percent of New York City families received (in 1979) incomes of $50,000 and more—a slightly lower percentage than in the nation as a whole.

So it makes a difference whether cities turn into caretakers of the poor or whether city economies will become sufficiently vigorous to provide opportunities for employment. As an optimist and a careful reader of the evidence, I conclude that cities are not obsolete. Cities that can adapt to changing technology will survive. *Change*, not *growth* in population, will be the key. And in our vast country there will be many variations in how the process evolves. If history tells us anything, there is no predetermined size or configuration that is the sine qua non for successful urban areas. Many cities—probably most cities—that retain or regain their vigor will be smaller in population than they are today. Some cities will not make the transition to smaller size with grace or with success, but those who think that cities will be replaced by bytes on a computer are wrong!

2

Can a Mayor Create Jobs for a City?

- Brooklyn Navy Yard loses contract to re-build the *Iowa*; Pascagoula, Mississippi, wins—1982.
- South Bronx Greenhouse, Inc., raises herbs in the South Bronx—1983.
- Agreement reached for Teleport on Staten Island—1983.

When I was Deputy Mayor for Economic Policy and Development for New York City, I was asked at least once a week, by a reporter or a community group leader or by Mayor Koch, "Why don't you get some high tech for New York?" Few people knew quite what it was that they wanted for New York City when they demanded some high tech. All they knew was that everyone else was trying to create jobs through high technology, so New York had better be part of the game.

As we entered the 1980s, high tech became the new buzz word for economic development. Every state and major city in the older regions of the United States began to look to high technology as a panacea for lagging job growth. If Massachusetts could revolutionize its economy with high technology on Route 128, why couldn't Mayor Koch and his deputy do the same in New York City? Of course, Mayor Koch wanted "high tech" for New York City, too. And

23

while I was working as his deputy, we started the process of targeting economic development to selected areas of high technology—such as telecommunications and biomedics—that meshed with our services economy. But it was a long leap from the "will" to a "way." The Mayor couldn't simply wave a wand, put together an attractive package of local government initiatives, and out of sheer determination *will* high tech to happen. To create jobs through high technology, in fact to create any kind of employment base in urban areas, requires that many ingredients, from geography, to entrepreneurial talent, to a bit of luck, fall into place. Well-conceived local economic policies have a role to play; but it is a rare case in which a mayor can act as a catalyst for creating jobs in the private sector if the conditions are not ripe.

Elected officials like to take credit for creating jobs in their city. We would send the Mayor monthly statistics on employment. He invariably would include them in his speeches, boasting, "We created 160,000 [or whatever the latest number was] private sector jobs in New York City since I took office on January 1, 1978." But when employment started to decline from its peak, in 1982, talk turned from the City's locally stimulated accomplishments to the influence of negative forces that were beyond the City's control. The reality is that a mayor works at the margins to create jobs for a city. An elected official inherits an economic and social structure that's been in place for decades; recasting that structure can take years of effort. It's easy to forget that cities have their histories—some longer than others—and that there is tremendous variation in just what made an individual city develop with a particular economic structure. The economist's explanation of locational advantage—access to supplies, to consumer markets, and to labor

—tells part of the story; but there's more to it than that. The risk-taking of an entrepreneur, the edict of a president, the act of a state legislature, the fads of consumers— they're all part of the past that confronts a mayor when he is attempting to create jobs for a city.

So we find cities like Rotterdam, whose fortune is tied to the locational advantage of its port, and cities like Pittsburgh, which developed as a manufacturing base close to supplies of iron ore and coal. Las Vegas, situated in the desert, gleaned its wealth from gambling; the strength of its cards changed in the 1970s, after the New Jersey legislature legalized gambling in Atlantic City. Brasília rose from an empty plateau in the center of Brazil as a monument to government because one man, Juscelino Kubitschek, President, wanted it that way. The decision of John D. Rockefeller, Jr., to proceed as an entrepreneur with the construction of Rockefeller Center shaped the skyline and the ambience of Manhattan for future generations. Mr. Rockefeller leased the property from Columbia University in 1929. But after the Great Depression hit, the Metropolitan Opera backed out of plans to build a new opera house on the site. "Father," as David Rockefeller explained on the fiftieth anniversary of the complex, "decided to go ahead with building Rockefeller Center. After all, Father had to start paying rent to Columbia, and he wouldn't let the land just sit there empty." Finally, some cities overflow with people and activity not so much because of their *positive* job-creating potential as because of their *relative* advantages compared with conditions elsewhere. Millions of the rural poor flock to the barrios of Mexico City and São Paulo, only to become the urban poor, presenting economic and social difficulties for their host cities.

These are the profiles, large and small, expanding or

contracting, that a mayor inherits at a specific moment. Whether the past turns out to be a plus or a negative will be heavily influenced by the national environment in which a local official operates. Cities do better in creating jobs (or minimizing losses) when the U.S. economy expands rapidly. Certainly, cities are more successful in job creation when their economic base is dominated by industries that are growing rapidly. Petroleum, electronics, business services, tourism—these were all "good" industries for a city to have in its economic base in the 1970s. Steel, domestic automobiles, textiles—these were "bad." But as many cities learn to their discomfort, a plus in one period can quickly turn into a negative—Houston's growth spurt ground to a halt after the oil boom collapsed in the 1981–82 recession.

Quality-of-life issues enter the picture, too. Americans can be fickle about the life-styles they prefer. A city has a better chance at job creation if it is located in a region to which people are flocking. My friends who moved to the Southwest delight in telephoning back East in February to find out how bad the weather is. They are part of a migration—of young and old—that has been attracted to warm climates. History has reversed itself. Strong economic growth used to be equated with temperate climates; changes in seasons stimulated the mind whereas unrelieved heat dulled the senses. Air conditioning altered all that. People can live in comfort in hot climates all year round and save money by spending less on heating, housing insulation, and warm clothes. Jobs follow people and people follow jobs and the potential for increasing employment is strengthened.

If city government has no control over the "big" forces—business cycles, technology, life-style preferences—what can a mayor do to stimulate job creation? Clearly, the *Village*

Voice muckraker approach, exposing the "incestuous" relationships between City Hall, contractors, and real estate developers who divide the job spoils at taxpayers' expense, exaggerates the power of a mayor to create jobs. A city's leverage on jobs is far more diffuse and more difficult to evaluate. What within the domain of city government makes a difference? Taxes? Crime? Clean streets? Infrastructure? Schools? A municipally supported convention center? A museum? A sports arena? A handsome mayor (John Lindsay)? A witty mayor (Edward Koch)? At any time, any of these elements can influence decisions concerning locations and the ability of a city to create (or hold on to) jobs. Sometimes it is the *perception* as much as the *reality* of local conditions that triggers decisions that carry employment implications. No matter how many times the mayor repeated that New York City ranked number seven among major cities in crime, no one paid attention. The media gleefully spread New York City's crime stories across the world. To the public, New York City *is* the crime capital of the nation.

I have no doubt that the highest priority for a mayor is to see that the city works: that the garbage is picked up, that crime is kept under control, that the subways and buses run on time, that the parks are maintained, that the schools (when they are within a mayor's orbit) are educating the youth. That's not a terribly original prescription —it is what mayors traditionally are paid to do. With businesses and individuals more mobile than ever before, the quality of the environment in which people live and work is becoming increasingly important in influencing location decisions. Is there no more to economic development than improving basic municipal services? Professor Richard

Netzer, urban economist at New York University, says, "Yes, get out of the way!" What he means is, if local government would only get out of the way, that is, reduce the proverbial red tape associated with licenses, permits, zoning regulations, and inspections, then business could function efficiently and economic development could proceed on its natural course. All too often, when government intercedes in a so-called activist mode, either everything grinds to a halt or, even worse, what government sets out to do turns out to be wrong. There's a lot of truth to this view, but I don't think it quite fits the real world in which a mayor functions, which is a world where competition for jobs among localities is not always fought according to the Queensberry rules or on home territory. As I see it, there are at least three areas where local government can exert influence on the job-creating process: watching out for local interests vis-à-vis other levels of government; building upon a city's strengths, at the margin; and cutting a city's losses, again at the margin. It's not easy to do any of these well. Risks of failure are high, but I think that careful, well-thought-out risk-taking can be worthwhile as long as one understands the pitfalls in the process.

"Keeping the Feds honest" is my phrase for it. What it says is that cities exist in a world where federal policies control much of their destiny. In the ideal world, federal policies are set for the broad national benefit, and it would be wrong for individual cities to lobby for their narrow self-interest. New York City *could* shut down its Washington office; the Mayor *could* curtail his air shuttle trips when he goes to Washington to testify before Congress. But often the federal government is not evenhanded in the distribution of pain or of benefits. Take the Interstate Highway

System, for example. Thousands of communities benefited from new highways built near them. But no one effectively made the case that the prohibition against using funds for reconstruction had severe consequences for older cities. New highways were built, ringing older cities; existing city road systems were allowed to deteriorate. It took years before local officials understood the cause of their "pain" and pressured Washington to introduce greater equity into highway aid allocations.

Pork-barreling, to benefit one's constituency, is a congressional art. Fighting for a larger piece of the federal spending pie became a preoccupation of big-city mayors when lagging national economic growth and accelerating job losses created fiscal difficulties for many cities. Economists may debate whether defense spending is an efficient way of creating permanent jobs for the nation as a whole, but there is little doubt that the fortunes of individual cities such as Seattle, San Antonio, and San Diego ebb and flow with shifts in defense spending. New Yorkers are babes in the woods when competing for defense jobs. Liberals by tradition, viewing themselves as internationalists, not narrow parochialists, they are accustomed to lobbying against, not for, defense appropriations. All of a sudden they woke up to the simple truth that once appropriations are approved, a specific locality will reap the benefit. And if the past is a guide, politics as well as competitive costs will influence decisions on *where* defense dollars are spent.

The prospect of obtaining a $400-million contract for the retrofitting of the battleship *Iowa* presented an enticing challenge to the City of New York in 1982. The *Iowa* was built during World War II in the Brooklyn Navy Yard. What could be more appropriate than to have the ship rebuilt at its original homeport! The Mayor made discreet calls to the White House. Top New York City executives visited with high Navy Department officials. The Port Authority tried to minimize damaging competition among the separate fiefdoms in the New York–New Jersey port area.

When Captain Stephen A. Coakley arrived to take over the Navy's skeleton force at the Brooklyn Navy Yard, he told us that Navy personnel felt ignored in the vast, impersonal city. So we tried to change their feelings about the city with a showing of New York hospitality. I called on every Navy ship that came into the harbor. Our local contractor was in close competition to the end, but eventually the contract went to a consortium of companies in Pascagoula, Mississippi, and in New Orleans. These cities' congressmen had a solid record of voting for defense appropriations. The lost contract meant forgoing, directly, nearly 2,000 jobs at the Brooklyn Navy Yard and probably, indirectly, twice that number through multiplier effects. Our loss proved to be a valuable learning experience. Over the next year, we improved our skills in the art of lobbying, and with the help of the Port Authority, the City obtained a federal commitment to homeport the renovated *Iowa* and its companion fleet at Staten Island. This "victory" in changing deep-seated attitudes of the defense establishment in Washington may look like a minor accomplishment in the context of New York City's work force of 3 million people, but I'm convinced that creating jobs succeeds and fails at the margins.

That same philosophy reflects my view of how a mayor should approach the challenge of building upon the economic strengths of his or her city. When the press or politicians badgered the Mayor or me, as his deputy, to create jobs through "high tech" industry, I knew we couldn't duplicate California's Silicon Valley or Boston's Route 128 in the rubble of the South Bronx or in the abandoned factories of Brooklyn. If we were to be successful at all, we had to find our own form of "high tech" that would complement our own economic strengths, and this isn't something that can be accomplished overnight. Nearly twenty-five years elapsed before high technology fully bloomed on Route 128, and the flowering occurred on the ring of the metropolitan area, not in Boston's central city. Boston's technological revolution blossomed not because government took the initiative, but because of an informal partnership between venture capitalists and Harvard and M.I.T. professors who wanted to become entrepreneurs by transferring their knowledge into profitable products. Route 128 was a convenient location, midway between the professors' university classrooms in Cambridge and their suburban homes. Silicon Valley's 3,000 companies lie spread out about forty miles south of San Francisco. In California's automobile-oriented society, that is close enough to the universities to the north, the Pacific Ocean to the west, and the mountains to the east to attract a new generation of young, mobile scientists and engineers.

When I thought about creating jobs for New York City through high technology, I started from the assumption that if New York truly held a competitive advantage, then high technology would already be clustered in the City. If it were not, then we would have to see what economic barriers could be removed and what indigenous assets could be strengthened. Clearly, New York City cannot duplicate the nonurban environments that the engineers and scientists who work for high technology companies prefer. Nor can the City compete with the low wages and low operating costs essential for the assembly of high technology equipment on a mass-production scale. As we studied the problem, we concluded that the City possesses strengths that can be utilized to increase high technology jobs: the presence of an extensive university and medical research community; access to a large pool of labor with a diversity of skills; an economic base dominated by a huge services sector utilizing high technology; and the potential for creating or renovating space suitable for the small-scale operations of the start-up entrepreneur. Two segments seemed likely candidates for the City's efforts: high technology industries related to the City's premier position as a provider of *medical services*; and *telecommunications*, serving the City's expanding business, financial, and cultural sectors. Economic theory was one thing; producing results was another.

We looked at high technology industry linked to the medical complex and discovered that bits and pieces are hidden within the huge fabric of New York City. Hardly anyone knows they exist.

Stanley Poler had just gone public with his company when we met in the summer of 1983. Starting his company in a loft, he had moved his expanding operation to a renovated commercial building in downtown Manhattan. Mr. Poler produces an intricate electronic component that controls eye movement and that has applications for other medical uses. Why is the company staying in New York City? "Labor," says Stanley Poler. "There's a unique pool of Oriental labor with the dexterity and the patience to do highly skilled work—not Ph.D. scientists, but painstakingly trained technicians." I was accustomed to hearing nothing but complaints about New York City's labor supply, but here was an entrepreneur-engineer telling me I was wrong. The key to the functioning of this small firm is adequate space in a location that draws on a pool of skilled labor. If the City can affect either element at the margins, it can exert leverage on the job-creating process. We worked on this theory when Columbia University came to the City and asked our help in locating a site for a biomedical research center. The Audubon Ballroom (where Malcolm X was shot to death), a onetime jazz center in upper Manhattan, was sitting abandoned and boarded up, close to Columbia-Presbyterian Hospital. The Audubon had fallen into City hands for nonpayment of taxes. The City's economic development commitment to "high tech" biomedics formally started in early 1983, with the signing of the sales contract between Columbia University and the City's Public Development Corporation. A small step in a very large city.

Biomedics is a highly specialized activity with a limited growth potential in New York. Telecommunications offers broad possibilities for linkages with economic sectors of strength. New York City's economic revival in the late 1970s and early 1980s was fueled largely by expansion in its business, financial, and entertainment sectors. With advanced telecommunications, those industries can remain concentrated in the City's core nerve center, linked to satellite activities all over the world. There is a downside risk that telecommunications will facilitate dispersal of secondary functions. The upside odds are that state-of-the-art telecommunications will strengthen the City's competitive position and provide employment from spin-off activities.

For a change, the City turned out to be in the right place at the right time. The City had acquired extensive acreage during the Lindsay administration. The Lindsay idea was to "land-bank" so that the City could build suburban-type industrial parks within its borders. The parks didn't get built, and for years, the land lay vacant. All of a sudden, a liability turned into an asset. The New York region is so densely developed that few available sites remain for transmitting satellite communications. By chance, the City's industrial park on Staten Island is ideal for setting up antennas that can receive and send transmission signals from satellite communications. The Port Authority of New York and New Jersey had commissioned a study on the feasibility of transforming the Staten Island property into an office park, based on telecommunications technology. Peter Goldmark, Executive Director of the Authority, came to my office early in 1981 and described the proposal. Merrill Lynch, Western Union, and the Port Authority would build an office complex centered on telecommunications on City-owned land on Staten Island. The Teleport, as the facility is dubbed, would be the site for antennas linked to the World Trade Center in lower Manhattan by a fiber-optic cable running through New Jersey and into Manhattan via the Port Authority's Hudson River subway tubes. Something in this picture made me uneasy. All I could visualize were "fingers" growing out of the cable in New Jersey with office buildings attached. Staten Island would host an "antenna" farm! New Jersey would garner all the new data-processing office jobs. This marked the beginning of a tedious process of multiparty political negotiations. The Mayor held the gold ring—a unique site on Staten Island. But there were limits to how hard we could press with our demands if we were to keep both New Jersey (whose approval was required) and the private developers in the venture. I pushed hard to protect the City's interests by pressing for office space at the Staten Island site and by obtaining assurances that the fiber-optic cable would run through Brooklyn and Queens as well as through New Jersey. My successor pushed even harder to nail down these commitments and to negotiate a share in the profits if the project proved successful. In June 1983, ground was broken for the Teleport.

Does the Staten Island Teleport mean that New York City can say with confidence, "We've succeeded with our version of 'high tech' "? The antennas, the satellites, and the fiber-optic cable will link Manhattan-based companies to their own operations and to related businesses all over the world. But the City cannot control where those other facilities will locate or how many new jobs will be situated on Staten Island, in Queens, in New Jersey, or farther afield, in Dubuque or Bali Hai. The Teleport is a calculated gamble, but the odds look good enough for the City to support the undertaking.

If uncertainties plague a strategy of building on a city's strengths, the obstacles to minimizing losses can be even greater. When a sector is in decline, is the best strategy just to let "nature run its course," or are there ways that a city, through its policies, can "cut its losses" or, more positively, transform a weakness into a strength? Again, the reality is that a local official's influence is at the margins. The experience with New York City's waterfront is an example. Its natural harbor formed the basis for the City's early economic ascendency. When the Erie Canal opened in 1825 and linked the Great Lakes to the Atlantic Ocean, New York City's economy prospered. More than a century later, New York City's port supremacy eroded. Expanding U.S.

markets and shifting patterns of international trade inevitably channeled shipping through other ports in the United States. Then the technology of shipping changed, and New York piers became even less competitive. After the introduction of containerized shipping in the 1960s, traditional methods of shipping, with their labor-intensive cargo handling, became outmoded. Containerports require large back-up space for storing containers and moving trucks. The crowded Manhattan piers could not physically accommodate the facilities. The longshoremen's union on the Brooklyn waterfront, where conversion was feasible, held out against innovation and concentrated, instead, on obtaining a guaranteed annual wage for its members. New York City bargained for and got a $40-million passenger terminal built by the Port Authority on Manhattan's West Side. The facility opened in 1974. The timing was perfect. High energy costs and inexpensive jet travel combined to make the Manhattan terminal noncompetitive. Almost precisely on the day the terminal opened, the cruise business deserted New York and shifted to Miami, Florida—an example of "if government does it, it will be wrong," or, more charitably, the public sector's version of a private marketing error, comparable to Ford's famous Edsel automobile! Today, most of the New York City piers, long since abandoned, are only a memory. A transportation asset has turned into an economic liability.

A mayor inheriting the scene of a crumbling port knows that a city cannot turn the clock back. True, Brooklyn and Staten Island may retain potential for shipping in the containership age, but the Manhattan waterfront cannot revert to its former use. Only by being developed for new uses will the Manhattan waterfront become an economic asset again. It has been nearly two decades since Governor Nelson Rockefeller proposed Battery Park City as a futuristic city, with mixed commercial, residential, and recreational uses. Battery Park City would rise on the Hudson River waterfront on landfill created by the construction of the adjacent, twin-towered World Trade Center. City and state politicians fought over the composition of the proposed waterfront development for years. Planning for the project ground to a halt during the fiscal debacle of the 1970s.

Mayor Koch and Governor Hugh Carey brought the project back to life, and a memorandum of understanding was signed in 1979 that gave the state Urban Development Corporation overall responsibility for Battery Park City. For all practical purposes, the City no longer had financial control over Battery Park City except for one critical element that came up in 1981, shortly after I entered the picture as Deputy Mayor. According to the memorandum of understanding, the City sets the terms for payments in lieu of real estate taxes that the developer of commercial space is required to make. I had the responsibility of recommending to the Mayor what those terms—with Olympia and York, the developer of 6 million square feet of office space— should be. The several months we took to reach agreement were like grains of sand in an hourglass. Eighteen years after the project was first proposed, Battery Park is becoming a reality. The waterfront is being transformed into a new economic asset, with office towers, apartment buildings, and a park, strengthening the City's business service sector and improving the quality of urban living. Mayors were part of the process of transformation, but many other officials, too, tugged at the strings, sometimes pushing the project forward, sometimes holding it back. No matter who pushed and who pulled, waterfront redevelopment wouldn't have occurred until, in the private sector's eyes, the time was ripe.

The years that it takes before "anything happens" frustrate the elected officials and the second-guessers who demand action. But sometimes the inability of the bureaucracy to move mountains quickly turns out to be a blessing in disguise. Today, Lowell, Massachusetts, is flaunted as a flourishing city risen from the ashes. "High tech" has arrived! The "ideal" combination of local government, federal aid, and private resources succeeded in attracting WANG, a computer manufacturer, to Lowell. But Lowell had lain fallow for decades. Earlier attempts to save the textile industry had failed. Was it enlightened policy or an accident of fate that earlier failure paved the way for subsequent rebirth?

This question has great relevance to cities where acres and acres are abandoned. The South Bronx became the symbol of urban decay when President Carter stood on Charlotte Street in 1977 and, sobered by the devastation he saw, pledged to bring federal resources to bear on the ruins. Two years later, mired in a political struggle, the grandiose plans were quashed after being voted down in the Board of Estimate. More modest goals were set to build and renovate housing on a less densely developed scale and to promote industrial development on sites that had been cleared and that had excellent truck and rail access and a large pool of blue-collar labor.

Well intentioned the goals might have been, but they did not prove easy to implement. Do cleared sites equal cheap land? Not in the South Bronx. The costs of removing debris from the foundations of demolished brick and concrete buildings proved excessive until a process of pulverizing the rubble was discovered. (Innovation is not dead!) Did subsidizing single-floor, modern industrial space make economic sense in the South Bronx? My initial reaction is—the South Bronx can work as an industrial location, but only if you find owners with the management skills and the products to operate a successful business! If you are just shoring up an inherently unprofitable enterprise, then your involvement is a misallocation of city resources. But if a relatively small investment can pave the way for others who follow and who progressively will require less (and not more) government aid, then the effort can be judged successful—once more at the margins.

By 1983, close observers of the urban scene detected signs that the South Bronx had turned the corner. The private market for industrial space appeared stronger; private property owners were tentatively investing in rehabilitation, and the Port Authority of New York was building three additional speculative buildings on the conviction that tenants were out there to be found, and they were: a printer, a generic drug company, and an art materials firm. By 1984, at least three more buildings were in the planning stage, each requiring smaller subsidies than the earlier "seed money" ventures. Perhaps the most successful operation evolved from a facetiously offered prescription for the South Bronx—turn the rubble into farms. South Bronx Greenhouse, Inc., started on city-owned land as a nonprofit youth-training program, now operates as a commercial enterprise. Using advanced technology "hydroponics," the community-based organization is the largest supplier of fresh herbs to restaurants in New York. The turnaround, if it proves to be real, suggests that local government can positively affect the economic development process, but job creation doesn't come quickly or easily or without costs. And if the South Bronx does revive, it will happen in large part because, beneath the rubble and decay, its location and its labor pool are pluses. However, the revival will be neither a return to the South Bronx of the past nor a dramatic high technology coup. It will be a South Bronx built on a modest redevelopment scale.

A mayor exerts little direct control over a South Bronx— or over the economic destiny of any city. Broad economic, social, and technological forces affect the job-creating process at any particular time. And the classic locational attributes—supplies, labor, consumer markets—shape each city's basic economic structure. But there is room for something special, and not quantifiable, in the process of creating jobs: preferences in life-styles, the risk-taking of the entrepreneur, and, sometimes for better and sometimes for worse, the hand of a hardworking, imaginative mayor. It's a sign of an inflated ego for a mayor to claim credit for single-handedly reviving a dying city, but at the margin, and over time, a local government official can make a difference!

3

Is the War between the
North and the South Over?

- Shell moves from New York to Houston;
  Johns-Manville moves to Denver—1971.
- Income in Wyoming posts the largest gains
  in the nation—1970–1980.
- Unemployment reaches 11 percent in California; settles at 6.5 percent in Massachusetts—Winter 1982.

Several years ago, I gave a talk entitled "Cities and the
Sunbelt: Growth, but Where?" In my conclusion I said,
"Substantial regional differences will surely remain, but
they should be expected to narrow as we move into the
1980s." The year was 1976. A lot has happened in the U.S.
economy since then—record inflation, deep recession, en-
suing recovery. But we're still troubled by that same question: Growth, but where?

I stand by my earlier convictions—the dates may be a
little bit off, but I think the conclusion is valid. Differences
in regional economic performance *will* narrow. There will
be winners and losers spread among the fifty states; contrasts *within* broad regions will be the new force to watch.

Why should we care if one region flourishes and another part of the nation wanes? After all, regional shifts
are a part of our history. The freedom for people and financial resources to move unimpeded across state borders is a

source of national strength. In economic terms, mobility maximizes economic growth. Is anyone hurt besides politicians, who lose their power base, and real estate investors, whose business it is to take risks? Is there any reason to pay attention? The answer, I believe, is yes. First, regional shifts do carry substantial economic and social costs—underutilized infrastructure, abandoned housing, empty museums, disrupted families. Second, government itself is part of the problem. Political power play, not just the invisible hand of Adam Smith's economics, influences patterns of regional growth. The challenge, however, is not the fruitless goal of regional homogeneity; rather it is to see that the advantages of differential growth are not outweighed by the pain incurred by the losers.

Disparities in regional economic growth became a matter of broad public interest in the 1970s. Suddenly, businessmen, labor leaders, and politicians from New York, Massachusetts, and Michigan found they had interests in common. Political and economic power was shifting to the South and to the West, and no one was doing anything about it. The Northeast-Midwest Coalition was formed to lobby in Congress: Investment banker Felix Rohatyn called for the establishment of a regional development bank; Governor Carey made a plea for a regional energy corporation to revitalize industry in the North. What happened to cause the agitation? Was the to-do about the Sunbelt versus the Frostbelt (or the Snowbelt) just a media event pushed into public consciousness by a few well-publicized books and articles? Or was a new force splitting the nation in a way that was becoming as divisive as the Civil War, more than a century earlier? As so often happens, neither extreme tells the story.

A little perspective is in order. To set the record straight,

Sunbelt versus Frostbelt is a misnomer, a label that caught attention, but that does not give an accurate picture of the existing situation. The growth conflict could be called East versus West, but that is not right, either. What really is involved is the northeastern quadrant of the United States, which comprises about one-quarter of the land mass and nearly one-half of the nation's population. Not everyone gives the region the same geographic boundaries, but generally we are talking about the Northeast from Maine to Pennsylvania, and the industrial Midwest, from Ohio and Michigan, on past Minnesota and Missouri—an area of slightly more than 100 million people. Population growth in this area totaled barely 2 percent between 1970 and 1980.

The rest of the nation, extending all the way from Florida and Maryland on the East Coast to California and Washington on the West, contains 75 percent of the U.S. land area and about 125 million people—over one-half the nation's total. Population in this vast area rose by one-fifth in the 1970–1980 decade. But the region is far from homogeneous. The Appalachian states are just starting to come out of a prolonged economic depression. Income in the poverty core of the Deep South (Mississippi and Alabama) lags far behind the national average income. The southern rim— Florida, Texas, Arizona, Southern California—has indeed experienced rapid growth; but the sparsely populated Rocky Mountain area, including such states as Utah, Colorado, and Wyoming, where winter temperatures fall well below zero, is the fastest-growing region of all. Hardly the Sunbelt, this region is where cowboys and ski bums congregate, where Ph.D. geologists search for mineral and energy resources for multinational corporations, and where major companies such as

American Express, with its data processing, and Digital Equipment, with electronic manufacturing, are staking their claims. Easy access to recreation and the outdoors seems to be the incentive that is drawing people in all regions to live and work in nonmetropolitan areas well beyond the suburban fringe.

A second observation is that the United States has long been a nation of movers. And whereas the general direction, as Horace Greeley said, has been to "Go West," the movement has not been completely one way. Starting in the 1920s, migrants from the agricultural South flocked to industrial jobs in the automobile factories of the Midwest. Banks, insurance firms, and public relations companies in the Northeast drew their executives and their well-scrubbed secretaries from an influx of respectable midwesterners. When I started with Chase Manhattan Bank, in the late 1950s, there were few recruits for the officer-training programs from the local Italian, Irish, or Jewish ethnic groups. The young college graduates who came East in the 1950s and early 1960s to fill the ranks of middle management were decidedly from small-town, middle America. Today, our society is increasingly mobile: two-way migration is a jet-age norm. Actors, writers, and film producers move back and forth between New York and California, shifting base with the availability of work and according to personal preferences—the prototypical commute is between the beach house in Malibu and the loft in SoHo.

A third simple "truth" is that for years and years growth rates have been higher in the South and the West. Industry shifts started before World War II, with the textile, apparel, and furniture industries seeking the low-wage non-union labor of the South. The broad picture looked clear at the close of the 1960s. The South and the West were growing faster than the North, but disparities were narrowing. And this is what economists expected. According to theory, the familiar pattern of economic takeoff, rapid growth, and maturity would repeat itself in the South and the West, and eventually growth rates there would converge around the national average.

So much for economic theory. That's not what happened in the 1970s. Growth differentials dramatically *widened* instead of narrowing. The matter was not just one for discussion in the learned academic journals, nor was it merely a case of overblown media reportage. We were witnessing not slow growth, but *no* growth. Population growth virtually halted in the Northeast and Midwest. Most of the established cities lost both residents and employment. Meanwhile, growth in the South and the Mountain States accelerated. It is one thing to expand less rapidly in one region than in another; it is another not to grow at all. A vision of the Northeast emptied of all but the elderly and the dependent looked uncomfortably plausible.

It is a matter of state pride not to lose population, but population trends tell little, if anything, about economic well-being. The bottom line is the standard of living. Are people better off or worse off than their neighbors? Trends in personal income—the broadest measure of economic vitality—confirm that disparities in economic growth became more pronounced in the 1970s. What makes these trends more than a numbers game is that the economic shift took place against a background of a weak national economy. The Northeast and Midwest were getting a shrinking share of a very slowly growing pie. The average New Yorker increased his own income by barely 1 percent a year (after adjusting for inflation) in the 1970s. When you work hard to stay in the same place while your neighbors are getting ahead (real income per capita rose 2.5 percent a year in the South), the abstract notion of regional growth disparities becomes painfully real.

What caused this shift in fortunes? Were the 1970s an aberration that will fade away as the 1980s progress, or did the 1960s, with the U.S. economy superheated from the Vietnam War–Great Society ventures, artificially pull the older regions along? These questions are not easy to answer without a longer historic perspective, but one thing stands out clearly: The combination of *low* economic growth with *high* inflation made the decade of the 1970s unique. The rare combination of recession and inflation had a particularly harsh effect on the ability of the industrial North, with its older capital stock, to compete. The energy situation bore down heavily on the Northeast, which relied on high-priced imported petroleum. The Northeast's energy price disadvantage didn't mean much when oil cost only thirty-five cents a gallon. But when the price tripled, the region was hurt. For manufacturing firms struggling to survive in the City's congested environment, spiraling energy costs added one more nail to the financial coffin. F. M. Schaefer, New York City's last brewery, shut its doors. Energy-intensive electroplating firms, long concentrated in Brooklyn, went out of business. We gave speeches and wrote learned papers on New York's energy advantage—low per capita energy consumption. Our economy revolved around office buildings, not aluminum mills; mass transit, not automobiles; apartments, not single-family homes. Even then, I wondered whom we were fooling. Offices, with increasing computerization, were turning into factories. And families bought small cars and insulated their houses before they altered their basic living patterns.

Meanwhile, the South and the West escaped the recessions of the early 1970s almost untouched. The region's energy-related industry prospered as increases in energy prices more than offset reductions in demand. Severance taxes, linked to retrieval of coal, natural gas, and petroleum, boosted the state treasuries in Texas and Wyoming. And industries, such as electronics, that were emerging in the South and the West, continued along a path of sustained growth.

Finally, a whole set of influences, not related to short-term economic conditions, came together to tip the balance farther away from the North, toward the South and the West. First of all, the children of the post–World War II baby boom grew up. The labor force ballooned. The prime working-age group—those 25–34 years old—increased by 45 percent in the 1970s. This is an age group that tends to be mobile, and this particular group of 25–34-year-olds is the one that revolutionized social attitudes during their college days in the 1960s. They carried their preferences for leisure and for less formal living styles into the 1970s as they started to settle down in jobs. The young, and the not-so-young who emulated them, found they could satisfy twin goals—jobs and comfortable living—by migrating to the South and the West, not only to large urban centers, but to small towns beyond the suburban fringe, where companies were setting up divisions. Recruiters at Chase Manhattan Bank and at other City firms couldn't fill their officer slots with the traditional midwestern college graduates. I watched as they turned to women and the products of local business schools (such as New York University and Pace

University) for future executives. An Italian Catholic from Secaucus, New Jersey, was appointed third in command at Chase in 1983—an achievement unheard of a decade earlier for a person of that background.

During the same period, the 1970s, the elderly population expanded by 25 percent. The retired didn't feel as much pain from inflation as did the rest of the population. Their Social Security benefits were adjusted upward with increases in the cost of living. So the retired moved in droves to warm climates, to Florida, Arizona, Southern California. And New York State, with its own peculiar death wish, encouraged the out-migration by "reforming," that is, raising, its inheritance taxes. I was about the only person of my generation I knew who didn't make an annual visit South—my parents were exceptions and had remained in their home up North.

Several metropolitan areas in the South and West had attained "critical mass" by the beginning of the 1970s. Their economies reached a stage where they could support multinational corporate headquarters. I used to track corporate relocations from New York as an economist at Chase Manhattan Bank. I found that corporations rarely strayed far from New York City during the 1960s—usually they moved to the suburbs in southern Connecticut or northern New Jersey. But the corporate relocation pattern changed in the 1970s: Shell moved to Houston; Cities Service to Oklahoma; American Airlines to Dallas; Coca-Cola to its hometown, Atlanta. Metropolitan areas in the South and West could now provide the services a major corporation requires, from a skilled labor force to good schools and, yes, even culture. Professional sports teams were established, reflecting metropolitan growth. Basketball shifted west with the Utah Jazz and Phoenix Suns; football flourished in Florida with the Tampa Bay Buccaneers. Ice hockey put its blades down in the Sunbelt with the Atlanta Flames, but apparently the warm climate was too alien, and the team retreated north to Calgary, Canada's western boom-town. Baseball, of course, had made the transition long before. New Yorkers date the beginnings of their problems to the end of the 1950s, when the New York Giants moved to San Francisco and the Brooklyn Dodgers fled to Los Angeles. Brooklyn's Borough President, Howard Golden, never forgave Robert Moses for allegedly driving the Dodgers out of Brooklyn so he could build a public housing project at Ebbets Field!

Weaknesses in the older areas fed back upon themselves. Losses in employment eroded the tax base. The educated labor force migrated to the new growth areas; the poor tended to stay right where they were. The net result was termed "fiscal distress." New York's new governor, Hugh Carey, took office in 1975, declaring, "The days of wine and roses are over." New York City reached the brink of bankruptcy. The situation was not as dramatic in other cities, but the response was similar—cutbacks in services and a deterioration in the quality of life while tax burdens remained high. When I asked corporate executives why they were taking their companies out of New York, they often replied, "I can't pay middle managers enough to convince them to come to New York."

As the contrasts between the Sunbelt and the Frostbelt sharpened in the public's eye, the cry went out that it was all the fault of the federal government, and that the federal government should make amends. Those of us who advised the influence-makers were asked to prove the case. We "massaged" the numbers until we made our point. The object was to show how much more "we" paid into the federal treasury in taxes than we received back in federal spending. If you wanted the balance-of-payments deficit of New York State to look big, you credited New York State with all federal taxes paid from New York City headquarters by multinational firms. If you wanted New York State's deficit to look small, you included as receipts the billions of dollars of federal interest payments flowing through the Federal Reserve Bank of New York that are eventually paid out to bondholders all over the nation. Senator Daniel Patrick Moynihan became an expert on New York State's "balance of payments." Says Senator Moynihan, "We quite dismiss the notion of a dollar-for-dollar return on our taxes. We are, after all, one nation. But we must not allow ourselves to be beggared by a federal government that does not know or does not care." According to the Senator's calculations, New York State paid $7 billion more into the federal government than it received back in outlays in fiscal 1982. The Government Research Corporation—an unbiased arbiter—estimated that the net outflow of funds from the Northeast and the Midwest totaled nearly $35 billion in fiscal 1979. For every dollar paid in federal taxes, the Midwest received only eighty cents; in contrast, the South earned a return of $1.22 on each dollar paid into the federal government.

Why is imbalance in the flow of federal funds a "bad" thing? For years, liberal congressmen of the North voted for programs that redistributed wealth from the rich to the poor. As it happened, more poor people lived in the South. What changed, I believe, is this: As economic conditions deteriorated in the North, northerners became more concerned about the effects of federal taxing and spending on their own well-being. Mayor Koch publicly atoned for his earlier congressional sins. "Mea culpa," he said. "I didn't realize what we were doing." As a congressman, he had joined with other liberals in voting his conscience for social programs, such as special education for the mentally retarded, without realizing how much it would cost in state and local taxes to meet federal mandates that were further compounded by the courts. Not only were we saddled with mandated costs, we also discovered a new truth—the urban North is *not* rich! True, per capita income, which forms the basis for many federal aid formulas, continues to be lower in the South than it is in the North, but if you account for differences in living costs, the tables are turned—and the North is poorer than the South, by nearly $1,000 per person. (The exact figure depends on what numbers you plug into the equation.) In this instance, as in many areas of social science, you can find statistics to make your case.

With a growing awareness of the shift in economic fortunes, northerners began to look at both the taxing and the spending sides of the federal ledger with an eye to their regional self-interest. Progressive taxation is a "good thing"; but wait a minute—northerners, with their high dollar incomes, pay a larger share of the tax burden than warranted by their higher cost of living. Investment tax credits and accelerated depreciation are supposed to act as incentives in our national interest to renew our capital stock; but their effect on the economy is to stimulate investment in the growth areas of the South and West, thus speeding up obsolescence of older industrial plants in the North. Few argue seriously that national goals should be subordinated to regional considerations, but the net result is that per capita taxes were higher in the North than in the South during a period when the economics of the North was lagging.

On the spending side, defense dollars are the big bucks

for which regions actively compete. There's no question that defense expenditures are weighted toward the South and the West, and, as the Northeast-Midwest Institute suggests, "the Pentagon tilt" is increasing. In 1981, three-fifths of all military prime contracts were awarded to companies headquartered in the South and the West. Undoubtedly, production is even more concentrated. Companies headquartered in New York received $1.5 billion in prime contracts, but that figure greatly exaggerates the amount of physical production in the City. Prime contractors will be headquartered on Park Avenue, but their defense widgets will be manufactured in factories all over the country. The South and the West garner three out of every four dollars spent on military payrolls and installations. But is warm climate the whole story? Sometimes I think our defense strategists are convinced that the Soviet Union is no longer a military threat, and that's why we don't place training facilities north of the Mason-Dixon line.

Shortly after I left city government, I was invited on the Twenty-first Air Force Base Civic Leader Tour. Major General Tom Sandler, commander of McGuire Air Force Base, in New Jersey, led a small group on a three-day whirlwind tour of facilities in Georgia, Florida, and Texas. I wasn't surprised to see that training facilities for new recruits and for fighter pilots are located in the South. I'm objective enough to realize that weather is an advantage of the South (even though we were almost hemmed in by a late spring snowstorm in Atlanta, and near-hurricane winds prevented a demonstration of the F-16 at MacDill AFB in Tampa). But I found it hard to believe that the U.S. Readiness Command and the U.S. Central Command, with their staff complements of 1,500 people, had to be headquartered in Florida because of weather considerations. These are essentially office facilities for logistics planning, and are not operating units. They are at the Florida site, I am convinced, because officers prefer warm climates and local government politicians did a good job of lobbying in Washington.

Given the Pentagon tilt in defense spending, it can be easy to put all of the blame for the regional problems of the 1970s on the back of the federal government. I think that would be a great oversimplification of a far more complex picture. First, the South and the West started pulling away from the northeastern quadrant at a time when defense spending was being scaled back. Defense outlays (after adjusting for inflation) reached a peak in 1968 and then declined until the end of the 1970s. During those years, federal outlays for retirement and social welfare programs more than tripled. The Midwest ended up with the short end of the stick. This older, industrial region received a shrinking share of a dwindling defense business *and* a relatively small allocation of the retirement and social welfare pie. At the same time, with its high wage structure in heavy manufacturing, the region continued to be burdened with high tax payments to the federal government. The net result was that the "balance of payments" of the Midwest deteriorated during the 1970s. The Northeast, with its large elderly population and its extensive network of social welfare programs, benefited in strict dollar flows from the federal spending shift. And that is the rub! More federal money flowed into the region. But welfare and retirement payments do not go directly into jobs the way highway, research, and defense money does. Rather, these monies represent transfers of income from one set of consumers to another. In the case of welfare and medical assistance, the inflow of federal funds carries with it a mandate for fifty-fifty matching from state and local taxes (compared with the seventy-five–twenty-five formula that applies to the "poorer" South). In other words, regional economies are affected not just by how much money flows to them, but also by what kind of money it is and what strings are attached.

When I put together the pieces of the puzzle, this picture of the 1970s emerges: Economic shocks converged with demographic and social trends to sharply alter regional relationships. Federal policies reinforced these trends, but these policies were not the sole culprit. Is the regional split going to widen? Is the momentum of southern and western growth so strong that northern interests should reconcile themselves to unrelenting lags? I see signs that the patterns of the 1980s will not be a carbon copy of those of the 1970s. Experience during the 1980–82 recession shows the folly of simply extrapolating from the recent past. Not surprisingly, the Midwest, with its automobile- and heavy-machinery-based economy, suffered severely. Yet, surprisingly, the Northeast held up well. New York State rode the crest of an economic revival that started in the business services complex and in the tourist attractions of New York City. The upturn looked so powerful that some of us raised the tantalizing prospect that New York had become "recession-proof," as *The New York Times* stated in a headline (slightly misreading a report I had written). This was not quite the case, but the momentum in its service economy did protect New York from the worst shocks of the 1980–82 recession. When overall U.S. unemployment soared to 10 percent, unemployment peaked at only 6.5 percent in Massachusetts, with its research and high technology base, and at less than 7 percent in Connecticut, with its defense contractors (the state ranks number one among the fifty states in military contracts per capita) and with its burgeoning new office facilities.

This time the Sunbelt did not escape unscathed. Earlier migration from the North shifted unemployment to the South and West. Unemployment reached 10 percent in Arizona and 11 percent in California. Houston had its "tent city," where unemployed migrants from the North congregated during the dismal 1982–83 winter. Energy production and exploration were curtailed. Demand for energy was so weak that inventories accumulated and petroleum prices fell. Texas banks reeled under the pressure of unprecedented loan losses. Tourism declined, and innkeepers in Aspen searched in vain for skiers in the winter of 1982–83. Layoffs came, for the first time, to companies in the electronics industry, with Atari video games lining storekeepers' shelves. And, in a stunning surprise to those who put their hopes for regional recovery on high technology, Atari announced in early 1983 that it would reduce the number of employees by 2,300 in California and start production in Taiwan. Even the new California growth wonder, biogenetics, experienced a shake-out when high interest rates put a crimp in capital financing.

The experiences of the early 1980s suggest that regional patterns are not fixed for all time. Perhaps just as significant, a broad picture of regional growth obscures the sharp contrasts that lie beneath the surface. If you look at subdivisions within the broad regions, you will find that some areas have developed specialized strengths, enabling them to buck overall regional trends, while others are experiencing a continuing decline. The resilience of the Northeast signals that its economy has made adjustments to the losses of the 1970s. Uncompetitive factories shut down for good. Wage rates lagged behind gains in growth regions so that costs became more competitive. New functions replaced the old. New York developed its specialization as an international center. Massachusetts revived after a lengthy incubation period of its high technology industries. Growth industries spilling over from Massachusetts discovered a tax haven in bordering New Hampshire. Eastern outdoors-lovers found paradise in Vermont, transforming abandoned dairy farms into stylish resort condominiums.

Do these newfound strengths mean that the regional troubles of the northeastern quadrant are over? Certainly not. The recovery in some areas is fragilely based and vulnerable to future shocks. And areas with revived economies abut on states with persistent weaknesses. The industrial belt of the Midwest—financier Muriel Siebert calls it the "Rustbelt"—will revive on a sustained basis only if the area becomes technologically competitive in *world* markets. Excess labor and outdated plants are drags. They can be turned into economic advantages, but if history is a guide, the process takes years. New England faces the question of whether its high technology industry is "maturing." As high technology firms along Massachusetts's Route 128 advance from a mode of experimentation and innovation to mass production, I am told, they spin off their expanded activities to new facilities in the South and the West, where space, labor, and tax costs are lower. The job-creating potential of established high technology centers is in danger of running its course—unless new forms of innovation enter the picture.

New York State is an economic conglomerate, in effect a holding company for subdivisions with greatly differing characteristics. The western portion of the state is closely linked to the Midwest's heavy industry and faces similar difficulties in revitalizing its plants and retraining a skilled labor force. Downstate is dominated by New York City's economy, where the strengths of its service economy could be undermined if support services, which are becoming increasingly footloose, locate in other, less-expensive, less-congested parts of the country that are linked to New York by computer and telecommunications technology. The banker can sit in his Wall Street office, mesmerized by his dramatic view of New York harbor, while loans are booked in Delaware's tax shelter and credit cards are processed in South Dakota. And much of the older northeastern quadrant must contend with social and economic costs rising from concentrations of the urban poor and a battle to maintain the crumbling infrastructure.

It is wishful thinking for a confirmed New Yorker like me to assume that the draws of the South and the West are going to fade away. The Sunbelt is favored by a base of industries slated for above-average growth. Unless we experience an extraordinary change in social values, the attractions of climate and life-style will continue to exert a powerful pull to the South and the West. More metropolitan areas are developing sufficient concentrations of wealth to support the diverse educational and leisure activities that a skilled labor force demands. Although New York's position as number one in the arts and entertainment is secure, Los Angeles, Dallas, and Atlanta will all provide competition in future years.

Why, then, do I think that regional growth differentials

will narrow during the 1980s? Essentially because economics and demographics point in that direction. Clerical wage rates in New York and Houston are nearly identical. Unionization won't become widespread in the South, but unions will make inroads in the Sunbelt, and unions in the North, through enlightened self-interest, will become more flexible in their wage and working condition demands than they were in the past. Energy cost differentials will be reduced (as natural gas prices rise relative to the cost of petroleum). The state-local tax gap will shrink. Fiscal pressures are growing under the strain of providing services and meeting infrastructure needs of an expanding population. Pollution plagues Denver, and California's population flows into the desert, away from the overdeveloped coast. Western water supplies are unpredictable and sometimes inadequate. As Mario Cuomo, New York's Governor, is fond of saying, "If we are just smart enough to keep our ample water supply clean, they'll soon be knocking on our doors for a cup of water." I don't expect full parity in all costs. But complete cost convergence is not required to reduce differentials in regional growth.

Demographics is also pointing to a slower migratory flow. The elderly population is not increasing as rapidly as it did in the 1970s. It's my guess that retirees will not flock in the same droves to the South and the West as they did in the 1970s. We are no longer in the era of largesse in raising Social Security benefits, and (I may be way off the mark on this one) I sense a greater willingness for mature communities to encourage housing for the elderly, in part as a way to *avoid* providing multifamily housing for the poor. Labor force expansion will moderate as the "baby boom" approaches middle age, and new, young workers shrink in number. As a result, we should be successful in reducing the national unemployment rate, and the pressure to migrate in search of jobs will be less than it was in the 1970s.

What about the federal government? Will federal policies operate to mute or to exaggerate regional disparities? On the taxing side of the ledger, the federal tax burden per capita in the northeastern quadrant will approach parity with that of the nation as a whole. Slower economic growth, reductions in the progressiveness of the income tax, and recently enacted tax incentives that encourage rehabilitation rather than investment only in new facilities all point in that direction. On the spending side, the South and the West will be favored, compared to the Northeast and Midwest, *if* policies of the early 1980s to increase defense rather than social programs continue. But pressures to distribute defense dollars more evenly will be great. If I am correct in my conviction that allocations are influenced by political leverage and personal preferences, then good lobbyists should be able to alter the balance. I do not believe that the federal government should place regional considerations at the top of its list of national priorities, and I do not believe that it will. But when federal policies negatively affect specific regions—whether through design or as an unintended byproduct then regional representatives are entitled to try to soften the blow or amend the policies. After the painful experiences of the 1970s and early 1980s, I'm convinced that congressmen of the North will become more skilled practitioners of the art of representing parochial interests. The danger is that competing jurisdictions within broad regions will engage in a form of internecine warfare as they fall all over each other in protecting their own specialized interests.

A strong national economy is the most powerful weapon for more nearly equalizing regional growth. I don't pretend to be able to read economic tea leaves with accuracy, but I do think the odds are reasonably good that our economy will perform better in the balance of the 1980s than it did in the 1970s. When I look at all the evidence, I come back to the conclusion that I reached some years ago. The South and the West will expand more rapidly than the northeastern quadrant, but differences in regional growth rates will narrow during the 1980s. There is a new wrinkle that I did not anticipate before. We are a large, diverse nation. Differences within the artificially defined megaregions will be the thing to watch in the 1980s as older, lagging economies develop new growth specialties and some of the recent leaders encounter obstacles to rapid expansion. Is the war between the North and the South (perhaps we should say the Southwest) finally over? Not quite, but the war will peter away, to be replaced by skirmishes within broad regional boundaries.

4

Is Gentrification Saving Cities?

- Median household income, city of Boston: $12,500; Boston suburbs: $20,469—1980 Census.
- Harlem residents protest sale by lottery of city-owned housing—1981.
- $3-million food emporium opened on Manhattan's West Side—1982.

"Gentrification" is a term I hear with increasing frequency. Depending on your viewpoint, gentrification is either saving cities or it is destroying them. The word "gentrification" isn't in my American Heritage Dictionary. The closest word to it is "gentry," defined as people of gentle birth, good breeding, high social position. That doesn't tell much about what is happening in parts of urban America. Barnhart's Dictionary of New English does include a definition of gentrification. To gentrify is to convert a poor or working-class property area to one that is more expensive or exclusive, especially to raise property values. It's not exactly my definition—the word "exclusive" does not characterize the neighborhoods I've seen gentrified. Webster's Ninth defines gentrification as "the immigration of middle-class people into a deteriorating or recently renewed city area." That's closer to giving a sense of what is going on in some sections of some cities in the United States.

I know gentrification from first-hand experience. I watched my West Side Manhattan neighborhood go downhill in the 1950s and 1960s and I saw it revive in the 1970s and 1980s. As Deputy Mayor, I learned quickly how gentrification raises political passions at City Hall. I have no problem taking a position on a question such as, "Is gentrification 'good' for cities?" My answer is a clear-cut 'yes.' I find it more difficult to answer unequivocally, "Is gentrification saving cities?" Experience in the 1970s suggests that gentrification was too limited in scope to have had a measurable influence on longer-term trends. Population continued to decline in cities; upper-income households, on balance, still left; the disparities in income between cities and their suburbs have widened; and per capita income in major cities such as Boston, Philadelphia, and New York is less than the national average. Gentrification has revived neighborhoods, but it did not pull whole cities up with it. And there is a sense that gentrification is sharpening polarization between a new "elite" of professionals who service the city's white-collar functions and the poor (mostly black and Hispanic) who are displaced.

My interpretation of the evidence is more positive. Yes, gentrification is limited, and there is no sign of a wholesale return to cities. Still, by the early 1980s population in a few older cities appeared to have turned up. Yes, gentrification raises issues of displacement. But without the creation of new, middle-class residential and commercial neighborhoods, cities would be worse off than they are today, and their outlook would be bleaker. Gentrification won't save cities, but those cities that provide options for "quality" living environments improve their chances for attracting the educated labor force that is essential to their economic survival.

Gentrification did not suddenly burst upon the scene. The Georgetown district of Washington, D.C., became fashionable years ago. SoHo (the loft area in New York City, south of Greenwich Village) was discovered by artists in the late 1960s. Society Hill has long been changing the face of historic Philadelphia. The first participants in such ventures were true pioneers. Young, middle-class, but not particularly wealthy, they sought inexpensive housing and renovated it largely with their own "sweat labor." Dinner was an adventure with friends who had bought a home in the late 1960s in the Park Slope area of Brooklyn. We ate by candlelight (the dining room had not been rewired even though our friends had moved in three years earlier); the pegged wooden floors were half-sanded, and the ceiling plaster not yet repaired. In time, the homes were renovated for comfortable living, and families became part of their neighborhoods, sharing pioneer experiences in self-help.

Today, gentrification is an industry. Construction companies specialize in historic restoration; real estate lawyers are experts in tax benefits and other forms of government assistance; unemployed architects are finding outlets for their talents. Associations are formed to protect the interests of their neighborhoods. What started unnoticed twenty-five years ago is today the subject of heated conflict, whether it is the proposed sale of abandoned brownstones in Harlem to middle-class, rather than to poor, blacks, or the conversion of factory space in Brooklyn to residential condominiums.

Gentrification takes many forms. It is not all exposed brick walls and hanging fern plants. The path that gentrification takes has much to do with whether it is attacked or welcomed. Turning factories into apartments sets up a different chain of economic events than does renovating existing housing for higher-income tenants. Putting abandoned buildings to economic use produces different reactions than does upgrading occupied buildings. When commercial revitalization provides neighborhood retail services, it is greeted differently from redevelopment that attracts outsiders to a neighborhood. Whether it is a large-scale commercial project such as Quincy Market, in Boston, or the result of individual entrepreneurial decisions on Manhattan's Columbus Avenue, gentrification that brings outside dollars to the local economy is an export industry creating new wealth, but that kind of gentrification displaces neighborhood services.

Gentrification causes little controversy when abandoned warehouses or unused factories are put to new uses. It's happened in New England towns, in Hoboken, New Jersey, and in Columbus, Ohio. There are no families to relocate and no local jobs are destroyed. At first blush, it all looks like an economic plus. But when there is competition for the space, then the story is different. New York City's SoHo tells something about how attitudes change when markets become stronger. The section of Manhattan south of Houston Street is made up largely of industrial loft buildings. Crowded, with little natural light reaching to street level, SoHo's chief architectural interest was its cast-iron buildings, which were a technological advance of the mid-nineteenth century, permitting prefabrication of columns, moldings, and even whole facades. Robert Moses tried to build the Lower Manhattan Expressway through SoHo to connect the East and West sides of Manhattan. The plan was defeated in the mid-1960s, and soon afterward SoHo was discovered by artists. Large floor area, high ceilings, and inexpensive space rather than design purity were the chief attractions.

The Lindsay administration encouraged reuse of these buildings by artists, for the lofts were rapidly being abandoned by manufacturers who could no longer operate profitably in the eighty- to one-hundred-year-old six-story buildings. Although not zoned for residential occupancy, SoHo was designated a special district for artists in residence. There were inconveniences in the lofts: Freight elevators were manually operated, so it took ingenuity to transport guests to your top-floor loft when the elevator operator left after the factory workday was over; lofts were not equipped with bathrooms, kitchens, or adequate wiring; and tenants had to install and pay for improvements themselves. Exposed pipes and freestanding columns were praised as design assets once the media began to publicize the artists' open-space renovation. Soon galleries, restaurants, and small shops were attracting tourists (and dollars) from uptown. So far, so good—imaginative public policy combined with a newfound market to add economic value to a neighborhood.

Then competition for the space built up. The middle class followed the avant garde. Accountants and advertising executives could not prove they were artists in residence. They simply moved into industrial lofts illegally. Landlords were happy to look the other way, for the space was either empty or, if occupied, earned rents of less than $2 a square foot, compared with the $10–$15 a square foot that residential tenants would pay. Distressed by the growing presence of illegal tenants, but encouraged by a demand for space that appeared, otherwise, to be slated for abandonment, the City administration added a new conversion carrot. Liberal real estate tax benefits were extended to permit residential conversion of industrial and commercial buildings. Until 1975, tax benefits under the J-51 program had been limited to renovations in existing residential buildings. With the blessings of local government, residential conversions of industrial lofts spread north to 34th Street and south of SoHo, to the southern tip of Manhattan.

I knew residential conversion was no longer the domain of artists and pioneering young couples when I overheard two impeccably tailored young men talking earnestly as they walked down Fifth Avenue. "I just made a killing on Wall Street," said one. Eager to benefit from a tip, I listened closely. "On a J-51," the well-groomed gentleman added, and then, with his companion, turned into Tiffany's. What the young man meant was that he had just invested in the residential conversion of a commercial building located in the Wall Street area. Tax shelters, real estate tax exemptions, an expanding market—conversion had become both big time and respectable. And along with the coming of respectability, conflicts arose as competition for space intensified. Illegal residential tenants, in true New York City fashion, sought protection for their property rights. They felt threatened by landlords who could dispossess them in favor of tenants who could pay higher rents and who would retain possession of improvements that the original tenants had made. After lengthy, acrimonious debate, compromise state legislation was passed in 1982, legalizing the status of illegal residential tenants on certain conditions.

Meanwhile, manufacturing firms occupying loft space began to compete for the same turf. Industrial tenants who had survived the economic shocks of the early 1970s wanted to stay where they were, paying below-market rents. The City was faced with a public policy dilemma. Should the City try to save manufacturing jobs (largely in the apparel and printing trades) or should it encourage conversion of property to residential uses that would bolster the City's service-based economy? Political pressure to save blue-collar jobs was great. One of the early mandates was to devise a tax incentive program for industrial renovation that would be as attractive as the J-51 program. There was no way this could be done. My advice (I was on loan to the City as an unpaid advisor at the time) was "Don't try." I felt the approach should be to reduce (or eliminate) residential conversion benefits and provide for relocation payments by developers to displaced industrial tenants who moved to other parts of the City. Eventually, this approach was adopted, along with a complex set of zoning changes that attempted to preserve some areas exclusively for manufacturing and to allow for the "orderly" conversion of others. The specific details were not as I would have designed them (government was trying to be far too precise in determining what should be where), but the approach was not unreasonable. Change was going to be "guided," not halted.

However, the machinery of government is cumbersome. By the time the new policy became effective, the forces shaping gentrification were changing. We had assumed that manufacturers displaced from Manhattan could relocate to empty industrial space in the Bronx, Brooklyn, or Queens. But by 1982 (when the program started), much of the desirable outer borough space, particularly in buildings on the waterfront, was being eyed by developers for residential or commercial conversion. Industrial tenants were often not welcome. Meanwhile, the economic permutations developed a new twist in Manhattan. Public relations firms, architects, and publishers who felt priced out of mid-Manhattan by escalating office rents "discovered" the lofts below 34th Street. Geer, Dubois, an advertising firm, took a full-page advertisement in *The New York Times* in November 1981 announcing its move from midtown Manhattan to Fifth Avenue and 17th Street, an unfamiliar outpost that advertising people equated with Siberia. The ad was written as a memorandum to "Fellow Movers and Shakers." The memorandum, "Kicking Midtown Cold Turkey," informally described the new location's virtues—a mixed-use residential, commercial, and manufacturing district with handsome architecture from the "Gilded Age" and old-time landmarks such as Paragon's for sporting goods, Barnes and Noble for books, and McSorley's Old Ale House as a possible "successor to the agency watering hole." (The advertisement did more for the image of the City than all the speeches I could give as Deputy Mayor.) The move by Geer, Dubois did not entail any intervention by the City. Under New York City's zoning laws, no special permits are required for commercial conversion and no relocation payments are due if manufacturers are displaced. But as commercial firms renovated space once occupied by manufacturing, commercial conversion began to be viewed as another form of gentrification, threatening, rather than improving, an existing neighborhood.

The political confrontations faced in SoHo and in nearby manufacturing districts built up gradually. In the early stages of gentrification, space was being abandoned by businesses in neighborhoods where people did not live. Conflicts become sharply defined when residential tenants

or existing jobs are involved. The celebrated Boston downtown revival went through a series of drawn-out conflicts.
As a naive but adventurous Radcliffe senior, I ventured to
Scollay Square in the spring of 1953 to visit the Old Howard, Boston's renowned burlesque house, which was about
to be shut down in the first stage of an urban renewal
project. Many years later, the Government Center was
finally built, and the new City Hall was opened in 1969.
The residential redevelopment, planned in the classic urban
renewal style of high-rise, upper-income apartments, was
stopped in its tracks. One high-rise apartment building
stands as a monument. Gentrification came in the late 1970s
to the waterfront in another form. The Rouse Company
transformed the Quincy Market into a commercial shopping
complex that opened in 1977. The complex draws thousands
of visitors each day from outside the area. Private companies built office towers in the nearby business district.
And demand mushroomed for close-by living and working
space for white-collar workers. Abandoned warehouses on
the piers, which had been acquired years earlier through
urban renewal powers, were sold to private developers for
conversion into professional upper-income offices and residential condominiums. Redevelopment moved inland from
the waterfront, and older residential properties became
targets for renovation. A sort of "no-man's-land," an un-
official "demilitarized zone," demarcates the area. On one
side, abutting on the waterfront, gentrification continues
unimpeded. On the other side, spilling into the Italian blue-
collar North End, opposition is strong. Potential upscale
buyers take the signal and stay clear—at least for the time
being.

In upper Manhattan, Harlem, too, presents an intricate

web of community conflicts. New York City owns about 40 percent of the buildings and empty land in Harlem because of nonpayment of taxes. Who would think gentrification would be an issue in a neighborhood where hundreds of abandoned buildings have either been sealed off to prevent entry or have been demolished, leaving blocks of rubble? But Harlem has many of the qualities that make an area a potential neighborhood for gentrification. Once sought after by the middle class (my father lived there in a family-owned brownstone house, with Richard Rodgers and Oscar Hammerstein as neighbors), Harlem is well located, north of Central Park, with broad boulevards. Its many brownstones that are still standing are assets. However, Harlem is torn by conflicts in development goals: between poor blacks and middle-class blacks now living in Harlem; between middle-class blacks living in the community and those who want to move in from outside; and between blacks and whites who are "rediscovering" the advantages of Harlem, with the unspoken objective (according to some Harlem spokesmen) of driving out blacks.

The City decided to offer brownstones that it owned for sale through a lottery. The conditions of sale were designed to ensure that the property would be bought by potential homeowners, not by speculators who would renovate the buildings and then quickly resell them at a profit. Community furor erupted: Outsiders would enter the lottery and take over Harlem. The Mayor indignantly responded that no one, rich or poor, had a God-given right to a particular neighborhood. The City would not discriminate between insiders and outsiders, between whites and blacks. The lottery, with its fixed terms of sale, was fair. Political pressures were great; the Mayor eventually modified his position to weight the lottery so that a Harlem resident would have a fifty-fifty chance of winning. In early 1982, after three years of controversy, the city sold twelve Harlem houses by lottery. Five of the twelve winners were Harlem residents. A difficult issue was addressed in a pragmatic way—a resident does not have an *inalienable* right to his neighborhood, but he does have legitimate concerns about its future.

The Chelsea district of Manhattan offers another variation on the theme of conflict. Chelsea, once a solid blue-collar neighborhood in the West Twenties, deteriorated during the 1960s and early 1970s. A good part of the housing stock—row houses built more than one hundred years ago—is essentially sound. Many of the buildings, although still tenanted, were taken over by the City for nonpayment of taxes. The Koch administration decided to resell housing to tenants who already lived in Chelsea. The City established a low sales price, $250 a unit. But the City acts with "deliberation." Between the time the policy was enunciated and the time the City was ready to sell, gentrification had made its presence felt, and the market value of the housing was clearly higher than $250 a unit. The City wanted to raise the selling price to reflect the new market conditions. All hell broke loose! Breaking a commitment! Selling out to the rich! Political alliances were forged. A compromise was struck. The Mayor agreed to retain the original $250 selling price to the tenants. But, if properties are resold, the City retains 40 percent of the profits. No one was entirely pleased with the outcome. There were those who felt betrayed—housing in the neighborhood should forever be retained for lower-income groups. And there were those who felt that the City had missed an opportunity to cash in on financial windfalls. If the City had sold the housing at market value, it would have acquired millions of dollars that could have gone to upgrade other residential property.

I think of the West Side of Manhattan, where my husband and I have lived since we married, as a laboratory for examining the dynamics of gentrification. The West Side is a neighborhood that went downhill and came back within twenty-five years, a short span of time in the swings of urban change. The area lies between the Lincoln Center cultural complex on the south and the residential West Side Urban Renewal Area, which stretches from 87th to 96th streets on the north, two urban renewal projects conceived in the 1950s. For years, our neighborhood was the dumping ground for low-income residents evicted from the bordering urban renewal areas. The "losers" settled into the SROs (single-room-occupancy rooming houses) and welfare hotels that lay between 72nd and 86th streets. Drugs, crime, deteriorated housing—all the urban ills descended upon the neighborhood. I heard Louis Lefkowitz, when he was running for Attorney General of New York State in the early 1960s, declare 84th Street (my street) the worst block in the City. (Many other streets have won that designation since then.) Some hardy souls bought brownstones in the late 1960s and renovated them for family use. A few entrepreneurs leapfrogged ten or fifteen blocks north of Lincoln Center and opened small restaurants. I sensed a turnaround was in the offing. My husband and I talked of assembling a site for a new apartment building. Like a lot of talkers, we never did anything. If we had, we would have been too early. It took more than a decade before the upturn gained enough momentum to support new multi-family construction.

Gentrification came to the neighborhood in the second half of the 1970s. And when it came, it moved on two fronts: with the upgrading of existing housing, and with the commercial development of Columbus Avenue. Columbus Avenue was a dreary commercial street that had never been fashionable. Darkened by the Ninth Avenue elevated railway until World War II, the tenements were home to working-class families living above the Irish bars and Italian grocery stores.

The West Side's version of gentrification differed from earlier approaches. Housing renovation entailed neither the bold interior design concepts that transformed the lofts of SoHo nor the carefully controlled architectural standards that restored Society Hill, in Philadelphia, to a modern version of eighteenth-century America. Rather, what happened on the West Side was a real estate market response to a perceived demand. As the City's economy began to revive in the late 1970s, employment opportunities expanded for young professionals working in finance, business services, and the arts. But suitable housing was scarce for singles and two-career couples. Home-ownership costs were escalating in the suburbs under the twin pressures of inflation and high interest rates. The benefits of suburban housing were not worth the costs for many childless, working couples. The conventional neighborhoods on the East Side were saturated. The time was ripe for development to spill over to the West Side, where mass transit, although far from great, was better than the legendary East Side "Lex." Property values were still deeply depressed from the earlier downgrading of the neighborhood, so there were bargains to be had. Developers stepped in, renovating buildings one by one, creating small rental and condominium units with the financial incentive of liberal tax benefits. Few design awards were won. I concluded that eating out turned into a growth industry, in part because the remodeled apartments are so small. Like their counterparts in Rome and Paris, young people escape their cramped apartments to spend their free time in cafés and restaurants.

The displaced poor left quietly in the early years of the process. Unlike the poor who organize to protect their interests when they see a specific project (usually sponsored by or requiring government approval) about to change their neighborhood, the welfare hotel and rooming house residents simply moved on. They had moved before and they moved again. One hundred percent turnover rates in classes of our neighborhood public school (which consistently ranked among the lowest in reading scores in the City) symbolized the mobility that was typical of the area *before* gentrification arrived.

By the 1980s, West Siders began to question where gentrification was taking the neighborhood. As the last SROs became targets for conversion, the same liberals who wanted to close SROs a few years earlier (the residents, former mental patients, or alcoholics, or drug addicts, were perceived as threats to the neighborhood) now wanted them protected. For, with the elimination of so many SROs as housing for the poor, these residents had no place to go except the streets. The City was being called upon to provide facilities for the homeless at a taxpayer cost of millions of dollars a year, at the same time that it was encouraging conversion and elimination of their housing through generous real estate tax benefits. In 1983, the rehabilitation tax program was finally revised after a long and bitter fight. Tax exemptions are no longer permitted for conversion of

SROs. Benefits were scaled down for residential rehabilitation aimed at upper-income markets and are completely
eliminated when assessed values in newly renovated units
increase by more than $40,000. Developers complained that
the limitations would inhibit renovation without curing the
housing problems of the homeless. Others complained that
the legislation introduced a new set of complex regulations
in what had previously been a smoothly working "as-of-
right" program. In my view, it was surely time to let the
market take care of demand for housing without the wind-
fall of tax relief in a neighborhood where the momentum
for development was so strong.

Commercial redevelopment sparked additional conflicts.
At first, commercial redevelopment was welcomed. Empty
stores on Columbus Avenue were filled for the first time in
years. The neighborhood felt safer with more people on the
streets. In the 1960s, my husband and I would carefully
plot an expedition to the movies, deciding what streets we
could safely walk on after dark. A four-block walk could
easily double in length once we mapped out a safe route.
Now people in the neighborhood are on the streets at all
hours of the day and night. Restaurants of every ethnic
persuasion, bookstores, antiques stores, and clothing shops
have flocked to the neighborhood. The ultimate in conspic-
uous consumption arrived in 1982, with the DDL Foodshow, a $3-million investment by Dino DeLaurentiis, the
Italian movie producer. A food emporium located in a
former welfare hotel, the DDL Foodshow transformed quick-
service take-out food into high-priced culinary creations.
Crowds come from all over to look and to be looked at. In
the "good old days," middle-class Jewish families drove in
from the Long Island suburbs on Sunday to buy lox and

bagels on the Lower East Side, and Italian families made the trip from the northern New Jersey suburbs to Little Italy, in lower Manhattan, to stock up on pasta, wine, and cheese. In 1983, Italian film stars were jetting from the Via Veneto, in Rome, to the West Side's Columbus Avenue. The neighborhood had turned into a tourist attraction. It was producing for New York what we economists call "export" dollars. Although DDL misgauged its market and "temporarily closed" in spring 1984, it had made its mark on the neighborhood.

But commercial revitalization on Columbus Avenue was also producing local conflict. The barber, the cleaner, and the druggist were disappearing, and outsiders not serving the neighborhood were taking their place. The cry went out: Save small business! Enact commercial rent control! We were able to convince the Mayor, a strong advocate of residential rent control, that commercial rent control was not in the City's interest. The media knew a story when they saw one and were harder to educate. An investigative reporter for a local TV news program would thrust a microphone in my face. "Mr. Smith has been at this location repairing shoes for forty years. The landlord is tripling his rent. What is the City going to do?" My answer, in one word, was "Nothing!" We had a difficult time explaining that most landlords are not big-time real estate operators but are themselves small business owners who had contended for years with vacancies and low rents in their buildings; that, with a few exceptions, the new tenants are small businesses and not big corporate conglomerates. We would help the old shopkeeper to find a new location, but commercial rent controls would be counterproductive.

As it happens, some neighborhood services disappeared;

others stayed. McGlade's, an old-time Irish bar, shut its gates
for good. As its neighbor, Zingone, the Italian greengrocer,
said, "I'll do the same when my lease is up. Why break my
back working for a landlord?" The shoemaker in my neighborhood moved off the avenue to a larger store on a side
street; the Polish immigrant cleaner retired and was replaced by a young Chinese. And the owner of Powers, a
fish store that had been in business for 100 years, agreed
to the tripling of the rent and passed the added costs on to
me, the consumer. She did not do her arithmetic properly—
about a year later, the fish store closed. Dislocation like this
is not new. Dugan's cupcakes were delivered to the back
door of my house when I was a little girl. I went to Saturday
afternoon movies and sat through a double feature, news-
reel, cartoon, serial, and coming attractions. Bottled milk
and diapers were delivered to the apartment when my children were little. These services have all but disappeared,
to the regret of those who enjoyed them and those who
profited from them. What we are seeing with commercial
redevelopment is another version of economic innovation
and change. And there is nothing permanent about the
process. When social habits change and eating out goes out
of fashion, the whole thing could collapse. And a new cycle
of change will commence!

Meanwhile, the big-time operators finally discovered the
West Side in the early 1980s. Developers assembled large
sites, and for the first time in forty years, construction
cranes for building high-rise apartments dotted the scene.
A 35-story luxury apartment tower rose on the site overlooking the Planetarium. This was the site that my husband
and I had daydreamed about ten years earlier. New construction altered the physical character of the neighborhood

as high-rise towers replaced brownstone houses and six-floor walk-ups. New construction also carried the potential for significantly increasing the population of the West Side. Gentrification reduced population density in its earlier stages as childless households displaced large low-income families. (Population on the West Side dropped from 300,000 in 1950 to 200,000 in 1980.) Gentrification in its latest stage could, according to City planners, increase population by 17 percent to 30 percent if development proceeds to the fullest extent permitted under existing zoning laws. Added population from the college-educated, affluent social strata produces new demands for municipal services. Whereas the poor utilized social services (welfare, medical assistance, bilingual education), the new high-income residents demand improvements in the quality of life—they want clean streets, functioning subways, security from crime, and good schools. The City, recognizing conflicts arising from changes in land use, unveiled a proposal in late 1983 that attempts to balance development pressures for new construction against neighborhood concerns for limiting change. The planners' proposal reduces allowable density in new construction and establishes design guidelines to "maintain the character" of the neighborhood. Initial reaction to the proposal was "cautiously positive," but if I know the West Side, with its cadre of informed activists, debate on community development will not end with passage of the zoning amendments in spring 1984.

It is important to see what we have learned about the process I've described in New York City, for it is being repeated in many variations in cities and towns across the country. First, the scale of gentrification has not been large enough in many cities to reverse the trend of declining population. Middle-income families have not returned to the center city in overwhelming numbers. Those who do come back from the suburbs are older and wealthier and their children are grown up. They tend to move to established neighborhoods, where they can live in comfort and security. Those who move to the newly restored neighborhoods tend already to live in the City. Many of them are two-career, college-educated couples working for banks, law firms, and advertising agencies. But many are also aspiring actors or actresses waiting on tables. Some of them are young people who migrated from other parts of the country to the City for jobs and settled first in established neighborhoods before they ventured to less conventionally accepted areas. To conclude that much of gentrification has been moving the pieces around on the checkerboard is not to conclude that it has been without impact. For without these shifts, declines would undoubtedly have been deeper. Will the gains disappear when couples mature, have children, then move to the suburbs in search of good schools and larger living quarters? I can't give a definitive answer, but if family size stays small, with two children at the most, and women maintain their careers, then a sizable proportion (not all) will stay in their new urban environments. (I see the signs of this with the opening of children's clothing and toy stores in our neighborhood.)

Has government helped or hindered the process? In spite of the dislocation and the mistakes in policy, in SoHo the new diversity is an economic plus. Manufacturing firms are moving from Manhattan to the outer boroughs, even if not on the scale the City had hoped for. The relocating firms are generally either older companies that would otherwise have closed down for good, or expanding operations that would have moved across the Hudson River to New Jersey. For the other boroughs, relocation from Manhattan adds up to renovated factories and blue-collar jobs. On the Upper West Side of Manhattan, Columbus Avenue, with its restaurants, fashion clothing stores, and gourmet food shops, has brought in new dollars and taxes and jobs, some of which reach the poorer segments of the population. It is not just a reshuffling of consumer dollars that are already being spent in the City. But government cannot fine-tune its policies or forecast their consequences accurately. Government, even when its policies are well conceived, has great difficulty in implementing programs in a timely manner and in determining the appropriate level of involvement. Of course, Lincoln Center helped buttress revival on the West Side, but it also caused a spillover of deterioration that lasted for years before other forces ignited the latent redevelopment potential.

One thing that is clear to me is that a city should look carefully at the special incentives it provides to encourage development. Too often, they are kept long after they are no longer needed; too often, they produce results that were not anticipated. Another conclusion is that we do not pay enough attention to dealing with adjustments to displacement. The traditional development pattern has been for lower-income families to move into older housing in urban areas after upper-income families leave for more desirable locations. This is the "trickle down" theory of housing and it has worked relatively well in this country. But when gentrification occurs, the direction is reversed and wealth moves into low-income areas. The United Nations buildings were built on the former site of Manhattan's meat-slaughtering houses, and within a few years, the surrounding area had turned into an upper-income, residential neighborhood coupled with office and hotel facilities servicing the international community. Stuyvesant Town and Peter Cooper Village, middle-income housing developments, were built in the late 1940s in what used to be Manhattan's notorious "Gashouse Gang" district, an area of tenements near the East River. These neighborhood transformations are now part of the City's history. The object is not to prevent all change, but to ease the stresses of adjustment for families and businesses that stand in its path.

5

Graffiti: Art or Anarchy?

The advertising agency executives arrived in the Mayor's office with flip charts to demonstrate the public-service advertisements they had designed as the centerpiece for the City's campaign to fight graffiti. The first placard showed the phrase "If you deface public property, be prepared to face the consequences" superimposed on a photograph of a jail cell. The second stated boldly, "Graffiti has been tough on us. Now we're getting tough on graffiti." The president of the agency and his associates ran through the series of advertisements to a silent audience. When the presentation was complete, we awaited the Mayor's reaction. I had a sinking feeling that I knew what it was going to be. "Get tough on graffiti?" said the Mayor. "I can't put rapists and murderers in jail! Who'll believe we'll give jail sentences to graffiti offenders?" So the advertising executives went humbly back to their offices, did more "market research" on graffiti, and a few weeks later came back with the campaign we eventually used: "Make your mark in society, not on society!" Role models who had started in poverty and, in young city kids' eyes, achieved success—a disc jockey, a basketball player, a boxer—were featured in the ads.

Why, in the spring of 1982, was the City mounting another effort to control graffiti? There are plenty of people who say that graffiti are an art form. Well, the Mayor believed, and I strongly concur, that graffiti are more like anarchy than like art. Although derived from a term describing a form of fifteenth-century Italian decorative art, today's graffiti are scrawls on a publicly visible surface—and no more than that! Some of those who execute graffiti may be skilled practitioners, but they are no more artists than are those who crack safes or forge $100 bills. Graffiti is more than a "quality of life" offenses and mere irritant to the senses. Graffiti carry incalculable economic costs. The City of New York spends millions of dollars for the prevention and removal of graffiti. When I was Deputy Mayor, I learned that business people view graffiti as another symbol of the deteriorating urban environment—they provide one more excuse to pack up and leave New York.

Of course, graffiti have been around in many places for a long time—political slogans painted on walls all over Europe and Latin America; sexual obscenities scrawled in public bathrooms; the World War II GI's "Kilroy Was Here" tagged on roadside fences; fraternity pledges' markings on the least accessible, most highly visible rock outcrops. Once in a while, the jottings display more than a trace of humor. My favorite (known by anecdote, not by observation) is the message written on the lavatory door of the Harvard Club men's room in New York: "Judge Crater, please call your office." Judge Crater walked out of his office on August 6,

1930, and was never seen again. A more current message cries out for graffiti—"It's a blessing to be a virgin," reads the sign posted in dozens of New York City subway stations. The temptation to add a word or two is overpowering. Although the shortest and most direct addition is simply the word "not" in the appropriate place, the variety of scrawls that have been added is testament to the imagination of New Yorkers.

But graffiti, whether in New York City or on top of the Rocky Mountains, are not a laughing matter. They have become more widespread in recent years and, like many other forms of antisocial behavior that are blamed on the postwar baby boom, did not disappear when that mass of teenagers grew up. I stopped to make a telephone call at an outdoor booth in a rural Connecticut town and I couldn't miss the message on the wall: "Want a good ———? Call 356–0034." Defacing telephone booths has become so prevalent that Western Electric has developed a special paint remover to wipe out graffiti in Bell System telephone booths. Sacred American Indian paintings were scrawled over with graffiti at Hueco Tanks, a volcanic formation on the prairie near El Paso. Judge John H. Cole ordered five days in jail for seventy-two members of three Los Angeles street gangs unless they cleaned up graffiti from their neighborhood. Prodded by the Los Angeles District Attorney to find a legally valid reason for this sentence, the judge ruled that gangs are unincorporated associations and can be held collectively responsible for their members' graffiti. So the gang members went to work and cleaned up their own mess with supplies provided by the business community.

There's no doubt about it: Graffiti are found in a myriad of places. Few parts of the country are immune. But graffiti in New York City are executed on a scale that has no parallel. Clearly, New York offers extensive graffiti opportunities, with its 6,000 subway cars, 4,000 buses, 850,000 buildings, and 37,372 acres of parks. However, the City is number one in graffiti not just because of its size but because it allowed graffiti to go unchecked during the fiscal crisis years of the 1970s. Once out of control, graffiti can become an intractable problem—new graffiti spring up faster than old graffiti can be removed. On top of this, efforts to stem graffiti are frustrated by New York City's unique position as a center of communications and the arts. "Graffiti are art," say the art cognoscenti. And the word that those massive "throw-ups"—large-scale works covering the outsides of entire subway cars—are "art" is broadcast all over the world. Displayed at a gallery in SoHo, these canvasses sell for up to $1,000 each. They're prominently featured in Park Avenue offices and not quite so prominently painted on garages in suburban Great Neck, Long Island. Television cameras followed gallery owner Joyce Towbin out to Great Neck to see her "masterpiece." "Why," asked a reporter, "if your graffiti are a masterpiece, don't you mount them on the *front* of your house rather than in back, on your garage?" According to Ms. Towbin, her upper-income neighbors "aren't ready for this kind of art *yet*."

It turns out that the so-called artists who are lionized are not teenagers. They are men in their early twenties who have been producing graffiti for ten years or even longer. It's a way of life for them. They go out together in the evening with beer and stolen spray paint and ply their "trade." They serve as heroes to youngsters who start on the graffiti route before they have even reached their teens. "Toys," the beginners, tag the insides of subway trains. Subway markings start out as names and addresses and turn into illegible scrawls covering subway windows and maps. Subway riders can tell neither where they are nor where they are going. Then taggers move from the trains, leaving their marks on station walls, up the stairs and onto the streets, where the whole urban scene is a potential canvas. Mailboxes, park benches, statues, school walls, storefronts, highway overpasses, sidewalk underpasses—there's hardly a surface that's not a target. Is anything off limits? Definitely. I don't see graffiti on private cars or taxicabs. I see public buses with graffiti, but private buses, no. Trucks, once in a while, but rarely. Apartment buildings—it depends on the neighborhood. There seems to be an underlying respect for certain kinds of private property, particularly the kind that youngsters see themselves owning or working with one day—or it just may be that youngsters are afraid of getting "beat up" if they're caught in the act by the owner.

Once the situation has gone as far as it did in New York, can anything be done to reverse the graffiti tide? That's the question the Mayor asked his aides in the early 1980s, when it looked as if every subway car was about to be covered inside and outside, and when a whole new generation of youngsters was on the verge of turning into "mature" graffiti practitioners. The Transit Authority was investing hundreds of millions of dollars in new subway cars and buses. The Mayor hoped to make progress in controlling graffiti before the new equipment arrived. And the City worked on many approaches.

Protect the subway yards. Make it hard for the graffitist to practice his trade. Most of the large-scale graffiti are sprayed on the outsides of subway cars at night, when they are stored in the yards. "Let's fence the yards and guard them with dogs," suggested the Mayor. "Then we'll paint the cars white so we'll know whether the system is working." Of course, some civil libertarians complained about the "inhumane" use of German shepherd attack dogs—Mayor Koch's "wolves." But the relevant question is, How do you evaluate the costs against the effectiveness? Enclosing nineteen subway yards with fencing topped with razor ribbon steel costs about $20 million. How many people are responsible for the large-scale graffiti damage done in the yards? 500? 1,000 tops? That comes to an investment of $20,000 to $40,000 per "perpetrator." Painting the outside of a subway car white with a polyurethane base that resists scrawls (that means the graffiti can be removed) costs more than $2,000. By early 1983, the Transit Authority had spent $3 million painting 1,400 subway cars. As graffiti began to cover the white surfaces, officials began to question whether the program was worth the cost. Even though some yards are fully secure, there is not enough room to store all the cars in yards, and some cars are defaced while in service. So it's possible to take preventive steps, but the cost is high and it's impossible to achieve 100 percent success, particularly once graffiti moves beyond subway cars to the vast array of paintable surfaces all over the City.

Punish the offenders. The Puritans made a public example of offenders by putting them in stocks. Why can't we apply the equivalent 1980s version? But in a criminal justice system as overburdened as New York's, where does one place graffiti in the priority of offenses? Above farebeaters? Below muggers? Above marijuana smokers? Below burglars? It takes scarce tax dollars to catch a graffiti scrawler, to try him, to jail him, or to supervise him while we make him wash off the graffiti. There are many who say,

"It is just not worth the cost, given our limited resources and higher priorities." Or, "Let them alone—better to be spraying subway cars than mugging grandmothers!" The problem is that a single graffiti offense may look like a minor misdemeanor, but the cumulative effect reaches major proportions. The Mayor initially thought there was no realistic way to "get tough on graffiti" and rejected that approach. But he had second thoughts and later proposed work camps where graffitists and other "quality of life" offenders could be assigned to work for up to five days on various urban Civilian Conservation Corps–type projects (the press unfairly attached the label "concentration camps"). A series of problems surrounded the program, including the difficulty of getting judges to sentence offenders, the high costs of supervision, and union opposition to offenders doing certain jobs. In the spring of 1982, Elizabeth Holtzman, District Attorney for Brooklyn, tried a different approach for subway crimes: Make first offenders clean up the subway cars. If the D.A. and the defense attorney agree, the case is discharged and the offender works off his offense. How long he has to work is determined by dividing the cost of repairing the damage by a transit worker's hourly wage. For example: $100 in damages divided by $12 per hour means eight hours' work cleaning graffiti from subway cars. About 450 subway cars had been cleaned after a year under the program, and other D.A.s in New York were following suit. A perfect solution? Undoubtedly not, but it is an approach that meets the criterion of balancing the punishment with the offense. In early 1984, the Mayor outlined a proposal advocating the establishment of special administrative tribunals that would replace the criminal courts in dealing with subway infractions such as fare evasion and graffiti. The

Mayor favored a civil fine for first-time offenders, sentencing to a work program for second-time offenders, and jail for third-time offenders. There might be variations in the "how-tos," but a consensus was growing that punishments can be meted out that fit the crime!

Educate the public. The Mayor achieved great success during New York City's water shortage with an advertising campaign. Surrounded by children, he appointed each of them Deputy Mayor for Saving Water. Corny? Much to everyone's surprise, water consumption dropped. "Why," the Mayor asked, "can't we do the same thing with graffiti?" So a group of us got together and convinced Levine Huntley Schmidt Plapler & Beaver, a New York advertising agency, to take on the job. We knew at the start that we were dealing with a complex social phenomenon and that designing an effective campaign would be difficult. An ad campaign could be only part of a multifaceted effort. It is common knowledge that most spray paint and markers are stolen, not purchased. Rejecting the idea that legislation outlawing sales to minors would be workable, we wanted to "educate" retailers that it would be in their self-interest to lock away or otherwise protect spray cans and markers. But it was hard to reach the thousands of retailers who conduct business in neighborhoods where graffitists rip them off. The ad campaign was to be the catalyst for bringing local communities into a "grass roots" educational effort targeted at graffiti "neophytes." We knew we couldn't reach the hard-core "professionals" through advertising. The concept was to appeal to impressionable youngsters who were not yet confirmed graffiti scrawlers. Show young people that there are constructive ways they can channel their energies, and use role models who come from their own environment to tell the story. The theme was "Make your mark in society, not on society." Boxers Joe Frazier and his son Marvis were pictured against a wall of graffiti saying, "We got where we are by messing up other fighters. Not by messing up our city's walls." Irene Cara and Gene Ray, stars of the movie *Fame*, were pictured with the line "Fame is seeing your name in lights. Not seeing it sprayed on the subway." The ads were done in English and Spanish, for use on radio and television and on posters in subways and buses.

When the ads were first shown, the cynics criticized, "Urban kids are sophisticated. They know they're not going to 'make it' like the stars. Their reaction will be: 'Who are you kidding?' " By and large, the reaction was positive— people thought the ads were on target. Did the campaign produce measurable results? When you enter the sales market with a new toothpaste or diet cola, your researchers can tell you precisely how effective your advertising campaign was. No one expected that we would instantly turn the graffiti situation around with public-service advertising (people have been educated for years in ads on the health hazards of cigarettes and still they smoke). Our problem was that we violated one of the cardinal precepts of advertising —we did not saturate the media and we did not have the resources for an extended prime-time ad blitz. The public-service spots were aired at 8:00 A.M. Sunday morning or after midnight, hardly the hours for drawing masses of preteen viewers. Education has a role in combating graffiti, but successful use of the media requires a continuing, oft-repeated effort.

The most effective approach, I've concluded, is quick removal. The London subway system, comparable in size and age to that of New York, is graffiti-free. I asked Anthony

Ridley, managing director of London Transport Railways, "You've imported American slang and American fast foods. Why haven't you imported American graffiti, too?" He replied, "Of course we have graffiti, but we remove it immediately. No car is allowed to start its run with graffiti in place." Boston and Toronto follow the same rigid rules. New York's own commuter trains and Port Authority subways (which ply the Manhattan–Newark route) are unmarked. The explanation according to officials: All graffiti is instantly removed. Graffitists know that their efforts will be erased. And that's the primary lesson. New York City, unfortunately, let graffiti get out of hand in the 1970s. It became so widespread that its removal turned into a monumental task. And a large part of the public became insensitive, finally accepted graffiti as a part of the urban scene.

Removal does work—and in New York City, too—when there's a system to identify new graffiti and make sure that they are erased. Sections of Central Park, which are heavily traveled and which have lots of walls, statues, and benches as targets for graffiti, have been cleaned and stay graffiti-free. Urban park rangers report graffiti as soon as they see it, and a follow-up cleaning force is assigned for its removal. The size of the transit system and the unfortunate reality that so much of it has fallen victim to graffiti makes controlling transit graffiti a much harder task. Sometimes it appears that the City takes one step forward only to fall backward by one-and-one-half steps when graffitists rise to the "challenge" and discover new opportunities for leaving their "marks." But if the City stays with those approaches which have the potential for success—with the primary focus on balanced punishment and rapid removal—the ratio between progress and slippage can be changed. David L.

Gunn, the City's new Transit Authority chief, newly arrived from Philadelphia, where he was successful in controlling transit graffiti, declared, on taking the job in early 1984, that that was just the approach he was going to follow in New York. For those towns and cities at an early phase of the graffiti peril, the message is clear: "Out of sight; out of mind." The initial costs of a punishment-and-removal program will be low compared with the economic and social costs of dealing with uncontrolled graffiti at a later date.

6
Historic Preservation:
Ill-Guided Nostalgia
or Economic Good Sense?

It was 2:00 P.M., March 22, 1982. The bulldozers started their engines, and demolition of the Morosco and Helen Hayes theaters, at the site of the future Portman Hotel, began. A few hours earlier, demonstrators protesting against the demolition had been arrested and issued summonses for trespassing (which Criminal Court Judge Bernard Fried later dismissed). At 10:00 A.M. that morning, the U.S. Supreme Court had lifted a temporary injunction against the demolition of the theaters. Only a few days before, the New York State Court of Appeals had refused to hear an appeal on a lower court's decision to permit demolition. As Deputy Mayor, I had spent several hours of the late afternoon of March 19 signing the legal papers for the financial agreements between the City, the New York State Urban Development Corporation, and the developer. Construction of the Portman (its new name is the New York Marriott Marquis)—a fifty-story, 2,020-room hotel, with a 1,500-seat theater—could start.

The Portman is a classic economic development–historic preservation drama—only it's one with more than three acts! John Portman first approached the City in 1974 with plans for a hotel. His architectural signature—a large-scale hotel with dramatic, open interior space—was visible coast to coast. But Portman had not "made it" in the Big Apple. With the City's deepening fiscal crisis, Portman was unable to obtain financing, and the project looked doomed. Plans were resurrected when Edward Koch became Mayor in 1978. The new Mayor, anxious for a symbol of the private sector's faith in the City's economic future, pledged to assist Portman. The City supported an application for a $22-million federal Urban Development Grant and enlisted the New York Urban Development Corporation as a vehicle that would enable the City to provide special tax treatment for the developer.

Opposition grew when word surfaced that construction of the hotel involved the demolition of the Helen Hayes and Morosco theaters. An architect developed plans to build the hotel *over* the two theaters. Preservationists attempted to put the Morosco on the National Register of Historic Places. Critics charged that the White House intervened improperly to influence a federal administrative ruling to permit demolition. Lawsuits were filed in state and federal courts. Joseph Papp, director of the New York Shakespeare Festival, organized demonstrations when court decisions began to go against the hotel's opponents. Some of the most illustrious people in the theater appeared on the sidewalks of 45th Street—Jason Robards, Lauren Bacall, Arthur Miller. What was the fuss about? Few people seriously argued for the architectural distinction of the theaters. The City's own Landmarks Preservation Commission had not designated the theaters as landmarks. Colleen Dewhurst pleaded, "Actors and audiences want the intimacy of small theaters, not the sterility of a 1,500-seat theater." Readings of Arthur Miller's *Death of a Salesman,* which premiered at the Morosco in 1949, rang with nostalgia.

Asked by the press what I, as Deputy Mayor, thought about it all, I felt a bit uncomfortable. I came into the picture long after the conflict started. I didn't accept the argument that plays live on through the preservation of particular theaters. The Greek plays and Shakespeare are performed in all kinds of theaters all over the world. As if underscoring this point, a year later, *Death of a Salesman,* staged with Arthur Miller in attendance, played in Peking, China, to standing ovations. I was not enamored of the Portman design, but I could not see stopping the development process and starting again with an awkward mating of two fairly ordinary theaters to a modern hotel. There would be another long delay—if the developer stayed around at all—and no certainty that some group wouldn't second-guess the new plans. The City, recognizing the special advantages of small theaters, included the rehabilitation of eight former legitimate theaters (most of which were then being used as theaters to show "porno flicks") as an integral part of its larger 42nd Street redevelopment plans. On balance, I felt, the benefits of economic development outweighed the merits of preserving two theaters. (Later, after the Portman controversy became history, the City worked with theater groups to design economic incentives for encouraging the preservation of existing theaters by permitting the sale of their air rights to developers of commercial property —an innovative but controversial approach to maintaining balance between development and preservation.)

It's not that I am a development-at-all-costs person. I have misgivings when I see important landmarks bite the dust. My husband and I used to walk along the waterfront of lower Manhattan, photographing the early-nineteenth-century shops that sold coffee, tea, and spices and that were about to fall victim to the wrecker's ball in the office building boom of the early 1960s. "We have no sense of history!" I lamented. The experts answered, "We are a young nation. New York City's ever-changing skyline is a symbol of our youth and vitality." Of course, the issue is not preservation versus development. It is, rather, how do you balance the two? Looked at another way, when is preservation ill-guided nostalgia, and when does it make economic and social good sense?

The preservation movement began to build up in the late 1960s as a combination of boredom with new sterile boxes, whether they were high-rise office towers or low-rise suburban shopping centers, and legitimate concern for the imminent destruction of our heritage under the push of new development. Rehabilitation of older structures began to make economic sense in the 1970s, when rampant inflation and record interest rates priced much new construction out of the market. The federal government fueled the preservation movement with changes in the tax law. Under the Economic Recovery Act of 1981, investment tax credits of 25 percent are allowed for renovations of income-producing property in nationally registered landmark buildings and districts. Smaller credits are allowed for renovations of other older buildings. In addition, owners can write off renovation costs over a period of fifteen years instead of, as before, over one of fifty years.

Today, every state and hundreds of counties and towns

have ordinances establishing procedures for designating buildings as landmarks. Thousands of private preservation organizations promote the specific interests of their constituencies. In the little town of Gaylordsville, Connecticut, residents formed a private, nonprofit corporation to restore the Merwinsville Hotel, built along now-abandoned railroad tracks in the early days when a train trip along the Housatonic River to the Berkshire Mountains involved an overnight stay. The privately funded Preservation League of New York State works for the preservation of vacation camps built in the Adirondack Mountains in the late nineteenth and early twentieth centuries by robber barons like Alfred Vanderbilt. Developers in Cincinnati struggle against neighborhood protests to obtain historic designation of the Over-the-Rhine district. The developers seek to restore its nineteenth-century Greek Revival and Italianate buildings as housing for middle-class professionals. The present lower-income residents fear gentrification. With cutbacks in federal housing and economic development programs, historic preservation has become, for many real estate developers, the only game in town.

The preservation movement began to gain public support in New York City after the demolition of Penn Station in 1964. Penn Station's vast waiting room, patterned after the Roman Baths of Caracalla, was called the "vestibule of a great city." The station was razed to make way for the new Madison Square Garden. Its thirty granite columns were removed from the rubble and dropped into the Secaucus meadows as fill. Today, the Giants (formerly of New York) play football in the sports complex built in the New Jersey Meadowlands. The New York City Landmarks Commission was established in 1965, shortly after Penn Station was demolished. In one of its early actions, the new commission designated Grand Central Station a landmark. In 1969, Penn Central, the owner of the station, applied to the commission for permission to demolish the station or to build an office tower over it. When the application was denied, Penn Central went to court, challenging the legal authority of the commission. The City and preservationists, with Jacqueline Onassis in the forefront of what turned out to be a long battle, won their day in court. In 1978, the U.S. Supreme Court upheld the City's right to designate Grand Central Station a landmark.

By 1983, the New York City Landmarks Commission had designated as landmarks about 700 individual buildings and forty-five historic districts containing more than 14,000 buildings. Landmarks cannot be altered without the commission's approval (not even the paneling on doors or the glass in windows). All new construction in an historic district must be approved by the commission. Critics of the commission say it has gone too far. New York City's former corporation counsel, Bernard Richland, says, "The commission's on a 'binge'—New York has more landmarks than are listed in the guidebooks for Rome." Advocates say, "The commission hasn't gone far enough. Less than 2 percent of the City's buildings come under landmark regulations." There's broad public support for many of the individual landmarked structures, for example, the Chrysler Building, the Flatiron and Woolworth buildings, Carnegie Hall, and the Radio City Music Hall's art deco interior. There's more controversy about historic districts such as Greenwich Village, the Upper East Side, and Brooklyn Heights—not so much about their designation, but about the broad regulatory powers the commission holds over any changes within a district. And many of the designations are surely not your ordinary "guidebook" historic buildings—seven sidewalk clocks, a sewage treatment plant in the Bronx, the interiors of twelve subway stations, the elevated viaduct of the Broadway IRT subway line running from 125th to 133rd streets in Manhattan.

The actions surrounding historic preservation can look more like *opéra bouffe* than serious controversy involving millions of dollars and conflicts among developers, government, neighborhoods, and personalities. Let's look at a few cases. These happened in New York City, but their counterparts take place—perhaps on a different scale—almost anywhere in the nation. The Biltmore Hotel, built in 1914 by the New York Central Railroad, next to Grand Central Station, was abruptly closed in August 1981. Wreckers began stripping the building to its skeleton for recladding in granite as the eastern headquarters of the Bank of America. Preservationists, aghast at the destruction of a "landmark" that had been immortalized in J. D. Salinger's *Catcher in the Rye*, obtained a restraining order. Accusations went back and forth. According to the preservationists, the Milsteins (the developers) came in the dead of night to dismantle the building before the appropriate hearings on its landmark status had taken place. The destruction of the Biltmore's Palm Court, with its legendary clock, under which generations of college students had met for their dates, was nearly a fait accompli. The developers countered that they had a valid permit from the Department of Buildings. Besides, according to their public relations spokesman, "Milstein informed the commission of his intentions months before and the commission did not act." As Deputy Mayor, I was delighted that the Bank of America was setting up shop with 2,000 employees in the heart of Manhattan. As an amateur critic of urban design, I could not see the architectural merits of the Biltmore. But the process for making a judgment on its merits simply had not worked. As I noted to the Mayor, "We're seeing the worst of both worlds in terms of the developer's actions and the City's role." Further charges were aired as the preservation groups tried to determine what at the Biltmore could be designated a landmark, now that the Palm Court was virtually destroyed. The developer and the Landmarks Conservancy, a private organization leading the preservation battle, reached an agreement. The conservancy would not seek landmark designation; the developer would restore the demolished Palm Court and return the clock to the lobby of the new building. The agreement, as many people suspected at the time, was unworkable. The Palm Court could no longer be restored. The developer eventually agreed to pay, and the Conservancy gratefully accepted, $500,000—a windfall reward for their watchdog role!

Question: What role should nostalgia play in the preservation process? The famed Palm Court at the Biltmore had turned seedy years earlier, serving third-rate buffet lunches to businessmen. College students, with their backpacks, nowadays congregate at airports and bus terminals. In recent years, few were to be seen waiting for dates near the Biltmore's clock. What most people were trying to preserve was not a physical landmark, but a sentimental memory, not even of their own experiences, but of Salinger's Holden Caulfield. "I told her to meet me under the clock at the Biltmore at two o'clock. I was early when I got there, so I just sat down on one of those leather couches right near the clock in the lobby and watched the girls. There were about a million girls sitting or standing around waiting for their dates to show up."

Different questions about the preservation process surround the Mount Neboh case. Mount Neboh Synagogue was built on Manhattan's West Side in 1928. Its congregation dwindling, the synagogue was sold for $375,000 to the Seventh-Day Adventists in 1978. The Adventists—shrewd businessmen or simply sitting in the right place at the right time—cashed in on the growing tide of gentrification and sold the building for $2.4 million in 1981. The new owner planned to raze the former synagogue and construct a seventeen-story apartment building on the site, which lay between two existing apartment buildings. Not so fast! A year later, the New York Landmarks Commission designated Mount Neboh a landmark. According to one commissioner, it "represents the important role played by the Jewish community on the Upper West Side and proudly exhibits a unique and unusual blend of stylish influences—a synthesis of Byzantine and Near Eastern influences." Kent Bartwick, chairman of the commission, voted against the designation, commenting, "Mount Neboh is not architecturally significant." He was too polite. I walk past the building at least once a week: It's an architectural bastard.

A year later, the owner was given permission to raze Mount Neboh Synagogue because of economic hardship. According to New York City's landmark law, if the commission agrees that the owner cannot make a 6 percent return on the property's assessed valuation, the owner must be allowed to demolish the landmark. Alexander Edelman, the developer, argued that the year's delay involved in the landmarking process had cost him $1 million, making a 6 percent return impossible to achieve. The commission agreed. The local community did not give up the fight. Neighborhood groups organized the Committee to Save Mount Neboh, obtained a court order restraining demolition, and held a benefit to raise funds to preserve Mount Neboh. Their efforts to "Save Mount Neboh" did not succeed although they surely delayed the project.

Question: What constitutes a fair return? How fair is 6 percent of assessed value as a standard of economic hardship, when assessed values in a city like New York can range from 20 percent to 100 percent of full value? Question: The Mount Neboh property no longer belonged to a religious institution when it was landmarked, but how can economic hardship be determined for properties owned by nonprofit organizations? Even more fundamental, as churches and synagogues argue in New York, is landmarking an infringement of the constitutional guarantee of "free exercise of religion"? (I don't think so, but a lot of antilandmark advocates do.) Question: How much weight should the interests of a neighborhood to maintain the status quo carry? I am convinced that the "Committee to Save Mount Neboh" was not interested in Mount Neboh as a landmark; the "committee" utilized the preservation process simply to keep a new high-rise building out of their neighborhood.

Lever House, built at Park Avenue and 53rd Street in 1952, was designated a landmark by the unanimous vote of the New York Landmarks Commission in November 1982. A few months later, the City's Board of Estimate upheld the designation. The chairman of the commission called the building "historic." The Mayor called it "dark and ugly," but he voted with the Board of Estimate in upholding the designation since both his landmarks and his planning commissioners supported the decision. Only thirty years old,

Lever House came in just at the minimum age required for landmark consideration. Lever House was the first building of its kind in New York City and provided the standard for the glass-skinned towers that followed. The building opened up Park Avenue to light, with its vertical tower constructed on a horizontal slab. Paul Goldberger, architecture critic, commented in his 1979 book *The City Observed, New York*, "Lever House is an historic structure in every sense of the word." But Lever House is far from perfect, and, as Goldberger also noted, "The open ground floor which seemed to be the very embodiment of enlightened urbanism—now seems dull and sterile, its public space little used. The glass that covers the structure is not structural honesty at all, but merely a modernist brand of ornament." Lever House, although important in architectural history, is a building with flaws. And the flaws involve not only aesthetics but construction quality as well. The entire glass skin requires replacing, and the original glass is no longer manufactured. The cost of repairs is estimated by Lever Brothers to be more than $12 million; it could well turn out to be higher.

Lever House was not built to the full size allowed under the zoning laws. This makes the property a prime candidate for developers who want to replace Lever House with a larger structure, or, if not that, to utilize its air rights for constructing a larger tower on the adjoining property. In New York City's extraordinary real estate world, there were a lot of parties with vested interests in the outcome. The Fisher Brothers held an option to purchase from the Goelet family the land underlying Lever House. Park Tower Realty held an option to purchase Lever House itself from Metropolitan Life Insurance Company. (Park Tower later sold its interest in Lever House to the Fisher Brothers.) Lever

Brothers rented the building from Met Life on a lease that had twenty-eight years to run. Under the terms of the lease, Lever Brothers is obligated to keep the building in good repair. Indicating that they intended to expand their New York operations, Lever Brothers commissioned an architect to design an addition for the adjoining property, which they own. Landmarks Commission approval is needed to break through Lever House's walls to connect the two properties. Confusing? A lawyer's delight! And New York City's top real estate lawyers with "political connections" were all involved. Interestingly, the developers did not challenge the landmark decision, but the drama swirling around control of the properties, repair of the building, and transfer of the air rights was far from played out. If New York City holds true to form, the drama could go on for years.

Whether the situation is resolved through the courts or by negotiation, the Lever House case embodies many of the issues that arise in landmarking. Most fundamental of all is, what are the standards for designating a landmark? Can a building with architectural flaws be designated a landmark on the basis of its historical significance? The law says yes, and I agree. If I could vote, I would support Lever House's landmark designation on that very basis—but my vote would entail a highly subjective evaluation. What standards govern renovation of a landmark? As more buildings and historic districts are landmarked, the veto power of the commission over changes, replacement, demolition, and new construction will become increasingly significant. What's the appropriate balance between remaining true to historic tradition and allowing a building to function with today's technology? Gene A. Norman, who was appointed Landmarks Commissioner in 1983, says, "The trick is to make sure that the changes do not affect the reason why the building was designated in the first place." A good guideline, but how do you implement it? When do the costs of restoration outweigh the benefits of preservation? The City spent nearly $1 million to restore Wyckoff House, a wood-shingled former farmhouse in Brooklyn that had been boarded up for years. Is $1 million too much to spend—the Mayor was appalled when he heard the cost—or is it an appropriate sum for restoring the oldest extant building in New York State? If a structure can be designated a landmark when it is only thirty years old, what incentives does a developer have to construct an architecturally distinctive building? If air rights belonging to a landmark can be transferred to other property, what standards determine how and where a developer can apply these air rights? Hard questions to which I certainly have no easy answers. But as I see it, we need to develop better standards so that the process will be more predictable and the interests between preservation and development well balanced.

The need for standards is even more important now that the federal government is so heavily involved in the preservation process. In mid-1983, nearly 3,000 historic rehabilitation projects had been approved for federal tax incentives. New York City acquired the former Brooklyn Army Terminal from the federal government in 1981 with $4 million of its own capital monies and a $4.5-million federal grant. This massive complex, built along the Brooklyn waterfront, was completed shortly after World War I, a little too late for its intended purpose as a storage point for war materiel. Its reinforced-concrete buildings were so sturdily constructed that, years later, the federal government discovered that it would cost millions to demolish the facility. The federal government looked upon the complex as a huge white elephant, but one for which the City had to pay when we decided that the Brooklyn Army Terminal held the potential for redevelopment. One building contains rail tracks running through its center and an eight-story atrium with a skylight topping its 640-foot length. What look like concrete balconies line the atrium along each of its floors. These protruding structures are not actually balconies; rather, they provided the space for hoists that lifted goods directly from freight cars to their storage floors above. The Mayor, at the press conference marking the transfer of the Terminal to the City, looked up at the "balconies" and exclaimed, "Perfect for luxury condominiums!" He was joking, we hoped. I had pledged to the new Reagan administration, which was on the verge of reneging on its grant, that we would convert the Brooklyn Army Terminal into a job-creating light manufacturing facility. And that was our intention. But it turned out to be more difficult to accomplish than we had bargained for. Negotiations between the City and the prospective developer broke down over financial terms. Left with a huge facility that was in danger of being vandalized, the City had to look at the project with a realistic eye to see what financial package would make it go. As analysts went through the numbers with our financial advisors, they latched onto a key piece that could be put into the equation—the recently passed 25 percent investment tax credit for the renovation of historic property. So, through our Public Development Corporation, the City began the application process to list the Brooklyn Army Terminal on the National Register of Historic Places.

I left City government before the revised development plan become a working reality. I am a cynical supporter of the City's historic-registration application. If everybody else is taking advantage of restoration tax incentives, why shouldn't the City of New York? The Brooklyn Army Terminal is old by American standards. It is unique in its architecture; and it has earned its place in American military history—during World War II, thousands of GIs were shipped to Europe from the Terminal. However, I cannot help but feel uneasy when I look at this widely used restoration vehicle in a larger context. A few years down the road, as the growing volume of projects is completed, someone will look at the tax losses and calculate that it's costing the federal government billions of dollars. A student doing research for his Ph.D. thesis will discover the uneven standards under which fifty separate state agencies make their nominations for the National Register of Historic Places. And an investigative reporter will uncover a few juicy scandals, such as a Revolutionary War–era tavern converted into a massage parlor or a 1960s supermarket falsely documented as an 1860s textile mill. What started as a program to provide incentives for historic preservation will be condemned as another "tax break for the rich." The danger then will be that we'll overreact and, in the name of reform, throw away the good parts of the program with the bad. We've turned preservationists and developers into partners—and that's a good thing in theory. The next question will be: Have we gone too far?

7

How Do Companies Decide
Where to Locate?

Question: How do companies decide where to locate? Answer: Bright, ambitious MBAs pinpoint a site next to the chairman's golf course. That's the folk wisdom that many New Yorkers believe who have watched an exodus of corporate headquarters from the City of New York. Sometimes the golf course is the key, but I believe, after many years of observing the corporate location decision, first as an economist at Chase Manhattan Bank and later as Deputy Mayor, that a combination of hard-cost comparisons and subjective value judgments intermingle in the corporation decision-making process. The weighting of individual factors changes over time and differs from one company to another. The public official charged with influencing the corporate decision faces a difficult task, often learning about an impending move after the decision has been made, rarely knowing what the company's true motivations are.

The mysteries of the corporate location decision became

my preoccupation when I was Deputy Mayor for Economic Policy and Development. The phone rings. A reporter abruptly asks, "What is the City doing about XYZ Company's leaving New York?" My stomach churns; that's the first I've heard of the company's decision to move. I haven't the faintest idea whether it's rumor or reality. One lesson I learned quickly: If the chief executive officer agrees to meet with you immediately, the decision-making process is over; your appointment will be scheduled for a half hour before a press conference announcing where the company is going. If the CEO tries to avoid meeting with you, the decision is not yet made, and the City has a fighting chance. That's the time to pull out all stops and involve the Mayor.

What triggers a corporate location decision? Typically, a particular event—the expiration of a lease, a decision to set up a new line of business, a strike on a commuter railroad, an electric power failure. Who presses the button to start the decision-making process? Sometimes a line executive who has responsibility for finding space for a new division is the one who does. Not infrequently, the chief executive officer himself is actively involved in the long-range planning for the corporation's future or the chairman, suffering from indigestion from being tied up in traffic after a two-hour lunch at the Plaza, declares, "I've had enough of New York."

What influences the ultimate decision? Everything from hard costs (rents, electricity, wage rates, taxes) to personal preferences and executive ego. Tangible criteria—access to supplies, unionization, markets, wage rates—carry considerable weight in the location decisions for a manufacturing plant. Intangible costs and benefits greatly influence the headquarters decision. Quality issues—attractions of the physical or cultural environment, the need for face-to-face contact, the perception of crime—can swing the balance. But whether we are looking at a machine-tool factory, a bio-medical research laboratory, a back-office data-processing operation, or a corporate headquarters, we see that a company can function effectively in many locations, and that a large element of value judgment enters the decision-making process.

A company may organize an internal task force or engage consultants at substantial fees to evaluate the options for a major move. More likely than not, an underlying predisposition will color the study's results. Pressure to deal with a short-run profit squeeze, desire to erect a monument to management's corporate ego, a wish to escape from the growing army of blacks and Hispanics—all these can influence the corporate decision and yet never be mentioned in written reports. And, as I discovered, executives are influenced by fads. There are fashions in corporate locations just as there are styles in widths of neckties and in automobile design. An executive who hears that "everybody else" is studying alternative locations knows that his board of directors will ask, "What are we doing about it?" It's time to think about making a move even though up to this point management has been content to operate just where it is. Does this mean that the process is irrational? No, because a corporation can operate from a range of economically viable locations.

Over the years, I've watched the pushes and the pulls that exert pressure on the location decision and have seen them change. I began, as an economist at Chase Manhattan Bank, to look at corporate location decisions in the late 1960s. Individual companies started to move their headquarters from the inner cities of New York, Chicago, and Philadelphia to their suburbs in the 1950s, but the number of companies that moved out was small, and there was no particular pattern to the flow. During the late 1960s, what started as a trickle looked as though it was turning into a flood. Headlines announced corporate departures from New York City with disturbing frequency. I began to keep score on the location of the Fortune 500 largest industrial companies in what my colleagues characterized as a slightly less than respectable form of economic research. For years, New York City had been headquarters for between 130 and 140 of the nation's 500 largest industrial corporations. The number fluctuated annually as firms moved on and off the Fortune 500 list because of sales performance, merger activity, and changes in industrial classification. Only a small number of companies actually moved their headquarters into or out of New York City. As the 1960s ended, relocations out of New York City far outnumbered moves into the City. New York City's share of the top industrial corporations fell below the 100 mark in 1974; the total sank to 66 in 1982.

I began to wonder what makes a corporation move and how a company fares once it reaches the promised land. Will company performance "prove" that the location decision was sound? I thought that Chase would be interested, because the movers, Pepsico, American Cyanamid, Olin, were prime bank clients. Chase corporate lending officers weren't particularly interested. Some officers wistfully admitted that they would move, too, if they could, but they weren't worried about the loss of customer base. Big corporations need big banks—they will always find ways to do business with each other no matter where headquarters are located. (By the early 1980s, Chase and other banks were following their customers and were establishing offices all over the country.) My boss indulged my whim, and account officers opened doors for me in 1971 to interview key executives of Chase clients who had relocated from New York City to nearby suburbs.

What did I find in my forays to the suburbs? First, the typical corporate headquarters relocation was spurred by a need for space. Headquarters staffs were expanding because of internal growth and the hectic pace of mergers during the 1960s. Office space in New York City was tight, and rents were rising. New York was on the verge of an office-building boom, but at the time that companies started their relocation studies, space was not yet on the market. This was also the period when commuter railroads appeared to be collapsing. Then, as now, most corporate executives commuted to the City by train from the suburbs. So, two prorelocation forces merged: a dollars-and-cents requirement for space and an emotional wish to get off the treadmill of commuting. Social observer William H. Whyte, surveying the scene, concluded that corporations moved their headquarters close to their chief executive's backyard. This was not precisely correct in terms of cause and effect. But once senior management started to think about a corporate move, the attractions of locating close to the CEO's home carried an extraordinary amount of influence.

As I sat in Pepsico's new corporate offices, looking out on a scene of artistically placed sculpture in a park-like setting, I asked my hosts how the move had turned out. Did the new location meet corporate expectations? That was undoubtedly a silly question, since I was talking to the same executives who, only a few years before, had made the decision to move. The reply was uniformly enthusiastic at

Pepsico and at the other companies that had moved. Executives did not regret their forgone two-martini lunches; middle management preferred driving from their suburban homes to commuting by train and subway; the clerical staff did not miss noon-hour shopping. Of course, time can alter perceptions. In 1983, more than a decade after our survey, American Can, one of the early movers to Greenwich, Connecticut, announced that the company was looking for a new headquarters site. According to Chairman William S. Woodside, a lack of "affordable" housing was a factor in the decision to move—some employees had to drive ninety minutes from their homes to the headquarters, in southern Connecticut. Of course, the press release explanation told only part of the story—American Can was cutting headquarters staff by more than one-half. Under Greenwich law, the company could not share its building with another company, so American Can had to move.

How efficiently do companies function after a move to the suburbs? According to those I interviewed, the move worked well. Management maintained contact with customers, suppliers, and corporate division heads—who did the added traveling depended upon power relationships. Usually, the seller traveled, the buyer stayed put. Primary loan and deposit relationships with leading big-city banks were maintained, but some secondary financial services and employee banking were shifted to local banks. The company president made such strong statements as "We don't miss New York at all." Sly winks and a sotto voce comment came from a middle manager: "Once a month, I dream up an excuse to make a trip to the City." Of course, the president is chauffeured into the City for board meetings, sessions with the underwriters, or the opera. The manager is tied to his desk.

What happened to employee productivity? The answer was unanimous: Productivity among the support staff improved. How did management know? I asked. Had the company conducted productivity studies? No was the answer. Couldn't I see for myself by looking around? This was a shorthand way of saying that the secretaries looked like me: they were middle-class white women, the newly discovered labor force of suburban housewives returning to work. These corporate location decisions were made in the 1960s, when the urban labor force was rapidly turning black in complexion, sporting Afro hairdos and speaking a form of English that middle managers could barely understand. Was the corporate reaction prejudice or common sense? Executives rarely discussed their views frankly, but a desire to leave the urban environment, with its potential for violence, entered implicitly into the decision-making process.

Did the move improve sales and profits? I conducted a follow-up survey in 1976. Sales of firms that stayed in New York increased more than did sales of those that moved. Rates of return displayed no clear-cut pattern. The strongest determinant of both sales and profits was industry, not headquarters location. New York–based firms such as IT&T were characterized by their dominant position in international markets; foreign sales and numbers of mergers were rising rapidly during those years. Escalating energy prices pushed up sales and earnings of New York–based petroleum companies such as Exxon in the early 1970s. That location does not significantly affect corporate performance should not be surprising, since headquarters costs for the typical multinational corporation comprise only a tiny fraction of total worldwide corporate expenses. Subsequent analyses by others confirmed our early findings, giving weight to what I think is a commonsense judgment: Companies can perform their functions from many different locations.

As the 1970s progressed and the City's economy weakened, rental costs and availability of office space faded as reasons for relocating. The combination of high taxes and a deteriorating urban environment moved to the forefront as the factors justifying corporate relocation. An underlying attitude of "Who wants to be on a sinking ship?" influenced corporate decision-makers in the dark years of the City's fiscal crisis. In 1977, Union Carbide announced its decision to relocate from Park Avenue to Danbury, Connecticut, sixty miles north of New York City. This unwieldly "dinosaur" of corporate move-outs placed the corporation's headquarters, with its 3,000 employees, on the far edge of exurbia. Executives living in southern Connecticut and staff employees scattered north and west of the complex drive long distances on inadequate country roads. Headquarters lies an hour and a half from New York City and the major airports. Union Carbide sold its Park Avenue headquarters at the bottom of the market (an astute real estate coup for Manufacturers Hanover Trust Co., the buyer) and started building its new facility during a period of inflationary increases in interest and construction costs. Why was the move made? Union Carbide complained, "Middle managers can't be dragged to New York with its high costs and unpleasant environment." Union Carbide seemed to have missed in its evaluation of several key elements. Given the long lead time between planning (the mid-1970s) and executing the move (the early 1980s), the cost equation changed with development costs far exceeding estimates; attitudes toward New York City turned more positive, and corporate organizational philosophy shifted toward decentralization rather than centralization in one megastructure such as Union Carbide's quarter-mile-long building.

Union Carbide decided to leave New York as the City's economy hit its trough. Other firms evaluating their headquarters location discovered that rents had become competitive with those in other areas and that the supply of office space was plentiful. (As usual, the real estate cycle was out of step with the market, so that millions of square feet of space were completed after hundreds of thousands of employees left New York.) W. R. Grace & Co., having outgrown its downtown financial district headquarters, conducted extensive studies of alternative locations in the suburbs of New Jersey, New York, and Connecticut, as well as further afield, in the South. In the end, W. R. Grace stayed in New York and pioneered a move to 42nd Street, across the street from Bryant Park, a notorious hangout for drug dealers in those years. Rumor has it that top management could not reach consensus on the competing sites outside the City. Whatever the motivation, Grace negotiated a long-term lease in 1972 at rock-bottom rents. And New York City praised Peter Grace as a local hero.

As we moved deeper into the 1970s, state and local efforts to improve the business climate began to pay off. Governor Hugh Carey, taking office in 1975, tried to counter negative feelings about the business climate by reducing top rates on state personal income taxes, the pet peeve of corporate executives, according to surveys commissioned by the state. The local real estate community, concerned about their empty office buildings, rallied behind the highly successful "I Love New York" advertising campaign. The Big Apple logo sprouted everywhere—on bumper stickers, T-shirts, and storefronts. Realtor Lewis Rudin, chairman of the Association for a Better New York, still tirelessly buttonholes businessmen, pinning symbolic gold apples in their lapels. Optimism, personified by the dynamism of Ed Koch, the City's newly elected Mayor, swelled. Smart investors saw there were bargains to be had. Firms stayed put in the City, taking space in gerrymandered fashion as their work forces expanded. Foreign companies, lured to the United States by weaknesses in the dollar and political instability abroad, competed for empty office space and invested in new residential and commercial buildings. Decision-makers realized that New York City was inexpensive compared with Europe and that New York City was rapidly becoming a world center of finance and business services. By the end of the decade, rents were climbing through the roof and prime office space disappeared from the market. Rents soared from $10 a square foot to $40 a square foot; in the choicest Park Avenue locations, leases were written at $50 and $60 a square foot. There seemed to be no end to the upward rent spiral.

Success sows the seeds for the next cycle, and a new wave of corporate relocation decision-making soon commenced. Once again, moves were triggered by space requirements. This time around, two new twists influenced corporate decisions. New York City's infrastructure had deteriorated badly as a result of its fiscal crisis, and this provided a new justification for relocating. At the same time, with the spread of computer technology, more and more corporations could separate operations from headquarters and decentralize divisions along functional lines. I knew when I agreed to take the position of Deputy Mayor that I was going to confront a new surge of corporate relocation. My predecessor, Peter Solomon, semiseriously warned me, "I took the job when the City was at its low point and I rode with it to the top. You're coming in at the peak and you'll have nothing but trouble!" He was right—almost. I had to deal with announcements of corporate move-outs from my first day at City Hall, but our official employment statistics continued to look strong. Executives were announcing corporate relocation decisions that would not exert their full impact on employment for another two or three years, when their decisions would be translated into physical moves. By then, I'd left City government.

Harcourt Brace Jovanovich, faced with expiration of the lease it had entered into in the 1960s, decided in early 1982 to decentralize its headquarters, principally to Orlando, Florida, and San Diego, California, two sites where the company already owned property. We tried to convince HBJ to relocate to a less-expensive Manhattan neighborhood, offering whatever financial tools the City had in its "incentive kit" to lower the costs of rehabilitating older commercial buildings. My powers of persuasion were not great enough. The HBJ move has extended the decentralization concept to trade book publishing, a field traditionally concentrated in urban centers. The move is based on the assumption that the celebrated face-to-face interchange of the publishing industry between authors and agents and their publishers will adapt to the era of jet travel, word processors, and telecommunications.

We won some and lost some in the corporate relocation game, and as often as not, we were not even sure just what role we played. Gibbs and Hill, an engineering company employing 2,200 people in its New York City headquarters, faced renewal of its lease. We'd heard that the company had refused to meet the landlord's "exorbitant" demands and was seriously considering a move out of New York. We met with Gibbs and Hill to see how the City might help. In the end, our function turned out to be mostly hand-holding. After negotiating for more than a year, Gibbs and Hill and Bernard Mendik, the building owner, agreed on the terms of a new lease. What, if anything, had the City done to influence the decision? I did not involve myself directly in the negotiations, but I did, with some persistence, try to keep the parties talking to each other over an extended period. My sense was that the real estate market was weakening a bit; and if the two sides kept negotiating for long enough, they could strike a deal. As far as the press was concerned, a lease renewal in an existing building—even if it contained 450,000 square feet and concerned more than 2,000 jobs—was a nonevent. It was only news when a company moved out.

The wife of one of our staff members learned that Sterling Drug, her employer, was about to move out of the City to Rockland County, New York. (We often heard rumors of moves from employees concerned about losing their jobs.) The decision looked like a strict dollars-and-cents proposition. Sterling Drug had moved into prime Manhattan space, on Park Avenue, when the building was completed in the 1960s. The company had outgrown its quarters and its lease would expire in a few years. Sterling looked like the perfect candidate to relocate to Blue Hill, an office complex forty miles north of New York City, built at the tail end of the previous office-building boom and never fully tenanted. Edward S. Gordon, Inc., a real estate brokerage company, put together an offer that Sterling Drug couldn't refuse. At least, that is the way it appeared. Move to Blue Hill at a rental far below what the company would pay if it renewed its lease and, in effect, sell its existing lease for four to five times the current rent for a handsome cash return.

I met with Sterling executives to see whether the deal was a fait accompli. "Yes," said the chairman. "Except for a few technicalities, the negotiations are complete." But I decided as long as I was enjoying the hospitality of his office to probe a bit further. How could Sterling abandon its ideal location at the nodal point of transportation, where employees could be drawn together from all parts of the city and the suburbs? "Ah, that was the problem," the chairman declared. The subways were falling apart; Manhattan's street traffic was snarled, and his secretary had to stand all the way on the commuter train from Stamford, Connecticut. A disturbing observation and undoubtedly true. "But how," I asked, "will your secretary get from Stamford, Connecticut, to Blue Hill, New York, when the only means of transportation is a fifty-mile automobile drive?" No answer from the chairman. I wasn't scoring any Brownie points with this line of reasoning. We then touched on the economics of the move. Sterling didn't divulge the terms of the transaction, but I knew that an important ingredient was the increase in value of their existing Park Avenue lease. I commented that I felt the New York real estate market had peaked and that the rent rises of the last few years would not be repeated in the next few years. Eyebrows were lifted. How high did I think rents would go? "Oh, no more than 10 percent above what they currently are." (This was mid-1982.) As I left, I remarked to an associate, "I should have said 10 percent *below* the current level. Sterling is clearly interested in what's going to happen to rents." I do not know what transpired afterward and what caused the deal to fall apart, but a few weeks later Sterling announced that it was, for the time being anyway, committed to New York. What did I learn from the Sterling Drug case? It reaffirmed what I've witnessed before: Relocation decisions that are long-term by their very nature are heavily influenced by short-term monetary considerations as well as by those intangible elements that color an executive's perceptions about whether the benefits of a location outweigh the direct dollar costs.

The recent tendency for corporations to segment their business and to separate operations from administrative functions adds a new dimension to the relocation decision-making process. When divisions are freestanding, it is much more likely, particularly in these days of pressures on profit margins, that each unit will be required to justify its contribution to earnings in measurable dollar figures. With data processing more akin to factory operations than to the headquarters executive suite, quantitative elements—rents, electricity costs, trained labor—will figure prominently in the equation. If the costs of a particular location are not clearly favorable, the intangibles will have to be demonstrably positive. We learned how hard it can be to make that case when we tried to attract back-office functions to New York City locations other than Manhattan.

In my first public speech as Deputy Mayor, I announced that our highest economic development priority was to attract back-office operations to the City's other four boroughs. It was easy to give speeches; it was difficult to influence decision-makers. I could talk myself hoarse explaining that downtown Brooklyn is five minutes from downtown Manhattan, linked by subway and rail transit. I could sing the praises of middle-income communities in Brooklyn Heights and in Jamaica Estates, Queens. I'd offer tax abatements, write-downs on the price of City-owned land, and reduced-cost interest financing so that office space costs would be comparable with those of other locations. I cheered when Lazard Frères Realty bought the former American Chiclet chewing gum factory in Long Island City, intending to convert the space for back-office use. The City pledged $4 million in capital monies to upgrade the surrounding streets, granted a nineteen-year partial real estate tax exemption to lower rental costs, and obtained a multimillion-dollar federal Urban Development Action Grant. But after a year of professional marketing, the private sector was no more successful than public officials in convincing corporations to cross the East River from Manhattan to the outer boroughs. Lazard Frères eventually switched its strategy, marketing the property as an interior design center, with showroom and office facilities. It looks as though the effort might succeed—the key, convincing a large anchor firm to move with the expectation that a group of related companies will then join a trek from the East Side of Manhattan over the 59th Street Bridge to Queens.

The fact is that business executives operate on herd instinct. No one wants to enter new territory alone. Corporate executives are supposed to be risk-takers, but I am convinced that at the heart of the arguments against the outer boroughs lies an inherent conservatism: Who would go all by themselves to the wilds of Brooklyn or Queens when it is safer to follow your corporate peers to Long Island or New Jersey? Changing corporate attitudes takes persistence as well as an economically competitive product.

City officials can attempt to influence the corporate decision-makers with a range of policy tools, from tax abatements and land write-downs to the hands-on boosterism of a chamber of commerce or a mayor who shows that the city cares. The use of specific incentives such as tax abatements that are targeted to individual corporate location decisions carries the attraction of measurable dollars-and-cents cost reduction. The danger is that a company can use these municipal "goodies" as a form of blackmail. "If you don't give us X, Y, and Z, we'll leave!" The city either knuckles under to the demands or calls the bluff. Mayor Koch didn't like being held hostage. Using well-chosen expletives, he would tell me where such companies could go. The problem was that sometimes they did go, and yet sometimes they stayed—and we had no reliable way of predicting what the outcome would be. We denied Smith Barney Harris Upham & Co.'s application for a real estate tax abatement to renovate facilities for data processing in Manhattan—Smith Barney proceeded with construction anyway. We denied the Bank of New York's application for a tax abatement to build an expanded downtown-Manhattan headquarters—the Bank of New York canceled its plans. We weren't sure whether the Bank of New York aborted the project out of pique with the City (top management was very angry, we were told), or because the project was no longer viable without the abatement (we doubted that), or because new senior management came in at the bank and didn't want to go ahead with expansion, with or without an abatement. My sense, after struggling with several similar situations, is that individually conferred tax abatements are a crude tool to use to sway corporate location decisions. You cannot be sure how significant they are in the weighing of costs and benefits, and you are under constant criticism by the second-guessers, who charge you are giving the city treasury away. Evenly applied, *predictable* incentives are, by and large, more effective.

The reality is that a great many elements, from the cost of rent and electricity to the availability of a skilled labor force to subjective judgments about the quality of the living and working environment, enter the corporate location decision. A corporate location decision can be triggered by an angry cry that a city doesn't care. One chief executive told me, "I've been trying for ten years to get the City to move the bus stop away from our building entrance and no one pays attention. You move the bus stop, and then we'll talk about our staying in New York." I couldn't change the bus stop. In the City's eyes, the bus stop is in the right place. This particular company did not move after all. They submerged their anger about a petty annoyance and evaluated the merits of moving or staying with other, weightier factors. We were lucky that time, but it doesn't always work out that way! In today's age of instant communications and rapid transportation, a company can locate *wherever* executives want to be.

PART TWO

POLITICS

POLITICS

Art of Survival

Economic and social conflicts among regions and within cities are fought out in the political arena. When economic growth lags, individual voters and businesses take a hard look at how well the political process works. Taxpayers rebel, not necessarily against paying their taxes, but against governments that do not perform effectively. In some states and cities that rebellion is silent—taxpayers simply move away. Or rebellion is organized in highly vocal self-interest groups that can slow or even halt the process of government entirely. In a city like New York, the political leverage of renters has perpetuated rent control regulations for more than forty years. The economic and social issues with which governments contend are more complex than ever before. Elected officials need both good people working for them and access to good information. Neither is easy to come by. Both are worth striving for. The private sector is asked to pick up where government has failed. Corporations can innovate successfully in social problem-solving if they carve out their roles realistically. Their actions cannot and should not be a substitute for the political process.

8

Why Do Taxpayers Rebel?

When Proposition 13 was passed in California several years ago, senior management at Chase Manhattan Bank asked me, as their "house" economist who followed social trends, "What does it all mean? Is Proposition 13 just a California happening?" I wrote a memorandum setting down my thoughts: "Proposition 13 clearly reflects attitudes that extend beyond California. . . . The drama speeded up a process that has been gaining momentum for the last few years —that is, a reevaluation of the role of government in an economy beset by inflation and limited real growth." Looking back at what has happened since 1978, I think that conclusion still holds. Proposition 13, which reduced local property taxes in California by 60 percent and then put strict limitations on the ability of state and local governments to increase or levy new taxes, took the specific form it did because of conditions peculiar to California. But there is no question that Proposition 13 represents a watershed, marking a broadly based taxpayer rebellion.

I was also convinced then, and I think subsequent events bear this out, that taxpayers do not rebel simply because taxes are too high by some absolute standard. Rather, the relationship between taxes and what you get for them is what counts—in an economist's terms, the cost-benefit ratio. Proposition 13 erupted on the national scene toward the end of the 1970s because inflation was pushing taxpayers into higher brackets, while the lack of economic growth was forcing Americans to look much more closely at what their tax dollar was buying. They looked—and they didn't like what they saw. A rash of tax cuts followed among state and local governments and, of course, in Washington, too, with the broad $600-billion tax-cut program passed by Congress in 1981. Then, there was a pause in the process as the recession of the early 1980s ate into tax receipts. The trade-offs between taxes and government services were evaluated in a harsh, clear light, and when push came to shove, it turned out that taxpayers valued what they saw as essential services—police protection, defense, clean air—more than they did tax reductions. Many government bodies once more turned—reluctantly, to be sure—to higher taxes. And this, I think, is the key down the line to the implications of Proposition 13. A continuing series of tax cuts and a dismantling of government will not be the rule. An extended period of closely weighing the costs and benefits of governments will mark the future.

Why aren't high taxes per se the explanation for the taxpayer rebellion? Because the real world is a complex place. We're not dealing with a simple equation that places taxes on the left side and government outlays on the right. The relationships involve, on one side of the equation, who pays, in what form, and with how much of their income; and, on the other side, who receives, in what form, and as how much of their income. Because it is so difficult to measure these multiple relationships, we sometimes fall back, in frustration, on simplistic explanations. But the single-factor explanation does not stand up to scrutiny. After steadily rising throughout the post–World War II years, state, local, and federal taxes reached 31 percent of the U.S. gross national product in 1970 and essentially stabilized after that. The tax rebellion that started in the 1970s emerged during a period when the overall tax burden was no longer rising. However, there was a continuing shift *away* from direct taxes on business *to* taxes paid by individuals and families. This may be good economics but it is politically dangerous.

The voter couldn't care less that the nation's total tax burden was no longer rising as a percentage of gross national product. All the individual taxpayer knew was that his tax bill was eating up a larger share of his own income. In 1970, personal income taxes and Social Security took 18 percent of the typical middle-income family's budget. Between higher Social Security taxes and inflationary increases in its income tax bracket, these taxes lopped off 23 percent of the middle-income family's budget in 1980. Even more important, increases in the personal tax burden occurred while inflation and the slow economic growth of the 1970s eroded the average family's standard of living and added to uncertainties about the future. It's one thing to accept higher taxes when your own real income after taxes is increasing. It is another matter when your gains are slipping away and your expectations are clouded with uncertainty. In that situation, you reassess your priorities— when to buy a house, where to go on vacation, whether, as a mother with young children, to seek a full-time job. Close questioning about what you are paying for with regard to government, compared with what you are getting in return, is a natural reaction.

Does a reassessment of the government cost-benefit relationship mean that taxpayers demand a direct dollar-for-dollar return on their tax money? No, but they do want value. The typical middle-income taxpayer looks for return in the quality of his children's schools, the cleanliness of the streets, and his sense of security against crime. The typical taxpayer also helps pay for the education of future generations, contributes to the nation's defense, and participates in the redistribution of income to those in need. The taxpayer does these things willingly when he perceives that the benefits are worth the costs—in plain English, when programs achieve results. But taxpayers rebel if they find the relationship is out of kilter—whether it is the Pentagon paying $1,185 for a $5 tool, or a welfare mother living in the Waldorf-Astoria Hotel.

Taxpayers resort to many forms of rebellion. They use the political process to cut programs, to prod the bureaucrats into more efficient delivery of services, to legislate tax reductions, and to shift the tax burden onto someone else by altering the form of taxation. And taxpayers frequently rebel outside the conventional political process. The growing underground economy reflects an aversion to paying taxes, whether it is the padding of an executive's expense account or the mechanic's unreported income from repair work he does on weekends in his own garage. Given government's poor record of tracking down tax evaders, the benefits of tax avoidance appear large in relation to the risks of getting caught. What couple, earning salaries in their professions, hasn't suddenly resolved, "We've got to find a tax shelter. We're the only people who pay taxes." My husband and I are not particularly interested in breeding cattle or investing in coal mines or renovating an old warehouse, but we felt as if we were bearing the entire burden of New York City, New York State, and the federal government on our shoulders while our friends with similar incomes were sunning themselves in the Caribbean. So we called our investment advisor one day and asked him to find us a tax shelter, our own personal tax rebellion.

Tax rebellions at the state and local levels are perhaps the most difficult to uncover. When state and local taxes get too high, taxpayers do not necessarily lobby through the political process. As often as not, they vote with their feet— they simply move to another jurisdiction. I know that most regional economists disagree. They've published study after study showing that taxes have nothing to do with business location decisions and that tax levels bear no relationship to the rate of state or city economic growth. I've read the studies and I think their conclusion is wrong. The trouble is that most analyses don't take into account the complex relationships between taxes paid and benefits received. Alaska has the highest taxes per capita of any state in the Union. Few Alaskans worry about high taxes because the taxes are paid primarily by oil companies, and benefits go to Alaska's residents in the form of both lower personal taxes and contributions of oil revenues into a capital account, which reduces Alaska's borrowing needs for building its infrastructure. In many jurisdictions, high taxes serve as a good proxy for value received. You can move to the boondocks and pay fifty cents in real estate taxes for every $100 of assessed value, but you risk finding that the schools are poor, sewers do not exist, the nearest hospital is twenty miles away, and public transportation to amass a work force is not available. Since state and local taxes ordinarily comprise a minor proportion of business or family expenses —and most of the taxes are deductible from federal taxes in any case—families and businesses will pay these taxes if they receive the services they want. However, if the relationship between taxes and benefits received deteriorates, many families and businesses can, and do, move. New York City provides a prime illustration of how the process can work. The beginning of New York City's taxpayer rebellion predates Proposition 13 by more than a decade.

New York City has been a high-tax town for a long time. Taxes per capita have been roughly twice as high as the average levied by local governments for at least forty years. In the "good old days," New Yorkers paid high taxes without much complaint. First, personal income was 20 percent to 30 percent higher in the City than in most other places, so the larger tax bite didn't hurt that much. Second, businesses, not individuals, paid a good portion of those taxes. And businesses anted up because New York City was where their market was. It was worth the high price—the taxes paid—to be at the center of finance, commerce, and culture. You pay your dues to be where the action is. The tax-benefit relationship began to falter in the 1960s, and for the next decade the City made a series of fiscal mistakes that contributed to its near-bankruptcy in the mid-1970s.

The City's economy looked to be in reasonably good health in the 1950s and 1960s. Population and employment totals remained essentially stable during a period when there was a decline in both of these areas in many cities. However, stability in the totals masked deep economic and social changes with the exodus of the white middle class and an influx of poorer blacks and Hispanics. Demands for social services increased while the tax-paying base of middle-income families diminished. Robert F. Wagner, mayor from 1954 to 1966, read the fiscal tea leaves and bowed out. John Lindsay, his successor, was filled with high hopes for achieving the Great Society in New York City. Going even further than a blue-ribbon commission's recommendations for broadening the City's tax base, the City and the state enacted a series of tax "reforms." Shift the tax burden to profitable businesses through a corporate income tax, thus replacing the former gross receipts tax, which weighed heavily on the low-margin garment industry. Levy higher taxes on "captive" industries such as the banks and the securities firms. Act as if you are the federal government and redistribute income from the rich to the poor through a graduated personal income tax. The tax "reform" initially raised lots of money and was a "success" on that basis, but the tax prescription proved to be a nearly fatal one over time.

In the "good old days," New Yorkers paid high taxes, and, by their own reckoning, they received their money's worth—good schools, subways that ran on time, safe neighborhoods. As the 1970s began, local taxes were taking up nearly twice as much of their income as they did in the 1950s, while at the same time the quality of services to the taxpayer declined. By the early 1970s, one out of four City budget dollars was allocated to welfare and Medicaid payments, compared with barely one in ten dollars a decade earlier. And New York City was one of the few cities in the nation that were mandated to pay 25 percent of their social service bill with their own tax dollars. It is not that New York City suddenly started pandering to the poor. New York City has a long tradition of social service—Bellevue Hospital's history at its present site goes back to 1816; City College had its origins in 1847; the City built the nation's first public housing project, First Houses, in 1935, with state funding. What changed was that budget priorities veered toward costly social services at a time when the City's economic base was shrinking.

With the shift in the relationship between tax costs and benefits, taxpayers began anonymously to rebel. The middle class and the mobile, typically more profitable, segments of the business community found justification to *move away*. Moreover, new businesses and new middle-class families failed to establish themselves in New York to take their place. John Lindsay's budget advisors used to say, "Our revenues go up only 5 percent a year but our outlays increase by 15 percent annually," as if the City were obeying a God-given edict. By the early 1970s, employment was declining by more than 100,000 jobs a year. Higher taxes could no longer close the widening budget gap. The City resorted to deficit financing on a massive scale. I don't believe that fiscal policy alone pushed the City almost to its knees in 1975. Actors on the City scene besides the politicians carry a portion of the blame. Both the municipal labor unions, which extracted costly wage and benefit packages from the City, and the money-center banks, which marketed the City's spiraling debt, share responsibility. At the same time, broad economic and social forces were weakening the economic base of most older cities. But short-sighted tax-spending policies surely contributed. I wrote at the time of the crisis, "New York City really has no 'public,' in the usual sense, to act as a prod or conscience to government. As a city of renters (who don't pay real estate taxes) and one which relies disproportionately on the business sector for taxes, New York City lacks a voting taxpayer constituency that carries political weight." In other words, there was no "public" using the political process to help maintain a viable balance between government costs and benefits.

The fiscal crisis educated New Yorkers on some basic principles of urban economics. First, a city without jobs has a hard time raising revenues to pay for government services. Second, a city that tries to redistribute income does so at its own risk—dissatisfied taxpayers can move away. Third, a city can't count on taxing captive industries. As far as I know, the only captive industries that can't pick up and move are those related to the oil and minerals in the ground or to unique natural wonders, such as Niagara Falls—and there are limits to how heavily local government can tax these activities without making them uncompetitive. After learning these harsh truths, New York City and New York State concentrated on trying to improve the business climate and, in 1977, began a program of tax reduction. But it is not an easy task to formulate a rational tax policy when someone is holding a gun to your head. The New York Stock Exchange threatened to prove that securities trading is no longer a captive industry. "Eliminate the stock transfer tax," the Exchange threatened, "or we'll move across the Hudson River and build a new exchange in New Jersey." (The stock transfer tax, a levy on each security transaction, had been raised 25 percent in 1966.) The City was afraid the Exchange would make good on its threat and agreed to phase out the tax over a period of five years. We were victims of our own shortsightedness. Everyone knew that securities transactions could be carried on outside New York. Many of us had heard stories of young law associates taking the ten-minute tube ride under the Hudson River, from Manhattan's financial district to the first stop in Jersey City. They'd get off the train, sit on a bench in the station, and sign and stamp papers. The stock transfer, transacted in New Jersey, escaped New York's taxes. This was peanuts compared with the tax avoidance we could see on the horizon with the spreading use of electronics. If we had had the sense earlier to face the reality that securities trading was no longer captive to New York, I think we could have reduced the levy to an acceptable level and would not have been forced to eliminate the tax entirely.

The stock transfer tax decision came back to haunt the City. The 1982–83 bull market began in August 1982. With securities trading at record volumes, City officials looked hungrily once more to the stock transfer tax. The hind-sighters mourned, "All those hundreds of millions of dollars that the City would have in taxes if we hadn't given the stock transfer tax away." The Mayor included a tax proposal in his preliminary January 1983 budget plan. By spring and the time of the formal budget presentation, the idea had quietly been dropped. Somehow the message was delivered that if the securities industry had been mobile in the mid-1970s, it was even more mobile in the mid-1980s. The Stock Exchange didn't need to move physically across the Hudson River to New Jersey to rebel against a tax. Traders just had to push a few keys on their computers to carry out their stock transactions beyond the taxing borders of the City of New York.

The reality that neither New York nor any other city has captive industries is difficult for public officials to believe. I discovered this when I tried to convince Mayor Koch that the commercial banking industry is no longer tied to New York. The banks were complaining that they are unfairly taxed. Financial tax rates were doubled in 1975. (Part of the federal government's price for helping out the City in its debt crisis was that the state and the City had to increase taxes—surely a counterproductive prescription. The banks, as "villains" in the crisis, were handed a much larger increase than any other sector.) Shortly afterward, the City implemented a program of selective tax reductions. But the banks (as punishment?) were excluded. The combined city-state financial income tax totaled 26 percent in 1981. By that time, taxes on other corporate businesses had been reduced to 19 percent. Anyone who has watched banks over recent years realizes that they are becoming more like other businesses (insurance companies, brokerage houses, equipment leasing companies) and other businesses (American Express and Sears, with their credit cards) are beginning to resemble banks. The old-fashioned banker greeting the neighborhood candy store owner by name and helping the elderly widow balance her checkbook is a thing of the past. The future of banking is in nationwide activities. From a banker's perspective, there is no point in locating offices physically in New York City, with its high taxes, when national market activities can be placed anywhere in the nation and can be linked to the head office by electronics.

I presented the banking situation to the Mayor in early 1981 and recommended that the City reduce bank taxes at least to the general corporate level. The Mayor posed a tough question: "How do you know that bringing taxes down to the corporate rate will make a difference?" The best answer I could give was "I can't guarantee that it will, but we don't have much to lose." The tax commissioner disagreed. He wanted to tighten up collections, not reduce tax rates. "New York City banks aren't paying taxes at anywhere near the 26 percent statutory rate. They find all kinds of loopholes to avoid paying taxes." There was no doubt about that. It was common gossip in financial circles that each bank decided its own tax liability—some paid and some didn't. "That's the point," I countered. "Our taxes are so high that we've given banks every incentive to transfer business out of New York, both physically and through paper bookkeeping transactions." The Mayor felt uncomfortable. No one wins votes by lowering bank taxes. He reluctantly agreed to support state legislation bringing the City and state taxes into conformity with the general corporate tax. But his heart wasn't in it, and the bill languished.

Time passed. In the meantime, the Chase Manhattan and Morgan Guaranty banks sent their lawyers to Delaware to write a tax law tailored to attract the New York money-center banks. Banks located most of their new national market activities outside New York and also started transferring some of their existing operations to out-of-city sites. I've been told that the chairman of Morgan came in to see the Mayor in early 1983 and stated the bankers' views bluntly: "You've just seen the beginning, unless you do something to reduce bank taxes." I think the Mayor now believes that the threats of a bank tax rebellion are real. In 1984, he once again supported legislation reducing bank taxes.

The issue is not easy to resolve. I feel pretty silly when I can't give definitive answers to very sensible questions: "What will happen if we reduce taxes? How many jobs will the city save (or create) for every $100,000 in tax reduction?" Econometricians can produce equations, but their predictive power is poor. And reliable answers are even more elusive to questions about how many jobs a city will *lose* if lower taxes lead to reduced city services. In the City's dark days, when jobs were disappearing, the City made a clear choice: Cut taxes and try to minimize the loss in services through improved productivity. The choice worked: Unions knew that they had to make sacrifices, and business sensed that the tax cost-benefit relationship was improving. By late 1977, the economic decline had bottomed out, and a strong recovery commenced. The local economy revived for many reasons, not the least of which was renewed confidence in the City as a place where people wanted to live and to work. However, by the early 1980s, the fragile cost-benefit balance was shaky once more. Breakdowns on the subways, potholes in the streets, muggings on the way to work symbolized the deteriorating quality of urban life. The City's hard-fought economic gains seemed in danger of slipping away unless basic services improved. The Mayor was convinced that taxpayers valued improvement in services more than reductions in taxes. He pinpointed his budget priorities on those services valued most highly by the middle class and business—education, personal safety, and infrastructure improvements (particularly the subways and roads).

In 1982, the Mayor sought and obtained a two-year surcharge on the personal income tax, yielding $100 million annually. The City rationalized the increase as a small offset to recently enacted federal tax reductions. As the Mayor put it, "The increase for a family with a taxable income of $25,000 is only $46.65—that's less than the price of two theater tickets! Aren't safer streets worth a pair of theater tickets?" He was right and he was wrong. The increase was small in incremental dollars, but the tax was added on top of a revenue base that is still high compared with that of other localities. Critics pointed out, "Maybe the increase doesn't look big to the Mayor. He's a bachelor, living in Gracie Mansion. Any increase is too big for a family trying to raise children in the City of New York." However, the Mayor kept his pledge and lifted the surcharge in fiscal 1985 as scheduled.

The Mayor confronts a difficult situation. Retaining middle-class residents and mobile businesses requires improving basic city services. Jaded taxpayers question whether an added dollar in taxes will return a dollar's worth of improved services. They want to see the City under pressure to use the existing pot of tax dollars more effectively —they want delivery on the City's much-discussed productivity programs. Meanwhile a large population of the poor, heavily weighted by blacks and Hispanics, views the City's approach as insensitive to minorities, with their needs for social services and their costly requirements for job training, special education, and housing. Satisfying the competing interests for services without igniting the fires of another taxpayer rebellion is no easy task!

New York City's experience over a period of nearly twenty years provides a graphic case study for the nation. If a city keeps on raising taxes without thought to the economic consequences, it places its economic base at risk, and then collecting taxes becomes even more difficult. If a city raises taxes without care to the efficiency of the delivery system and to the composition of government services, taxpayers can, and will, rebel. Taxpayers are willing to pay for government, but they want government to carry out its functions effectively. This simple truth applies to cities and states and the federal government. Americans want a strong national defense; they'll pay for it, but they don't want to pay for 200 percent cost overruns. Americans recognize the need to improve the quality of education, but they are wary of approaches that simply throw more dollars at the problem. The taxpayer rebellion that looked so straightforward at the end of the 1970s—cut taxes, get government off our backs—will continue in a different, more complex form in the 1980s. Taxpayers, weighing the costs of government against the benefits, will rebel when government does not perform.

9

Special Interest Politics:
New Force or Different
Twist to an Old
Political Tactic?

We are being inundated by special interest groups. Each day, I learn about the demands of groups interested in their own special causes. Special interest groups cover the alphabet from abortion (pro and con) and agriculture to zero population growth and zoo reform. Are we simply more aware of single-issue groups today because the media instantly bring their messages into our homes, or has there, in fact, been a change in the nature of special interest politics?

Special issue politics is not a 1980s invention of the New Right, with its pro-life, pro-death penalty, anti-gun control advocates. Special interest advocacy has been the political tool of "liberal" reformers for a long time—Nader's Raiders for consumer safety, Gay Rights for homosexuals, bilingual education for Hispanics. Of course, going back far enough, the concept of special interest politics is engrained in our history, with Jefferson's agrarian Republicans and Hamilton's budding-capitalist Federalists. Third-party candidates are not a rarity. William Howard Taft garnered more than one of four popular votes in the 1912 Woodrow Wilson–Teddy Roosevelt campaign. The American Medical Association and the AFL-CIO are old hands at lobbying Congress on behalf of their constituents.

The line can be hazy between the constructive actions of a special interest group in educating the public and the obstructive role of a group that succeeds in enforcing its will on the larger society. How we label the role depends on where we as individuals come out on that issue. I've seen "living-room liberals" transform themselves into near-fascists when they think their ox is being gored (for example, West Siders protecting their rent-controlled apartments). I've watched Orthodox rabbis physically attack homosexuals during a City Council debate on a Gay Rights bill. I've also seen special interest groups develop issues that eventually achieve broad national support. Having started as a small movement, environmental protection is recognized today as a legitimate national concern, although there are deep differences about how to balance the costs and benefits.

If single-issue politics is all part of our past, what, if anything, is different today? The answer lies, I believe, in the proliferation of special interest groups, with funding and professional ability to get their message across. The media play a critical role, dramatizing for millions of viewers issues that start with a small base of support. The result is less need for the traditional political party intermediary. Let a TV camera show a helicopter taking off near a children's playground and you've made your case for why the heliport shouldn't be located near your neighborhood. With computer technology, we can quickly identify potential allies and contact them individually through direct mail. And the Political Action Committee, blessed by the legislation of the 1970s, provides an organizational structure for funneling money to the right candidates and causes.

We've become deeply, often emotionally, involved with a whole new set of social and economic issues—first, the social upheaval of the 1960s, with the civil rights and women's movements and the protests against the Vietnam War; then, later, the reaction against what many perceive as disruption to the moral base and social stability of the nation. Self-interest—looking out for *número uno*—intensified with the slow economic growth and rapid inflation of the 1970s. Perhaps just as significant, government now enters so many phases of our lives, from *before* the cradle until well *after* the grave, that the old political patronage system no longer serves its purpose.

Does this mean that we're on the verge of being pulled apart by special interests? I'm more optimistic than that. But I do think the business of carrying on government will become more time-consuming and frustrating with the potential of single-issue groups to obstruct the process. My experiences come mostly from the local scene, but, as I've observed, both small-town and big-city politics can be microcosms of large national tendencies.

Sherman is one of Connecticut's fastest-growing towns—the population was 2,281 in 1980, up from 1,459 in 1970 and 250 in 1950. Its conflicts are not far different from those in other fast-growing communities, from East Hampton, Long Island, to Hilton Head, South Carolina, to Irvine, California. We bought a house and land in Sherman in 1966 (bemoaning our luck of hitting peak interest rates with a 6½ percent mortgage). For all its small population, Sherman is a diverse community made up of old-timers left from the days when western Connecticut was primarily agricultural; onetime "bohemian" expatriates such as Malcolm Cowley, the literary critic, and Peter Blume, the painter, who made their way from the City in the late 1920s and early 1930s, when houses without electricity and indoor plumbing could be picked up for a song; New Yorkers such as ourselves who buy homes for weekend and summer use (often maintaining their voting address in the City); and the lowest caste of all, summertime renters of the lake houses. After southern Connecticut burgeoned as a center for corporate headquarters, a new type of resident emerged in Sherman—white-collar workers who lived there year-round with their families.

Sherman, a haven for New England town meeting democracy, airs issues with heated discussion in its local town hall. Sherman votes solidly Republican in elections—First Selectman Kenneth Grant has held office for more than twenty years. But passions run deep and cross party lines on specific issues. In May 1982, Sherman led the vanguard in the nation's debate on nuclear arms and voted 142 to 98 in support of an immediate nuclear arms freeze. The single issue, however, that consistently dominates Sherman town meetings is land development—this is the issue that touches on the direct self-interest of every Sherman resident. We're *for* open space (we won't finance our purchases with federal money because there are federal strings attached that require letting outsiders in to use the space). We're *against* cluster development and multifamily housing; we're *for* two-acre, single-family zoning. The anti-development factions marshal evidence on inadequate sewers, ecological imbalances, and lack of road facilities. Essentially, the "antis" are the "haves" who want to keep Sherman as it is: an oasis of green, an hour and a half's drive from New York City. The "pros" are the voteless developers, a small cadre of voters in the building trades, and a few die-hard liberals.

I often find myself in a "plague-on-both-your-houses" position. I love our bit of semirural paradise and would like to see it stay just as it is. But I also feel that change is inevitable, and I'm not convinced that long-term salvation for Sherman or other semirural towns lies with uniform, two-acre zoning—it is neither good land use in a region as scenically beautiful as the southern Berkshires nor does it deal with the needs for alternative housing, not even for the town's present elderly residents.

The 1,000 acres of the Timber Trails Club in Sherman were bought by the Farley family in the 1930s, before cluster housing entered our vocabulary. The Farleys developed their property slowly, building homes on small lots along winding dirt roads. Lakes, trails, tennis courts, and ski-tows turned Timber Trails into an ideal weekend and vacation development—for a small, self-contained community. In 1970, the owners sold the land to Henry Pascarella, and fourteen years of special interest arguing began. At the time of the sale, Timber Trails boasted 107 homes. Theoretically, about 900 single-family homes could be built on its undeveloped land under the one-acre zoning regulations. Pascarella pledged to maintain a 60 percent open space, but to no avail. In a record four months, the Planning and Zoning Commission upgraded Timber Trails to two-acre zoning. Pascarella sued the town and won. The town appealed the decision and lost. But the fight didn't end. Sparring among the special interests—the town, the developer, and the Timber Trails residents—continued. In 1978, Pascarella presented a master plan. In effect, he gave the town an ultimatum: Allow him to develop 580 lots on a grid pattern under one-acre zoning or allow cluster housing on 150 acres for 900 rental units. I assume that Pascarella viewed the grid plan, which his own representative termed "distasteful," as a prod to induce Sherman to accept some form of cluster housing. But Sherman didn't rise to the bait and in late 1978 voted to upgrade all remaining one-acre zones in the town to two-acre status.

What did special interests accomplish in the fourteen years years since the land changed hands? Rapid development was stopped in its tracks (although development would not have proceeded rapidly in any case, given the poor economy and high interest rates in the late 1970s and early 1980s). Rumors that decisions would soon be handed down by the courts surfaced periodically; but as of early 1984, five lawsuits were pending, involving development of this unique tract, with its streams and woods and views of the Berkshires. In the meantime, Timber Trails residents, unable to resolve their own differences, watched their private community deteriorate: The lake beach is closed, the trails are no longer maintained, and all traces of the clay tennis courts have disappeared, overgrown with grass.

Sherman is a small town of 2,300 year-round residents. New York City is a metropolis of 7 million residents, give or take a few hundred thousand. But New York City is a city of neighborhoods. And the same kinds of conflicts arise between those whose turf it is and those who want to impose change—whether a developer, an outside group, or government. Special interest groups seek out their allies. Sometimes the result is a constructive effort to make government rethink its posture; sometimes the process simply grinds to a halt. But all too often these episodes create a major source of frustration for those with responsibilities at City Hall.

The Lincoln West development provides a Kafkaesque lesson in how tortuous it can be to work a project through the roadblocks of special interest groups. Robert Wagner, Jr. (former Deputy Mayor for Policy), calls Lincoln West a "Paradigm of the Process." In 1980, Lincoln West Associates, a development group controlled by Argentine investors and bankrolled partly with Italian money, took an option with Abraham Hirschfield, a New Yorker, to buy the Penn Central Railyards, seventy-six acres stretching along the Hudson River. As rail freight use declined over the years in Manhattan, several developers presented proposals for large-scale residential development of the Penn Central site. All earlier plans foundered, victims of economic or local community opposition. Now Lincoln West Associates unveiled plans to build a platform over the railyards and construct Lincoln West, a residential complex of 4,850 units, together with a hotel, shops, and a waterfront park. The developers did their homework. They knew they would enter a lengthy, acrimonious approval process. So they retained John Zucotti, a lawyer and former chairman of the City Planning Commission, and Judah Gribetz, a lawyer and former Deputy Mayor, to shepherd the project through the approval maze.

The City's leverage: The project needed zoning changes. In New Yorkese, this means going through what we call ULURP (Uniform Land Use Review Procedure), a procedure requiring City Planning Commission approval, local community board hearings, and, as the last step, Board of

150

Estimate approval. In most situations, an Environmental Impact Statement (EIS) is necessary, detailing the adverse and positive effects the project will have on its site and the surrounding community. Lincoln West's EIS weighs five pounds and is filled with fascinating tidbits: Lincoln West will utilize 1.9 million gallons of water and produce 34.7 tons of solid waste a day, generate 4,538 outbound subway trips each morning, and cause violation of the one-hour standard for air pollution at Tenth Avenue and 57th Street.

ULURP was adopted in 1976 to provide a fixed timetable for developers and to establish a process that balances the special interests of local community groups against the rights of the City as a whole to control its future. That's the theory. How does it work in practice? The developers spent hundreds of hours building their case with community groups. Although the project was less than half the density of an earlier proposal, the developers realized that West Side community groups are among the best organized in the City. They expected that the bargaining over the balance between density and open space would be tough. The developers knew that the City held the final trump card, so they played their own cards with finesse. I first met the development group in the spring of 1981. They arrived at the meeting with a ten-foot model of the project. Dr. Carlos Varshavsky, the project director, solemnly vowed, "We don't want any tax breaks," and then in a pointed aside added, "unless you make unrealistic demands on us." So the game was set with the three traditional players—the City, the developer, and the local community—to determine what the developer would have to give up as the price for his prized zoning change. Everybody tried to forget about a fourth player—the rail freight interests. They knocked at my door for entry into the game. "If the City doesn't reserve the railyards for TOFC, you'll be a partner to writing off 300,000 manufacturing jobs in Manhattan. Do you want the death of the garment industry on your conscience?" (TOFC is an acronym for a freight facility, whereby loaded truck trailers are placed for shipment onto rail flatcars.) A study had been commissioned many months earlier to evaluate the demand for TOFC at the railyards. But the study was not yet finished. The developer insisted on his right to start ULURP; the City Planning Commissioner himself was anxious that ULURP proceed on schedule so that that he could show the world that New York City had an efficient review process. We fashioned a messy compromise, allowing the developer to submit his application, with the understanding that he would withdraw it if we decided after the study was finished that we wanted TOFC. Then we might ask the developer to redesign the project, including a rail facility *under* the residential complex, and to submit a new ULURP application. I don't know why Lincoln West did not walk out at that point— they surely wanted to make their mark as big-time developers in New York!

The completed rail freight study projected a potential economic demand for TOFC at the site. I was uncomfortable with the study's methodology and dubious about the conclusions. Rail access did not seem to be the key to whether manufacturing could survive in the heart of Manhattan. But *there* was the study, with the rail freight advocates demanding action and the director of the City's new Office of Rail Freight at my door, making a strong case that the TOFC option be fully explored. Well, we debated among ourselves on what to do next. The Mayor's reaction was "10,000 people living on top of cranes lifting 300 truck trailers a day. Men and women and children will die from cancer!" His instincts were not far off the mark. But we couldn't ignore the TOFC issue. The City decided to undertake two more studies, one to evaluate the environmental and physical compatibility of a combined TOFC–Lincoln West development, and a second to examine alternative sites. The studies turned out to be predictably inconclusive, but they gave me the opportunity I was looking for—the feasibility of an alternate TOFC site in the Bronx.

In return for approval, which came at a politically charged Board of Estimate meeting that lasted from noon until 2:00 A.M., the City obtained a series of commitments— the extracting of a few million dollars from the developer for investment in the Harlem River Rail Yards in the Bronx, along with many millions more for subway station improvements in the neighborhood and full responsibility for building and maintaining a waterfront park. The rail freight advocates were not happy. They didn't trust the City to follow through on the Harlem River Yards, and I could hardly blame them for their cynicism—the City should have dealt with the special TOFC issue head-on before the developer was allowed to submit his application. The community won a slightly scaled-down project, reduced to 4,300 housing units, the setting aside of 200 units for low-income residents, and the elimination of the proposed hotel. Although the project ultimately received approval through the established political process, special interest groups in the community remained unsatisfied. So they went to court to block Lincoln West. The court eventually threw out the suit. Four years after the original proposal, it looked as if the project would get under way. Did the process work? Yes, in terms of compromises rendered. No, in terms of the time lost, the added costs, and the unpredictability of the results when so many special interests compete for leverage through an unwieldy political process.

The $1-billion Lincoln West project is a larger-than-life version of special interest politics—well-trained community activists with their political representatives, rich developers hiring the savviest lawyers, garment manufacturers lobbying their business interests, and City Hall juggling them all in the midst of a primary election campaign.

The homeless, in contrast, is a people issue, a matter that tugs at the heartstrings. Organized activity is anathema to homeless men and women. For years, the homeless were familiar sights—the "Bowery bum," the "shopping bag" lady, remembered at Thanksgiving and Christmas and then ignored. Then, in the early 1980s, advocates for the homeless organized to lobby for legislation and filed court suits on their behalf. The homeless became a special interest of the media in the recession winter of 1982–83. The story had good press in Los Angeles as well as in Boston, in the well-heeled suburb of Westport, Connecticut, as well as in the bowels of Penn Station. The issue took on added dimensions in New York City. The Community Service Society had issued a report in early 1981, estimating that 36,000 homeless people wandered around New York each night, but that the City could house only 3,000. The City disowned the statistics. Most observers agreed that 36,000 exaggerated the situation, but no one could develop better figures, so 36,000 became The Truth, repeated, unchallenged, in each news story. And no one could deny that the homeless were turning into a highly visible problem. Rooming houses and welfare hotels were being "gentrified"—renovated as housing for the middle class. Their existing tenants, many of them former mental patients released from state hospitals, had no place to go but the streets. As the recession deepened, the homeless seemed to be everywhere—keeping warm over subway gratings, lying in doorways, or sleeping in bus and rail terminals. The City was under a 1981 court order to provide "clean and safe shelter to every man who seeks it." In November 1982, Judge Richard Wallach rejected as a "cruel and unacceptable hoax" the City's plan to let homeless men sleep in armories and to bus them elsewhere for showers. At first, the Mayor railed against the court. Then he decided there would be no advantage in going that route. The media had taken up the cause of the homeless. The Mayor could use the media, too. He appeared in the middle of one night at Grand Central Station with his Human Resources Commissioner at his side—and newspaper and television reporters close at hand—importuning a "shopping bag lady" to come with him to a warm city shelter. But for all his kind words, the woman wouldn't go with the Mayor, and the City had no legal authority to force her against her will.

The administration searched for facilities that would meet the court's standards. Never one without an imagination, the Mayor badgered his aides, "Why can't we put showers in National Guard armories? When I was in the army, we used portable showers in the field." The Park Avenue Armory, where an antiques show is held each year, isn't exactly a World War II battlefield, but his assistants scurried around for an answer. Soon afterward, portable facilities were installed to meet the court's standard of one toilet for every six men and one shower for every ten men.

It turned out that the matrons of Park Avenue were in fact more willing to accept overnight guests in "their" armory than were groups in other parts of town, where the familiar cry was heard: "Yes, of course, the homeless must be housed, but not in my neighborhood. Alcoholics, former mental patients, drug addicts—they'll undermine the morals of our children." Finally, even the Park Avenue residents protested when, about a year later, the City tried to double the Armory's quota of the homeless.

Special interests—protecting your own against a public intrusion—took an ugly political turn with racial overtones. The City tried to house homeless men in a former elementary school in Harlem. The local minister, leading the neighborhood protest, complained, "Another sign of the Mayor's racial callousness, dumping the homeless in Harlem." The Mayor riposted, "You, a minister, with Christmas approaching, you're telling me, 'There's no room at the Inn!'" (He repeated that line, which he loved, for days.) The Mayor had already made a broad appeal to ministers and rabbis: "Put up ten homeless men in each of the City's 3,500 houses of worship. The City will provide beds, food, and medical care." The response was less than overwhelming. Everyone had an excuse—high heating costs or inadequate sanitary facilities (and many of the reasons were valid). He then threw down the gauntlet to the neighborhood planning boards. (New York City is divided into fifty-nine community planning districts.) "You don't like the sites we select. Then you suggest buildings in your neighborhood that can be used." After several months, only six boards wrote back with specific suggestions; and of these, only two sites were new proposals. So we had an issue, The Homeless, with the media exploiting it as their issue of the month; neighborhood interest groups protesting, "Take care of them, but somewhere else"; religious institutions, caught in the middle, asked to shoulder what they viewed as government's problem; and the City responding to a combination of legal, political, and humanitarian pressures. Was anything accomplished? At winter's end, in March 1983, the City was caring for more than 5,000 homeless men and women a night; nearly fifty religious institutions had pledged a total of 500 beds.

The homeless did not fade away in the summer of 1983, as one would expect, when warm weather arrives. Instead, a new constituency, homeless families, mostly welfare mothers and their children dispossessed from burned-out apartments, was added to the growing numbers relying upon the City to provide shelter. The more attention and the greater the resources devoted to the issue, the larger the demand appeared to be. The City, incurring costs running into tens of millions of dollars, was caught in the middle: on one side, organized special interests fighting through the courts and the media for additional facilities and services for the homeless; on the other side, special interests protecting their neighborhood territory from undesirable outside elements.

The conflicts are repeated over and over again—where to locate a prison, an airport, a highway, a resource-recovery facility. Whether it is small-town, big-city, or national politics, we contend with special interest groups, and they go about their business with more sophistication than ever before. They slow the political process—and this costs us both time and money. They can bring the process to a complete halt through counterproductive means. We cannot and should not try to eliminate special interest groups, as they identify issues that government would prefer to ignore. But it takes strong leadership at each level of government to prevent the negative aspects of special interest politics from gaining the upper hand.

10

Do Good People
Work for Government?

"Do any good people work for government?" My answer, after serving nearly two years in City government, is an unequivocal yes. The problem is that it is hard to keep the good people in, and it can be even more difficult to get the bad ones out.

I wouldn't have answered that way a few years ago. Until recently, I thought most people fit the stereotype of the civil service drone, feet up on the desk, reading a newspaper, fixed in that position until retirement day. Yes, anyone who has tried to retrieve a birth certificate or renew an auto registration or obtain a building permit knows that there are plenty of drones. But as I learned firsthand, that picture is distorted. Good people *do* work for government, attracted by the desire to perform a public service, to change the system, to be part of the circle surrounding a dynamic elected official. But all too often good people leave important jobs in government after two years, or maybe four years, tired of daily crises aired in public or frustrated by the difficulty of implementing change or lured by the pull of earning more money in the private sector.

You can get good people in and you can get bad people out at the very top levels of government. That's what elections are about. What's the measure of a "good" person at the top? Few elected officials possess backgrounds as experienced administrators. And fewer still bring to their jobs an understanding of the economic environment in which they operate. And certainly few big-city mayors or state governors are introspective, brilliant thinkers. Men and women who work their way to the top of the elective process must be comfortable with the press of people and exposure to the media. They do need a good head on their shoulders if they are going to be successful as the chief executive of a large city or state, and they do need a commitment to a political philosophy. Former Governor Hugh Carey, Governor Mario Cuomo, and Mayor Edward Koch are poles apart in personality—the moody Irishman, the Italian family man, the on-stage Jewish performer—but they share common traits—they are quick learners and they have excellent memories, not only for names and faces (the trademark of a politician) but also for the detailed arguments underlying complex issues. No, a successful politician does not need to be the all-round Leonardo da Vinci. "Good" elected officials need to understand issues and the temper of the times. And they need to attract men and women who can carry out their mandate, or sooner or later they will be voted out.

One key to an elected official's success lies in his or her

160

ability to attract good people into government. The mayor who is a product of a political machine may divide the "spoils" among political hacks who may be knowledgeable in the political process but may have neither the expertise nor the motivation to change the system. The mayor who is sensitive to the demands of special interest groups will be certain to include blacks, Hispanics, and women in visible positions, but unless appointments are made with an eye to qualifications, neither the administration nor the individuals will benefit over the longer run. The mayor who is out to reform the structure of government will look for management experts who are skilled in the business of efficiently running an organization, but these experts often turn out to be ineffectual because they do not understand the political process. Most administrations will be a mélange, combining sophisticates in the political world who breathe and sleep politics, long-term career administrators who rise from the ranks and who move with ease from one government appointment to another, and outsiders who are lured to government from the private sector. Typically, the outsider's tenure in government is short. These men and women leave voluntarily when they have had their fill, or they are unceremoniously dropped when it appears that their private-sector skills do not mesh with the requirements for success in the political environment.

Make no mistake about it, the attractions of taking a top-level job in government are real. First, a government position provides an opportunity for public service, and, as old-fashioned as the concept may seem, that can be *the* raison d'être in and of itself. We all have our ideas about what government should or should not do. Most of us never carry our convictions further than cocktail party conversation and voting in elections. Some of us are exposed directly to the world of government when we are enlisted for pro bono efforts—to serve on a commission, to provide "on-loan" advice to a government agency, or to devote time to a civic organization. But it is one thing to second-guess government as an outsider; it's another to test your ideas in the political arena. Public service can beckon as a strong challenge whether your personal mission is dismantling building department regulations or creating a new public welfare agency.

Second, working closely with a dynamic political leader adds a new dimension to one's life. Most of us know government officials only from watching them on television, or from shaking hands with them on street corners at campaign time, or, if we are business people, from sitting through a civic or political dinner, occasionally sharing the dais. "What's Koch *really* like?" everyone from the chairman of a New York City bank to the elevator man in my apartment asked. (Answer: He's just what you see on television— there's no hidden side to Ed Koch.) And that question was followed by, "Are you having fun?" No one asked whether I was having fun when I worked at Chase Manhattan Bank. Almost everyone posed that question when I worked for Mayor Koch. People sense that there is an aura of excitement at the nerve center of government.

Of course, New York City provides an extreme example because of its size, its diversity, and its unique position as an international city. It is fun, not formal duty, when you meet a panoply of influential people in the informal, nearly small-town setting of City Hall or Gracie Mansion. City Hall, completed in 1812, was built when New York City's population was only 100,000. Meetings there take on a personal flavor. The Mayor sits in his shirt-sleeves in a worn leather chair. Nearby, on a sagging sofa, the Mayor of Tokyo or Senator Alfonse D'Amato or David Rockefeller balances a coffee cup on his knee. Miss Universe contestants arrive at City Hall. "That's yours," the press people tell me. "The Mayor will never show up for this." But he does, and to please the television cameras, he kisses nearly every one of the contentants. Eighty-six-year-old President Alessandro Pertini arrives from Italy for a reception at Gracie Mansion. A tiny man, the Italian President sits next to the Mayor in Gracie Mansion's slightly shabby living room and chats for a few minutes with each guest. Gillian Sorenson, the City's Commissioner for the United Nations, arranges a luncheon for ten ambassadors at a small French restaurant. The Mayor provokes his guests with comments praising recent Israeli actions. Gillian cringes in embarrassment, but the Mayor smiles and says, "Isn't this fun? What can be better than good food and stimulating conversation!"

But it is more than rubbing elbows with celebrities that makes government service an exciting job. It is the diversity of activities and the range of issues that an official confronts in a day, with quick shifts between frivolous events and matters that potentially carry great weight for government. A typical schedule for the Deputy Mayor would look like this: a ten-minute breakfast speech at a mid-Manhattan hotel, welcoming a travel agents' convention; a ground-breaking ceremony for a city-aided industrial facility in Brooklyn; a staff meeting to discuss negotiating tactics for an economic development project on Staten Island, followed by a session with the developer and his attorneys; a gathering in the Mayor's office to review his testimony before Congress; an emotionally charged meeting with community representatives protesting helicopter landings at a city-owned heliport near their children's playground; testimony before the City Council on tax abatement legislation; signing letters, answering telephone calls (no writing of memoranda—that's done on weekends); and, the high point of the day, a dinner hosted by the Bronx Chamber of Commerce—boxers Joe Frazier and Muhammad Ali are guests of honor, and I am seated between them!

If the attractions of working in government are outsize in a City like New York, so are the drawbacks. The pay, of course, is an obvious shortcoming. It is not so hard to bring good people in to top levels as it is to keep them, especially in a City where executives in the private sector can earn $200,000 a year and more. For a person of independent means or for an established executive secure in a high-salaried position, a relatively low government salary will not be a deterrent for a *short* stint in government; it may be for a long-term stay. Salaries of $40,000 to $80,000 are sufficient for the stars in their thirties—a bright, energetic breed of commissioners and their deputies, often single or part of a childless, two-career household. These young people exercise more independent responsibility than most of their peers in the private sector. However, after a few years on the job, the best receive offers from the private sector at two or three times their government salaries and most of them will go. Seasoned executives in mid-career are the most difficult group to attract to government. In their forties, with college-age children, these men and women often find government service an immediate financial sacrifice. Or they think a two-to-three-year interruption in their career will cause financial penalties at a later date. They may be insecure about leaving a position within the corporate hierarchy, fearing that once they step off the fast track in their companies, they will lose out in the race to advance. But seasoned professionals and managers are just what the City needs. Robert McGuire remained Police Commissioner for six years. That's a long, near-record tenure in a grueling job. The Commissioner, a lawyer by training, entered city service at age forty-one and left at forty-seven. "I was turning into a civil servant—without the pension," he said. "It's time I thought of my kids and the costs of their education." Loyalty to the Mayor and the challenges of the work kept Commissioner McGuire from leaving sooner, but leave he did, to go to Pinkerton as chief executive at a hefty increase in income.

My sense is that money is not so much a problem in attracting good people as it is in keeping them, and that salaries are not so critical for those at the upper echelon of government as they are for those positioned in the middle ranges of the bureaucracy. The political *environment* is probably more important than strict dollars and cents in deterring "good" people from extended government service. Along with the excitement and diversity of experience come long hours, public exposure, and the frustration involved in getting the system to respond. A few weeks before I officially reported to work for Mayor Koch, the telephone rang in my apartment just before 7:00 A.M. "This is Ed. Have you read the story in the *Times* on President Reagan's budget? I'd like to issue a press statement this morning. Can you come down to City Hall now to work on the draft?" I quickly learned to read the *Times* and the *Daily News* before I arrived at the office (most "pros" read the early edition the night before) in preparation for a day that typically stretched until ten at night, when I'd return home from a "rubber chicken" dinner and spread memoranda on my bed, reading through the papers as quickly as possible.

Don't business executives follow the same packed schedules? Many of them do, but the conditions under which they work are markedly different. You don't have to be very high up in management at a large corporation to eat in the executive dining room, travel first class in airplanes or occasionally accompany the chairman in the company jet, stay overnight at the best hotels, exercise in a corporate-sponsored physical fitness program, or attend conferences at expensive resorts and entertain clients in private clubs where the company pays the fees. Few of those perks, designed to make life more comfortable and more productive, are duplicated in City government (one major exception: Commissioners are supplied with cars, simple black Fords, and drivers, who are never called chauffeurs). City Hall is a classically designed early-nineteenth-century building—with no waiting room for visitors and no conference rooms with up-to-date office equipment. Rat poison is discreetly placed in the corners of all offices. A constant procession of people wander through the halls, perching on secretaries' desks as they await a meeting with the Mayor or one of his aides. My office, located in the basement of City Hall, came equipped with a shower—a unique luxury (which the Mayor sometimes utilized) dating from the days, rumor has it, when Mayor Jimmy Walker kept his mistress close at hand.

I accompanied the Mayor on a one-day trip to Washington shortly after starting to work for the City. We stood on line before boarding the 7:00 A.M. shuttle plane (a good politician wants no special treatment). When we landed in Washington, I tried to match the Mayor's long-legged stride and headed straight for a waiting black limousine, with a chauffeur holding open the door expectantly. The Mayor caught my arm and laughed. "You're working for New York City, not Chase Bank; the City can't afford to rent limousines." A small, battered Volkswagen appeared, driven by Julian Spirer, the City's Washington representative. The Mayor stuffed his 6'2" frame onto the front seat and we drove off anonymously to testify before Congress. The parsimonious style reflected the Mayor's personal preferences as much as the strained financial condition of the City. But aides took note and the pattern set by the Mayor was strictly followed. A small sacrifice for the privilege of working for New York City? Of course, but it probably takes its toll in productivity on those who work intensively at an unremitting pace.

The pressures of life in the public sector are not necessarily greater than those in the private sector, but they are of a different quality, and many private-sector people do not adapt easily or want to put up with them for long. From the day you accept a government job, and the official press release prints your salary and your age, you know you are in a different world. Then come the investigations and the financial disclosure forms and, at some levels of government, public hearings before confirmation. Once you have received your appointment, the press and television are constant presences—certainly in New York, the communications capital of the nation. And you must be responsive if you are going to be successful in government. State capitals and city halls are located physically close to where voters live and work. When something unusual happens, elected officials are expected to show by their presence that they care—the Mayor of New York, photographed at the bedside of a wounded policeman; the Governor of Connecticut, photographed looking at the gaping hole where a bridge section collapsed and three people died; the Arizona legislator, shaking his head unbelievingly at the havoc caused by a flood! Because elections come up with regularity, a political leader's job tenure is highly uncertain. He'll want to show with great frequency that he cares if he intends to run again or to seek higher office.

The elected official sets the tone for press relations, and aides take their cue, being accessible but careful not to overshadow their superior, and remaining anonymous and leaking stories as an "unidentified, reliable" source, when that course is more prudent. Are things different in the private sector? In degree, yes. A business executive must personally answer the press when profits fall, when there's an explosion at the plant, or when dioxin is found in the vicinity. But typically a business executive can be shielded from unwanted interviews; the "must-do" situations occur rarely and the corporation has the financial resources to develop positive public relations stories an executive wants to see placed. True, a business executive cannot rely on 100 percent job security—a company president can be fired because of a corporate takeover or even an indiscreet romantic affair—but the odds for staying on until retirement age, if that is what he or she wishes, are high for an executive who reaches the upper levels of management.

Certainly government *is* different in terms of public exposure, but why should that difference present a problem? It's a good ego trip for those who like to see their names in print and their faces on television. No, the problem doesn't come so much from the interviews per se, or even from the unsettling fact that reporters often err in their haste to be first with a story. It is the need to be always accessible, taking precious minutes or hours out of an already crowded day. Even more important, press reporting and anticipated public reaction become part of the decision-making process. Under the press of a reporter's question, an official makes an on-the-spot decision about an issue on which the administration is really not prepared to take a position. Then, later, the decision has to be undone because the "intuitive" response can't be implemented or, upon reflection, should not be (or, worse, it is implemented, just because the decision is "on the record"). And items will be pushed forward or held back for ultimate decision, depending on the political timing. A mayor does not need to say openly, "We're not going to do this; it will look bad in the papers." (In fact, the Mayor I worked for more often said the reverse: "——— them; we're going to do it anyway!") But all the way down the line, aides are sensitive to how it will read in the paper tomorrow or how it will look on the evening news.

Here's a small but not atypical illustration. Cultural organizations in New York City were complaining that their continued viability was threatened by the Mayor's policy of taxing organizations that had traditionally been exempt from paying real estate taxes. The Mayor set up an internal task force to look at the issue. We recommended that the Mayor ease up on his hard-line policy. Our reasoning was that the short-term gains to the City from imposing taxes were minimal compared with the potential losses to the City from weakening its base by imposing new taxes on the City's nonprofit cultural institutions. The timing of the report was poor. First came a primary election in the fall; later, in the winter, a budget squeeze prompted the City to consider raising additional taxes. How would it look if the

Mayor reversed his position of being "tough" on nonprofit organizations and granted tax relief to museums and libraries, the darlings of the rich? The report was held under wraps for months. After the press finally started asking questions, the Mayor scheduled large-scale public hearings to "aid" him in his decision. Ten months after the report was completed, the Mayor announced his decision, accepting the recommendations of his internal task force. A newcomer to government will be frustrated by the tendency of government officials to be swayed by short-term political considerations when making decisions on longer-term issues. A pragmatic elected official will claim that this is the only way to achieve desirable longer-term goals.

The bottom line is accomplishment. Can "good" people achieve results? Will the external political environment and the internal management structure of government respond to constructive suggestions for change? The answer to both questions is yes. But the on-the-job training for the neophyte from outside can be filled with pitfalls. A business executive functions in a world of external constraints— petroleum crises, high interest rates, competition from corporate rivals, consumer protection advocates. Government officials work under the same kinds of external constraints. On top of these, a multitude of legal barriers, designed to "protect" the citizenry, inhibit their decision-making latitude. Independent legislative and regulatory bodies limit how much government can spend and for what, setting out procedures that must be followed and controlling the flow of financial resources. This does not mean that state and local government officials operate in straitjackets. It does mean that the newcomer must learn a new set of operating rules. He or she cannot give orders to underlings and expect that they will be carried out. It takes perseverance and an understanding of who the external key players are— and then a lot of time-consuming telephone calls, hallway buttonholing, and shaking of hands at political functions.

State assumption of a larger proportion of local Medicaid costs is worth millions of dollars in tax relief to New York City, but the Mayor could not get this measure through the state legislature without convicing Upstate New York counties that they, too, will benefit financially. Federal aid for mass transit is worth millions of dollars to New York City, and during a Republican administration, a Democratic Mayor becomes very friendly with Alfonse D'Amato, New York State's Republican Senator. A major commercial development like the South Street Seaport project in lower Manhattan involves a kaleidoscopic array of parties, external to the direct control of the Deputy Mayor's office. The Landmarks Preservation Commission (mayoral appointees, but theoretically independent) and the Board of Estimate, both at the local level, have approval responsibilities. At the state level, the Urban Development Corporation, financed by appropriations voted by the state legislature, is charged with responsibility to restore historic buildings in the area. At the federal level, the Housing and Urban Development Department holds approval power over a key multimillion-dollar Urban Development Action Grant for pier reconstruction. Then, there are the South Street Seaport Museum, a nonprofit organization with a vested interest in the project; the Fulton Fish Market, long-term tenant on the waterfront property; and the Rouse Company, the private developer, which provides the vast majority of the financing and the entrepreneurial drive to make the South Street Seaport project happen. That's a lot of external parties for a City administrator to negotiate with, to obtain approvals from, and later to work with in implementing a project, and the list does not include the City's own internal departments—economic development, ports and terminals, highways, general services (public works), city planning, buildings, corporation counsel, fire, and police.

Which is harder to move, the external process or the internal bureaucracy? The answer depends on the personalities and on the project. One contends on a day-to-day basis with an internal management structure constrained by tradition and by regulations. State-imposed civil service rules and pension requirements overlay City municipal labor union agreements, setting the parameters under which managers operate. Career public servants are suspicious about business people (they're "greedy profiteers"), and business people come to government assuming all employees are incompetent (or lazy or, worse, "on the take"). Mutual distrust stands in the way of accomplishment. The obvious solution is to put your own people into key positions, just as you would do in the private sector when taking on a new job. That ensures loyalty, shakes up the bureaucracy (a little job insecurity can be a great motivator for middle managers), and enables you to introduce change fast. A "midnight massacre" is practical advice (which I did not follow as aggressively as I should have), but it is not easy to implement effectively in a government bureaucracy. John Simpson came with an excellent record from Denver to run New York City's Transit Authority. After four years, he left. "The job eats you up," he found. The entrenched bureaucracy was near-impervious to change.

The upper levels of management in a city like New York combine political appointees who can be let go at will and long-term career civil servants who cannot easily be fired. If one indiscriminately fires the political appointments of one's predecessor, government may lose its best administrators. You can bring in capable, energetic innovators, but by the time they learn their job, they themselves may be on their way out when you leave, when a new deputy mayor or commissioner comes in and shakes up the bureaucracy again. Meanwhile, the old-timers stay on, nod their heads, and wait for another bright young genius to learn the ropes. There will have been lots of short-term changes but few lasting benefits.

The outsider who enters government assuming that all civil servants fit the stereotype of a do-nothing paper-shuffler can make a damaging miscalculation, for dedicated, capable long-term employees do work side-by-side with the drones. Some years ago, I served on the Public Service Award selection panel of the Fund for the City of New York. The Fund makes tax-free cash awards of $5,000 each to six career public servants, in the Fund's words, "Celebrating the Unsung: Excellence in City Government." Typical award winners have been Edith Spivack, for nearly a half century a lawyer in the Corporation Counsel's office, an extraordinary woman in her knowledge of real estate law; Charles Brady, assistant director in the Office of Management and Budget (when I was at Chase Bank, I knew him as a faceless voice on the telephone who patiently explained the intricacies of the City budget to me each year when the City's annual budget cycle began); and Paul Casowitz, a man in his thirties, with fewer than a dozen years of government service to his credit, who struggled to bring the

173

Department of Sanitation into the modern age of resource recovery.

Spotting individual capable career employees is not difficult. They stand out from the masses. Providing the motivation and the skills so that management in government improves on a broad scale is something else. The private-sector carrots of upward management mobility and monetary rewards are limited in government. The internal selection process for key openings is still largely an "old boy" network. When I was with the City there was no centralized city roster with the names and qualifications of potential candidates among the up-and-coming managers throughout City agencies. The typical business management technique of identifying "fast-track" winners and exposing them to outside schooling while moving them, systematically, from position to position to broaden their management experience is done rarely in government. There's more "management science" now than there used to be, but commissioners can be paranoid in their fear of stepping away from the political environment even for a few weeks of private-sector experience or university training.

The unimaginative or, even worse, the incompetent, manager or deputy commissioner who has worked up the civil service ladder cannot easily be fired. He or she can be moved out of a job, sometimes placed in a slot paying a lower salary, or have all meaningful responsibilities taken away, but except in the most extreme cases of proven culpability, he or she cannot be summarily fired. The sergeant can be stripped of his stripes, but he won't be court-martialed. The City carries the financial burden of a non-productive employee whose continued presence can poison the air of those working around him. The disease of "make work," of putting in one's time, spreads and a whole division can be marked with inefficiency, cynicism, and obstructionist attempts to teach newcomers a lesson.

The person who comes into the political environment must focus simultaneously on two priorities: personnel and policies. Unless the outsider can affect government processes and government programs, personnel changes will be cosmetic rather than enduring. It takes patience and special skills to do more than shift the faces at the top—an administration has to negotiate with unions to alter work rules, push through legislation at the state and local level, and develop programs and agency organizations that can outlast an individual administrator's tenure. The tendency is to look for quick victories—the highly visible easy winners. The reality is that substantive change takes a long time, while the public is a fickle thing.

Pressures to produce short-run results at the expense of longer-run achievements are not unique to government. Business executives face similar conflicts when they are asked to maximize bottom-line quarterly profits at the same time that they are expected to move their company toward its long-range objectives. The difference is that in most companies top management sets the standards, which are measured in dollar profits; then management judges itself. In government, results are not easily quantifiable. Oh, one can develop measures—reading scores, arrests per patrolman, jobs created per dollar of government aid—but such yardsticks are not accurate measures by which to judge the short-term performance of an administrator. Furthermore, government does not enjoy the luxury of self-appraisal—the judge and the jury are external—daily media reports, special interest group demonstrations, and, ultimately, the elective process. Some newcomers to government will find the pressure to produce quick results for deeply entrenched problems just one more challenge to a career aleady notched with successes. They'll mark up a few more victories and then leave when they are ahead. Others may find the frustrations are greater than their ability to move the system.

I stayed with the City for nearly two years—about par for a Deputy Mayor for Economic Policy and Development but probably too short a period for producing much substantive change. I nudged a few projects to completion, started a few more on the long road through the development process, and, I believe, helped clarify where the City should concentrate its development efforts. I suffer twinges of jealousy when I see my successor garnering publicity on projects started under my tenure, but I conveniently forget that I benefited from efforts begun by those who preceded me five to ten years earlier. I left having accomplished less than I had hoped, in part because of what I brought to government (was I an economist too inexperienced in the harsh world of politicians and real estate developers?) and in part because of the limitations of the job. After observing and participating in the process of government, do I think it is worthwhile for government to search for "good" people who will come and then go—after two years, four years, six years at most? The answer is yes. Government needs to attract outsiders who bring fresh ideas and who can impose change on the bureaucracy. There is no way of holding on to them forever. But I'm not sure that's a terrible thing. The hangers-on who can't find their way out of government almost always suffer from burnout no matter how good they are at first. I wouldn't pursue the futile goal of trying to corner the market on "good" people. I would try to encourage more movement in both directions—government to the private sector and the private sector to government. The exposure of each to the other's world is good medicine for both camps. The alternative—leaving it all to the drones who can't be forced out—is far worse!

11
Why Can't Economists Say, "I Don't Know"?

Practical men who believe themselves to be quite exempt from any intellectual influences are usually the slaves of some defunct economist. Madmen in authority, who hear voices in the air, are distilling their frenzy from some academic scribbler of a few years back.—John Maynard Keynes

Economists have fallen from grace. Keynesians, supply-siders, and monetarists all failed the policymakers with their projections and prescriptions for the economy in the late 1970s and early 1980s. The White House chides Martin Feldstein, chairman of the Council of Economic Advisors, for his gloomy forecasts. Mayor Edward Koch derides his staff economists for their inaccurate tax revenue projections. "Savants," he labels them. "They are *always* wrong!"

The golden age of economists was the 1960s. The mating of economists with the computer produced a new breed, the econometrician. Academic theories were put to work, producing near-instant forecasts from hundreds of equations for almost any question a policymaker posed. "Garbage in, garbage out," the old-timers cautioned, initially staying with their judgmental forecasts scratched out on yellow legal pads. But the old-timers didn't hold out for long. Either they learned to use the computer themselves or they hired the bright young econometricians spawned by the universities. Every major corporation, every sizable government agency employed a stable of economists. Their forecasts—judgmental or computer-driven—weren't very accurate. But with the economy on a path of strong, stable growth in the 1960s, nobody paid much attention. Then the days of high inflation, high unemployment, and low economic growth exploded on the scene, and economists, with their forecasting failures, bore part of the blame. Not that they were fired— the greater the uncertainty, the more policymakers look to experts for help.

It is not that economists are less capable than they were in earlier days. I'm sure they are better trained. But they operate in a more complex world, where change spreads rapidly. They have access to far more information than their predecessors dreamed possible, but much of the data is inaccurate and of little use in forecasting events. Neither human behavior, nor the weather, nor technology, nor political change can be predicted accurately. Yet all these exogenous events influence the economy, and in our world, linked internationally by rapid communications, the ripple effects are transmitted more widely and more quickly than ever before. Good economists understand that they are not scientists working in a controlled laboratory environment. They treat their computers with respect. But many of today's economists, enjoying the spotlight, oversell their product—and that is why they fail. They invent numbers where no data exist, and then the findings take on a life of their own. This is not terribly important when economic conclusions are hidden in obscure journals and, at most, discussed at the annual meeting of the American Economic Association. But when they become the basis for policy-making and for daily exposure on the television news, their validity takes on a new importance. Pierre Rinfret, economic consultant, says, "I shudder every time I think of industrial planning. How can we hope to plan if we don't even know where we *are*?"

It's easy to become a number inventor or a manipulator of data that your common sense tells you shouldn't be trusted. It's more difficult to tell those who rely on your advice, "Be careful, these numbers aren't 'real.' " I started out as an economic researcher at Chase Manhattan Bank and soon became involved in an exercise in economic invention. The Rockefeller Brothers Fund was sponsoring a series of reports looking ten to fifteen years ahead. The America at Mid-Century series was one of the first "think tank" efforts that tried systematically to evaluate long-term trends in the United States. The Rockefellers amassed panels of experts in several key areas (Henry Kissinger, then a young Harvard professor, was enlisted as executive director and so began his close association with Nelson Rockefeller). I was research assistant to William F. Butler, Chase economist who prepared the national economic projections for the report, *The Challenge to America: Its Economic and Social Aspects.* The Rockefellers, with their family tradition as masterbuilders, were intrigued with the potential role for urban renewal as a tool for revitalizing metropolitan areas. "How much private money is invested for each dollar of public expenditure in urban redevelopment?" was one of my research assignments. Urban renewal had no brick-and-mortar track record in 1957, nor did hard data exist on how much the private sector was investing on its own in urban areas. But one didn't tell the Rockefellers, "I don't know," so I put together what bits of information I could find on urban renewal land write-down costs and projected development costs for urban renewal projects and adjacent properties. The "facts" were immortalized in the Rockefeller Brothers study. "At the present time, the ratio of private to public expenditures is running about five to one."

Nearly ten years after the report was published, Nelson Rockefeller caught presidential fever. Thinking of campaign material, he wanted to know how accurate the Rockefeller panel reports had been. My assignment was to check the real world against the economic projections. As it turned out, the economy expanded about in line with the earlier 4 percent post–World War II growth trend. But the real world was not an exact replica of the projections. Defense spending and private investment grew more slowly, whereas government transfer payments expanded more rapidly than the study panel had recommended. The social upheavals of the 1960s, involving the women's movement, minorities, and youth, were entirely missed. My little piece, investment in cities, what happened there? I checked in Washington at the Housing and Urban Development agency. After a decade's experience, HUD should be able to answer the question: "How many private dollars are being invested for each public dollar?" The reply it gave was "You'll find the answer on page forty-six in *The Challenge to America*." My invented number had taken on a life of its own. It was printed in a respected book; it must be correct. Does it make any difference? Probably not, in a ranking of cosmic events. But for years, the "experts" turned the data around and claimed that one dollar of public money stimulated, or brought forth, five dollars of private investment. Some time passed before the "experts" began to dig more deeply and ask, "What does the number mean?" How long does it take for one public dollar to generate four or five private dollars? Ten years?

Fifteen years? What happens to private investment in urban areas while we wait?

The "How Much Is Your Wife Worth?" campaign started out as a fun project dreamed up by the public relations people at Chase who were looking to attract retail customers to their branches. Jack McCroskey, a Chase economist, was assigned the responsibility of researching that question. Those were the days when the suburban housewife was queen. Jack asked his wife how many hours a week she spent on household activities. As a well-trained social scientist, he knew that his wife might be atypical, so he broadened the sample and asked three of his economist colleagues to ask their suburban wives how they divided their time each week. The answers came back: six hours on laundry, three hours shopping for food, five hours chauffeur-ing the children, ten hours cooking, fifteen hours cleaning the house, two hours sewing, three hours gardening, twenty-four hours baby-sitting, five hours tutoring math, three hours on miscellaneous repairs, five hours dispensing medicine to a sick child. Then he telephoned the local Department of Labor to find out the hourly wage rate for cook, chauffeur, baby-sitter, laundress, gardener, refrigerator repairperson, and nurse, multiplied hours times wages, added up the results, and arrived at a total. The conclusion: A wife, because of the long hours she worked, was worth more than her husband earned at his salaried job. Posters, printed with Jack's calculations and placed in Chase branch windows, were an immediate hit.

The trouble was that Jack left Chase shortly afterward, but year after year, the inquiries came in. "How much is a wife worth adjusted for inflation in today's dollars?" In-surance claims agents, divorce lawyers, and feminists lobbying for legislative reform were all using our numbers to justify their cases. We knew that "How Much Is Your Wife Worth?" hardly qualified as research, but how could the bank disown its findings? Fortunately, with the women's movement and the growing role of women in the paid labor force, interest in the subject increased. Today, a mass of research fills the libraries. Women's advocates and sharp lawyers defending their clients can choose their evidence. Economists still do not agree on the best way of measuring a homemaker's economic value.

There are times when you know there is no way to produce reliable numbers, but decision-makers don't want to hear about your research difficulties. The Chase Real Estate Division had been financially hurt by the collapse of the New York City office market in the early 1970s. Before re-entering the market, the bankers wanted to know how long it would take to absorb the existing overhang of office space. My assignment in the spring of 1976 was to look five years ahead and assess the outlook. The key to the outlook rested on whether the City had made sufficient adjustments to its fiscal crisis for its economy to revive and to enter a growth phase. There was no way that this could be proved with statistics. I reached an intuitive judgment, based on my views about what had caused the City's difficulties in the first place, and concluded that the odds in favor of a turnaround were fairly good; whatever expansion did take place would be concentrated in the Manhattan office sector. The report was only a few pages long and couched with caveats about the supporting numbers: "If you don't believe the underlying assumption that the decline is bottoming out, the numbers that follow are meaningless." However, middle management couldn't go to senior management and ask for a reversal of policy on the basis of a ten-page report that disowned its supporting data. The Real Estate Division did what corporations typically do in that situation: They hired a consultant. The consultant accepted my conclusion as his beginning premise and for tens of thousands of dollars produced a bound report with hundreds of pages and scores of statistical tables. Now management, armed with volumes of data, felt comfortable taking action.

The economist walks a tightrope between the dangers of giving bad advice based on inaccurate data and acting so cautiously in reaching judgments that his counsel is of no use at all to policymakers. I have sympathy for the frustrations faced by policymakers when they ask for economic analysis as a guide to policy decisions and their economists tell them, "The data don't exist," or, "We can give you numbers but we don't know what they mean—history doesn't repeat itself." The problem arises at the national level, whether we're dealing with inflation, productivity, the balance of payments, or the federal deficit. At the state and local levels, uncertainties about what data mean are even more severe. Population is so basic that you'd hardly think that numbers of people could be an issue. But the truth is that our population counts, even in the decennial census, are not 100 percent accurate. Census experts acknowledge that people are missed—demographers cannot reconcile the number of recorded births and deaths in specific age groups with the population counted in the census. The census shortfall tends to be particularly pronounced for young black men. It does not make much difference for national economic policy if we fail to count 4 million people out of 227 million, but it makes a substantial difference in the accuracy of the tally for individual places where minorities concentrate. After the 1980 census, New York City officials initially complained that between the undercount of minorities and the failure to enumerate illegal aliens, one New Yorker was missed for every seven New Yorkers counted. That adds up to one million uncounted people. Later, they shaved down their estimate of those who had not been counted to more than 500,000. But how do you track down people who don't want to be found? If the undercount is sizable, New Yorkers lose legislative representation and forgo dollars in government aid. But there's more to it than that. We plan for the City's future on the basis of an inaccurate picture of the economic and social makeup of the city in 1980. And we will take distorted readings for the next ten years. The decennial census forms the basis for continuing household surveys that provide up-to-date estimates of such measures as unemployment, earnings, education, and occupation. If we start out wrong, we will perpetuate and possibly exaggerate those errors for the next ten years.

Take one example. Every month, the U.S. Department of Labor announces the unemployment rate for the nation—the fifty states and large urban areas. The unemployment rate, one of the most closely watched numbers in the government statistical arsenal, is based on surveys of households, profiled from the 1980 census. Every once in a while, around election time, someone charges that the numbers are "massaged" to make the administration look good. But Labor Department statisticians are as straight as can be. They report the numbers as they find them. The problem lies with economists, politicians, and the media, who read meaning into changes of even one-tenth of a percentage point in the monthly unemployment rate.

At the state and local levels, the possibilities for error in the reported numbers are uncomfortably large. For many years, New York City's unemployment rate fluctuated between 9 percent and 10 percent; the number of New York City residents who told the survey-takers they were employed remained almost unchanged. Meanwhile, *employers* located in New York City reported, through a different monthly survey, that the number of *employees* on their payrolls had increased by 160,000. How could one survey indicate a substantial gain in employment while another survey showed almost no change? Economists provided a reasonable interpretation: Commuters are not included in the labor force survey of City residents, so commuters must be taking the new jobs reported by employers. But what were all those young black men and illegal aliens doing who were never counted by the census in the first place? Their status is not reflected in the monthly surveys. Are they working in the underground economy as street peddlers, sewing-machine operators, or dishwashers, not counted officially as employed residents, but nevertheless working and pumping money into the economy? Are they engaged in a life of crime, draining income away from the gainfully employed and then recirculating it through their own spending (on designer clothes, box stereos, or drugs)? Are they truly unemployed, congregating idly on street corners, adding to the numbers of the homeless, but not included in any official statistic as either employed or unemployed? If the uncounted—mostly men—actually are working, then the city's unemployment problem is not as serious as official statistics portray. If they are not working, the situation is far bleaker. We don't know the answer, so we do the best we can with the 9 percent to 10 percent figures reported. Each month, when the unemployment rate is released by the U.S. Department of Labor, local economists will be asked what the latest reading means. Most of us—not wanting to remain speechless—seriously hold forth on why New York City's rate is higher (or lower) than the national unemployment rate even though the margin for error is so large that we don't know how we are performing at any particular time.

If we can't be certain of our population and employment totals, we know even less about other economic activities at the state and local levels. Yet, we must make judgments about what is happening and why. New York City's economy is larger than that of all but a handful of nations. However, policy advisors do not have access to the equivalent of a gross national product in their array of regularly published statistics. Some economists do prepare estimates of the value of goods and services produced in the City, but the figures are based on so many unverifiable assumptions concerning relationships between the city's economy and the nation's that they are only very rough gauges of short-term changes in economic activity. We fall back on the employment numbers as proxies for overall economic activity because they are the best current data we have. But if we take the numbers too literally, we can badly misread the economic climate. I remember how strong New York City's economy looked in the late 1960s on the basis of its employment totals. Each month, payroll employment rose, breaking away from a pattern of near-stability that had lasted for almost two decades. But what were those employment numbers actually saying? First, one-half of the expansion occurred in the government sector—the ranks of city and state government employees swelled with the burgeoning of social services. Yes, government employment was rising, but a city needs a healthy private sector to provide tax dollars to pay government salaries. And the private sector was not as healthy as the employment totals suggested. Employment was expanding, but employment growth was not so much a measure of increased economic activity as it was a symptom of a breakdown in productivity. We called it "the back-office crisis." Banks and securities firms were drowning in paper work in the late 1960s—their computer systems lacked the capacity for processing their transactions. In attempting to unjam the backlog, firms hired more and more employees, who turned out to be less and less prepared for the job. An astute observer could discern difficulties lying beneath the surface optimism projected by the employment statistics, even though no economic yardstick existed for precisely measuring what was taking place. However, economists hesitate before giving an "on-the-one-hand, on-the-other-hand" answer based on intuitive reasoning rather than on provable facts, particularly if their client—an elected official—wants clear-cut policy guidance or an upbeat, positive story for the evening news.

The harsh reality is that soft data surround almost every question on which a policymaker needs guidance. How many jobs will be saved if a city reduces taxes? On what kinds of industry should a city concentrate its scarce economic development dollars—manufacturing, tourism, biomedics? How large is the illegal drug trade? *New York* magazine published an estimate of $45 billion for New York City's drug trade in 1982, a figure nearly twice as large as all legitimate retail sales. The numbers portrayed a city overwhelmed by illegal activities, but the estimates were based on such a loose string of assumptions that they could be wrong by a factor of two or three, or even more. Clearly we do not know the full dollar value of the illegal drug trade in New York City. What we do know is the amount of illegal drugs seized and the number of arrests. "Experts" blow the figures up to arrive at a "street value" and then make an educated guess about what proportion the "known" activity is of the total. Or they scale down an estimate made by federal authorities of the national trade in illegal drugs, assuming that New York counts for x proportion of the U.S. total—in other words, an estimate of an estimate, which is itself a crude approximation (inflated by bureaucrats anxious to increase their department's budget). Dramatizing an issue can raise public consciousness, but if the problem appears to be outsize, the response can be despair rather than an objective analysis of the economic consequences and a realistic assessment of the resources needed to deal with the situation. Economists do not invent all trumped-up numbers, but economists often forget their professional credentials and take guesstimates as gospel once they appear in print.

A few years ago, New York City was struggling through a subway strike. Peter Solomon, then Deputy Mayor, was besieged by the press: "What is the economic impact of the strike?" Peter turned to his economic aides, who searched through the newspaper clips to find out what city officials had said in 1966, the last time New York endured a subway strike. They took the 1966 number—$100 million a day—and doubled the figure for inflation, and Peter Solomon had an instant answer. But reporters wanted more details. I worked with the City's economists to put flesh on the numbers. After a little research, we realized that the 1966 estimates grossly exaggerated the strike's effects. We gave the Deputy Mayor a revised set of numbers, roughly half the earlier estimates. The new numbers were still "soft." We cautioned that there was no way to measure accurately how much economic activity would decline in a strike. And we also pointed out that much of the lost activity would be regained once the strike was over. The Deputy Mayor fumed about the stupidity of economists. As a government official, he was in a difficult position—low loss estimates could minimize the economic harm to the City and its businesses and their employees; high economic loss figures would feed into the hands of those who wanted a quick settlement, no matter what the price in increased transit wages. The Deputy Mayor did what public officials rarely do. He simply shrugged and admitted, "The earlier estimates were wrong."

Are economists, then, just an unnecessary weight that policymakers drag around, burdened by their imperfect knowledge? Of course not. But economists need to show a bit of humility when they give advice. And they ought to be out there fighting for better data and for research that will link the academic theorists with the pragmatic sphere of decision-makers. While we are waiting for the paradise of perfect knowledge, we economists should have the courage to be honest about what we know and what we don't know—in statistician's terms, our margin of error. Policymakers themselves should take a crash course in Ec. I! If they understand the strengths and limitations of the "dismal science," maybe they will make more decisions based on commonsense judgments, and tempered, rather than driven, by the computer printouts of their economists' equations. Our policy mistakes, I'm convinced, will then be less extreme.

12

Why Is Housing a Political Issue?

Summer 1983: Our daughter wants to be on her own. She's looking for an apartment, willing to share, since she knows that, just starting fresh in her job as a physical therapist, she can't afford to live alone. The pickings are slim in New York City's tight apartment market and the rents are high ($800 per month for a 2½-room walk-up). A friend with a daughter in similar circumstances suggests half-seriously, "Why don't we buy a building as an investment and rent apartments to our children and their friends?" An acquaintance buys a weekend home in western Connecticut. At 13 percent, mortgage rates are down from the peak of 17 percent a year earlier. This two-career couple, in their late thirties, joins the herds reentering the housing market, fearful that rates might turn up again. "It's a nice lake house with a cathedral ceiling," Barbara says a little wistfully, "but the kitchen needs redoing and the bedroom floors are *linoleum!*"—for a cool $275,000. New York State legislators extend the Emergency Tenant Protection Act for two years, turning responsibility for administering New York City's rent regulation programs *back* to the state, twenty-one years after the state relinquished its role and ceded responsibility to the City and *forty years* after emergency wartime rent controls were first enacted in New York State.

Forty years is a long time to be in a state of emergency. Why does housing continue to be a political issue, not only in a major metropolis like New York but also in many communities all over the nation? After all, the United States has made extraordinary strides in improving the quality of housing since the end of World War II. Two out of three American households own their homes, compared with only two out of five in the 1940s. Families are smaller and houses are larger than they were in the early postwar years. We constructed nearly 18 million housing units in the decade of the 1970s, an all-time record. True, the combination of recession and inflation sharply cut into housing markets in the early 1980s, but anyone who steps away from the swings of the business cycle and takes a longer view can see that the U.S. record in housing is strong. And by and large, the American public is satisfied with the quality of its housing. When polled about issues that concern them, most Americans put housing low on their priority list.

Why, then, does housing continue to be a political issue, fought over in Washington and debated heatedly in the smallest town halls? The answer, I believe, lies in the alliances between constituencies among the producers and consumers of housing. The *producers* of housing (along with their suppliers of credit, material, and labor) bring a chain of special interest groups to lobby for measures supporting housing. They've spent years lobbying for a steady stream of low-interest-rate, long-term credit to finance single-family housing construction for middle America. And they forged alliances with *social activists* to produce subsidized housing for lower-income families. Although the "trickle-down" theory of housing supply generally works over time—let the marketplace supply new housing for middle- and upper-income families, who then pass on their older housing to lower-income families—there are gaps in the process—particularly for minorities, who face discrimination, and for residents of older cities, plagued by heavy concentrations of deteriorated housing and high costs of construction. The producers of housing, in uneasy partnership with lower-income interests, were the primary architects of housing subsidy programs, from the early days of public housing in the 1930s to the "Section 8" rental supplements of the 1970s. It's only recently that their influence in Washington has faded as costs of subsidies mounted and a conservative administration stood firm on reducing future federal commitments. With Washington's direct involvement lessening, producers and their partners looked closer to home, attempting to spread limited subsidy dollars further by focusing less on the poorest segments of the population and more on moderate-income families. Thus, the New York City Housing Partnership, a civic group headed by David Rockefeller, lobbied in 1983 to meld federal, state, and city subsidies with private-sector money to produce housing for the middle-income market. The subsidies on an $80,000 to $100,000 house total $20,000 a unit—a lot of money, but far less than for low-income housing.

Americans, as *consumers* of housing, acknowledge that, for the most part, they are well housed. However, they are protective of their status. If there is to be a change in their housing status or in their neighborhood, Americans expect the change to be for the better. In the short, five-year span, 1976 to 1981, interest rates on mortgages rose by 50 percent and housing prices increased by 80 percent. The result was a doubling in monthly mortgage payments for the average home buyer. Meanwhile, family income increased by barely 50 percent. For men and women brought up to believe that the quality of life inexorably improves, the early 1980s were a rude awakening. Nearly one out of ten Americans normally moves each year—that adds up to more than 100 million people in five years. A lot of discontented middle Americans—disappointed home buyers and sellers—write to their congressmen when housing expectations aren't fulfilled. The strength of housing as a political issue ebbs and flows with changing market conditions, but it never disappears.

Homeowners bring their special interests—property values and taxes—into the local political arena. A house is frequently a homeowner's largest single financial asset, so an owner has a financial stake in what changes in the neighborhood mean for property values. The legal obligation of paying local property taxes goes along with the privilege of home ownership. A real estate tax bill provides a sharp, direct link between the homeowner and the process of government. The suburban homeowner knows that for every $1,000 paid in real estate taxes perhaps $500 will go for public schools, $75 for police protection, $50 for roads, $25 for sewers. The homeowner has a vested interest—a personal tax bill—to weigh before supporting measures that could raise real estate taxes in his community. And the homeowner makes his views known.

Even in a city like New York, where renters outnumber

homeowners by nearly three to one, homeowners carry a disproportionate weight in deliberations affecting local taxes. One of my first lessons on entering city government was just how strong the homeowner bloc is on an issue that threatens their purse. Homeowner properties in New York have traditionally been assessed at lower rates than have income-producing properties such as apartments and office buildings. Even though assessors were supposed to reappraise all properties each year, they rarely got around to increasing values when neighborhoods improved or reducing values when neighborhoods went downhill. The upshot was that assessed values varied from 10 percent to more than 100 percent of full value. Everyone agreed on two points: The system was a "non-system," and the middle-class homeowner, the lawyer in Forest Hills, the doctor in Brooklyn Heights, or the plumber on Staten Island, came out ahead.

The state was under pressure from the courts to change the system. Otherwise, localities would be subject to judgments levied on behalf of injured property owners—in New York City, the judgments could run into billions of dollars. The state legislature struggled to devise a solution that would satisfy both the equity criteria of the courts and the political pressures of homeowners. Governor Hugh Carey proposed a fairly straightforward approach: Assess all properties annually at 100 percent, and then let individual communities set tax rates for separate types of property. Communities could favor homeowners, but differential tax rates would be sanctioned through an open political process. The system would be phased in over five years. I thought the Carey proposal made sense, but I was untutored in the world of politics. The "pros" concluded that homeowners would not accept the concept of a 100 percent assessment and the possibility of large tax increases. As time allowed by the courts to reach a legislative solution ran out, the City became more concerned with warding off legal judgments than in the substance of the bill. The final bill was a convoluted compromise, protecting homeowners from large changes in tax status while insulating communities from court challenges by setting out an explicit process for assessing and for setting tax rates. One lesson I learned was that the homeowner is not to be toyed with lightly!

The renter is a different animal. More than seven out of ten New Yorkers are renters. That makes New York City unusual among U.S. cities and towns. (Newark and Boston are close in their percentage of renters; in San Francisco, two-thirds are renters.) Still, variations on the New York renter mentality surface wherever there is a concentration of rental property. Renters, as a group, earn lower incomes than homeowners. Renters cluster at the extremes of the age spectrum—they tend to be younger men and women, starting out in careers, and older people, often retired and widowed. Renters are disproportionately women without a husband, who live with their children, and women who live alone, either widowed or divorced. The renter is more concerned with government social services (medical care, day care, public assistance) than is the homeowner, who looks to the quality of neighborhood life (schools, roads, parks). Since the renter does not pay real estate taxes directly, he or she does not have the same restraint on demands for government services as the homeowner.

Several years ago, I tried to fathom how New York City could find itself on the brink of bankruptcy. I became convinced that the dominance of renters contributed to our problems. There were just too many people who wanted something out of government, but who did not ask, "What is the cost?" And government succumbed to pressures by the people. Of course, additional government services carried a price tag. But the tenant didn't care. Taxes were hidden in the rent bill. If the landlord complained that he needed higher rent to cover higher taxes, the tenant ran to government to strictly enforce the rent regulations that were first instituted in World War II. And government paid attention. Tenants outnumber landlords by a large margin!

Any person of normal intelligence understands that the costs of food, clothing, and electricity increase each year, and that wages move up more or less in tandem with inflation. But, somehow, operating costs of apartments are supposed to stay unchanged or, if they rise, the New York tenant convinces himself that landlords can absorb the increases in their profits. Some years ago, I asked several building owners, "Why don't you list your real estate taxes on the rent bill? Then tenants will realize that taxes eat up a quarter of their rent." But New York City landlords are a peculiar breed, turned bitter after years of rent regulations. They all gave basically the same answer: "Tenants won't believe our tax figures; the next thing we know, we will have to open our books to everyone." Was their attitude a paranoid concern with privacy?

Irrational behavior and distortions in the operations of the marketplace are offshoots of years of rent regulations. I know. I have lived in a formerly rent-regulated building for more than twenty years. Our building, bordering on Central Park, was built in the gracious style of the 1920s. Oriental rugs covered the marble lobby floor, and doormen wore white gloves when we moved in during 1962. When our two-year lease expired, the landlord asked us to sign a new lease with a 15 percent rent increase. We were entitled, under existing rent regulations, to stay in our apartment as "statutory" tenants without a lease and without paying any increase. My husband and I, a lawyer-economist couple, understood the evils of rent control. We offered a 10 percent increase. The landlord tore up the lease and settled for zero. That was my initiation into how rent control distorts behavior. The landlord's decision was irrational— his gamble that rent control would be terminated within two years was based on a wishful reading of the odds. We knew that the landlord "deserved" the full 15 percent increase, but how far could we go when the rest of the world thought we were irrational to pay any additional rent? A bit of the rent-control tenant mentality had brushed off on us.

A few years later, we began to feel confined by our apartment. We considered moving to an apartment with a view, but we couldn't find a rent-controlled bargain. New apartments cost twice as much as ours. We made a decision, one distorted by our rent-control status. We bought a weekend house in Connecticut. Together, the cost of our rent-controlled apartment plus the mortgage on our country house equaled the market rent of a new apartment. In effect, New York City subsidized us to the benefit of the state of Connecticut. True, we would have bought a country house at some point, but bargain rents influenced our timing and how much we paid. But bargains in rent are bought at a price—deterioration in services. The Oriental rugs and the white gloves disappeared. More important, maintenance faltered, and boiler breakdowns, water-pipe leaks, and elevator stoppages became weekly happenings. The tenants went on a rent strike. "Rent strike—Landlord Unfair" appeared, painted in bloodred paint on sheets hung from windows overlooking Central Park. I tried to explain to our fellow tenants that services were bound to decline if the landlord didn't receive adequate rent. Their verdict—I was ostracized with silence in the elevator. We'd witnessed another form of aberrant behavior. Tenants are pitted not only against landlord but also against one another.

The situation came to a head, as it did in many apartment buildings, when the landlord finally wanted out and filed a proposal for converting the apartment building into a cooperative. Disagreements among tenants were acrimonious. The allocation of cooperative shares determines both the purchase price and the monthly carrying charges for individual apartments. Years of rent regulations had produced a crazy-quilt pattern of rents. A five-room apartment rented for $200 a month more than did an eight-room apartment. An apartment on the fifth floor rented for more than an apartment on the twelfth floor. Some apartments facing the rear rented for more than apartments with views of Central Park. The rent of each apartment depended on when a tenant moved in and on what form of rent regulation governed the apartment. (New York City has two forms of rent regulation: the original rent control program instituted in 1943, and a rent stabilization program, enacted in 1969. The rent stabilization program regulates rents in both apartment buildings constructed after 1947 and in formerly rent-controlled apartments that have been vacated and rerented.) Under the cooperative proposal, shares were allocated by a formula based on square footage, floor height, and view. The result was that some tenants faced substantial increases in their rent, while other tenants enjoyed the prospect of lower charges. And that was the rub! Tenants were so conditioned to their below-market rents that they could not accept the reality that the existing rental pattern was irrational. They were the beneficiaries of a bargain that they had converted into a "right." Yes, there were hardships. Some tenants could not afford to pay higher rent or did not have the assets to purchase their apartments. Older tenants, their children married and gone, were living in grand isolation in seven-room apartments. They were conditioned to their "right" to live with more square footage than the typical apartment dweller at the same stage of life. Sell the apartment, pocket the capital gains (which turned out to be four to five times the insider purchase price), and move to smaller quarters—that sounds like a great financial windfall for a tenant. From an economist's viewpoint, the turnover results in a more efficient allocation of space, since a move-out releases an apartment to a larger family with children. But the thought of moving was wrenching for the tenant who had lived in the same apartment for thirty-five years. Tenants in apartment buildings made their fears about conversion known. And politicians, always sensitive to the voting power of renters, passed state legislation making conversion more difficult and restricting the ability of owners to evict tenants in place.

Three years have passed since our building turned co-op. We're investing in building systems and upgrading maintenance. But renter mentality dies out slowly. Even though tenants are painfully aware that they own a building that suffers from years of undermaintenance, some old-timers are frustrated that they cannot vent their anger at a greedy landlord or demand that a government agency force the landlord to make repairs. The lesson that it takes money to maintain a building in good condition is painful for those who have been conditioned to years of rent controls.

The moral of this story is not that people are bad, but that rent regulations, extended for years, lead to aberrations in personal behavior and to distortions in the housing market. "But," say advocates of rent regulations, "isn't rent control necessary to retain the City's shrinking middle class?" There's little question in my mind that middle-income families *are* the primary beneficiaries of rent regulations. The wealthy live in cooperatives or condominiums or in newly constructed apartments, where first-time rents are at market value. Many of the poor are elderly or on welfare, with statutory allowances for rent. If rent controls were eliminated, landlords to the poor could not obtain much more in rent from low-income tenants. Yes, if there is a beneficiary, it is the middle class. But what middle class? My sense is that New York City subsidizes some middle-class families to remain in rent-regulated apartments at the expense of other middle-income families who would take their place. We remained in our apartment for years, rather than move to the suburbs or to a new market-rent apartment. So did the widow whose children had married and moved away. If rents had been allowed to rise freely, either we would have paid additional rent or we would have left, and other middle-income tenants—perhaps newcomers to the City—would have moved in. Instead, those middle-income families not lucky enough to be in apartments subsidized by rent controls competed for the relatively small pool of high-rental new apartments or gave up and moved to the suburbs. Meanwhile, buildings deteriorated, whole neighborhoods suffered from blight, and the City's very attractions for the middle class diminished.

The ultimate stage for the least fortunate buildings is abandonment and eventual demolition. Between 25,000 and

30,000 apartments are abandoned each year in New York City—landlords simply walk away. "That's not rent control's fault," say rent regulation supporters. "Housing is abandoned in cities without rent controls. Housing is abandoned because middle-income families move out of cities and the remaining residents are too poor to pay the rent." This argument has a ring of truth. No respectable economist would argue that eliminating rent controls can solve problems related to inadequate family income. The relevant question is: Does rent control make housing problems worse? Common sense says that investors will shy away from building rental apartments if they know that rents will be regulated—I am told this time and again by the banks and insurance companies that provide the financing. And landlords will cut back on maintenance if rent controls cut into their profits. According to George Sternlieb, an economist and urban expert who has studied the situation in New Jersey, controls depress the value of rental property and thus lower the amount of taxes a community can collect on regulated apartments. Nonregulated properties are saddled with higher real estate taxes, further reducing a community's ability to attract new investment.

The "real world" situation out there is complex. We cannot conduct "controlled" experiments in a large metropolis over a period of years to test what happens with and without rent controls. Fortunately, rents are no longer rigidly controlled in New York City or in most other jurisdictions with rent regulations. (New Jersey, Massachusetts, and California all permit various types of rent regulation.) Debates in most communities center not on whether rent increases should be permitted, but on how large the rent increases should be. Rental housing is becoming a form of regulated public utility. And, as with other utilities, decisions about price increases pit economic considerations against political pressures. In the "real world" out there, development costs are so high that it is extremely difficult to build housing that low- and moderate-income renters can afford. And also in the "real world" out there, housing does not operate in a free-market economy. In New York City, perhaps an extreme case, more than one in five renters benefits from direct housing subsidies, either by living in low-rent public housing or middle-income housing built with government aid or by receiving housing allowances (such as welfare) to help pay the rent in private housing. The City itself is a major landlord, operating 40,000 rental units that came into City ownership because landlords failed to pay taxes.

So, given the many forces that shape a community's housing environment, I can't unequivocally conclude that instantly eliminating rent controls would unleash a flood of new construction. But I do believe that the negative distortions produced by rent controls far outweigh their questionable merits. What policy conclusions follow from these views of the rental situation? First, I would reduce the artificial distinctions between renters and homeowners that spring from local assessment practices and income tax policies favoring homeowners. Tax benefits that accrue to homeowners—for example, the deductibility of mortgage interest and real estate taxes from income taxes—create a financial disincentive against renting and limit the potential pool of upper-income renters. If we put renters and homeowners on a more nearly equal tax footing, we would have an economically stronger group of renters, and renters who are more aware of the tax costs of providing government services in their communities. Congress could either permit renters the same federal tax deducations allowed to homeowners, or, more difficult to accomplish politically, reduce the tax allowances accorded to homeowners.

Second, any jurisdiction that has rent controls should phase them out. New York City missed a golden opportunity to eliminate controls during its fiscal crisis of the 1970s. Housing markets were looser than they had been for years. The federal government sought to force the elimination of rent controls as one of the conditions for guaranteeing the City's debt. Bowing to federal prodding would have been a face-saving way out of the web of rent regulations. But state and local officials attuned to the political power of the renter felt differently, and rent control stayed. In the early 1980s, housing markets tightened as the supply of rental housing shrank through abandonment, at the bottom of the stock, and from conversion to cooperatives or condominiums, at the top of the stock. The chance of easing regulations with a 2 percent rental vacancy rate was nil. But if inflation abates for an extended period or if housing markets should weaken, I would push for vacancy decontrol. Apartments would enter the free market when a tenant moved out. In ten to fifteen years, nearly the entire rental stock would be free of rent regulations. Government's role would be restricted to protecting tenants against harassment, ensuring that services are maintained (at the risk of reductions in rent), and providing rental information so that tenants are fully apprised of market conditions.

Third, I would stretch limited housing production subsidies as far as possible. This means that little new housing would be built exclusively for low-income families. Rather, housing supply would be increased primarily through new units constructed for middle- and upper-income families, while the moderate rehabilitation of existing housing would help prevent deterioration and abandonment. This is probably the most cost-effective way of ensuring a supply of housing for lower-income families. That still leaves a real problem in New York City and other urban centers with concentrations of lower-income families whose income is inadequate for renting or buying existing housing. The issue of "inadequate" income is not a trivial matter, and many people have strong views about whether, and in what form, income should be redistributed. Whether the vehicle of redistribution should be housing vouchers or food stamps or a broad, guaranteed minimum income—we have been debating the issue for years. But by now we should know one thing: The problems of poverty cannot be dealt with effectively either through rent controls or through deep and costly housing production subsidies.

Why do we bother about renters? After all, we are a nation of homeowners, and homeowners possess the political leverage to look out for their own interests. Homeownership indisputably brings benefits to a community, if only because homeowners have a stake in maintaining the value of their largest financial asset. Why not aggressively promote conversion of rental buildings as a matter of policy? New York City has found that tenant ownership can be a viable option in returning city-owned buildings to the private sector even in low-income neighborhoods. But there are a lot of "ifs" attached—if a strong tenants' organization stands ready to work hard, if the building's basic systems are in proper working order, if the tenants earn enough to cover expenses. I am quite sure that ownership will become a significant mode in multifamily markets. However, there is a place for rental housing, too. A dynamic community needs variety in its housing supply. It should be able to accommodate not only a stolid, middle-aged middle class, but also the young, the elderly, the newcomers who reinvigorate a community, and the mobile, middle-income earners who move from one part of the country to another. Rental housing provides fluidity to housing markets. If rental housing is hamstrung by misguided state and local regulations perpetuated to satisfy a powerful voting bloc, and if renters continue to be disadvantaged by tax policies that pander to homeowners, then rental housing will not fulfill this important role.

13

Whatever Happened to
Corporate Responsibility?

The phrase "corporate responsibility" (and its synonym, "social responsibility") entered the business lexicon nearly twenty years ago. Cities were burning in the aftermath of racial violence. Massive federal Great Society legislation had been enacted to right social wrongs of the past. What was business doing as its fair share? Corporate leadership publicly embraced the concept of social responsibility, and a whole new breed of instant experts emerged to advise corporations on how they could implement their chairman's corporate responsibility commitments. Inflated expectations were soon dashed by disappointing results. And it wasn't long before we were looking back and asking, "Whatever happened to corporate responsibility?"

Chase Manhattan Bank was at the forefront of those early corporate responsibility experiments. Like many corporations, Chase established a special department in the late 1960s to deal with urban affairs, assigning support staff and a vice president as director. But it was simpler to set up a department (eventually retitled Corporate Responsibility) and draw an organization chart with lines connecting the new box to other bank units than it was to deal with substantive policy issues—just what does a corporation do under that broad rubric, corporate responsibility? And, as I discovered to my discomfort, it was a lot easier to say what was wrong with what Chase and its corporate colleagues were doing than to prescribe programs that had any realistic chance of being "right." Many of those early programs that we started with the naive belief that we'd see fast results bit the dust when the first corporate profit squeeze came. By the late 1970s, corporate responsibility looked dead. Corporate responsibility departments became the place to fill your affirmative-action goals—and no ambitious career officer sought the assignment. Glossy brochures detailed corporate efforts, but the spirit was gone and nobody much cared; in any case, most of the programs were failures.

But corporate responsibility did not fully expire. It received a new lease on life in the 1980s, with a conservative administration's tentative blessings, under the name of Public-Private Partnerships. The new name, although awkward, is an improvement over the old. The earlier notion that business has a corporate responsibility to spend shareholders' money as a *debt* to society never made any sense. The question, rather, was and still is: Can a corporation bring resources to bear on social issues in ways that will return profits in the longer run? Put another way, can corporations do some things more effectively in the area of social problem-solving than can their counterparts working in isolation in government or nonprofit organizations? If so, the short-term profits sacrificed will come back in the future in the form of lower costs (e.g., taxes to pay for social programs) and larger markets in which to sell their products.

Of course, these days it is fashionable to damn corporate do-gooding. "The business of business is business," according to Friedmanites. Corporate profits should either be reinvested in a company or distributed to shareholders to spend or to save as they wish. The workings of the marketplace guarantee the most efficient allocation of resources. Anything else raises costs and reduces output. An individual corporation "investing" in social causes is inviting financial disaster. Its competitors don't carry the burden of social responsibility costs, but they will share in the longer-term benefits without putting their ante into the social responsibility pot.

The anti–corporate responsibility arguments are powerful, but they are too one-sided. Corporations can perform effectively in the realm of social problem-solving. They will do best if they craft their role carefully, drawing on their own corporate expertise in those areas where they have a strong interest in the outcome. They can't be all things to all people, dabbling a little here and a little there, and they must be prepared for a long haul before seeing results. Otherwise their efforts—whether alone or in partnership with others—will be at best ineffective and at worst counterproductive. How do we wend our way between the extremes of blindly strewn corporate conscience money and complete abdication of any corporate role? Here are a few examples of what works and what doesn't work, gleaned from nearly twenty years of trial and error.

The failures, of course, were heavy in the early days,

when many companies fell victim to knee-jerk responses to inner city violence, a combination of guilt and fear that society as they knew it was about to be destroyed. The National Urban Coalition, formed in the late 1960s, was a noble effort, bringing together leaders from business, labor, and nonprofit organizations. But it turned out to be mostly a debating society, its constituency far too diverse to develop workable programs. Its greatest benefit was to bring people of different backgrounds together in the same room for the first time. David Rockefeller was on a housing committee with Whitney Young (the late president of the Urban League) and Walter Reuther (the late president of the United Auto Workers). As part of the support staff, I was one of the middle-class beneficiaries of the new social consciousness. Asked to join luncheon meetings in New York's most exclusive clubs, I met the movers and shakers of the corporate and union worlds. (I also discovered overt discrimination for the first time, when, as a woman, I was barred from the private dining room of the University Club and was asked to use the enclosed elevator and not the elegant open marble staircase at the Knickerbocker Club. David's newly hired personal assistant, a black active in community development, and before that, a professional basketball player, entered both enclaves with no problems.)

Our housing subcommittee developed a good idea. Almost every day, someone would announce a new cure for the nation's housing problems. Each program involved government subsidies; numbers would be tossed off showing why the new program was less costly and more effective than the old. At that time, we had no way of quickly estimating the full costs of alternative housing subsidies or the savings that could be realized through reducing the costs

210

of construction. We proposed developing a computer model with IBM for systematizing the analysis. We'd have a tool to aid in rationally selecting least-cost approaches for subsidized housing. The model would be made available to government agencies, community groups, and developers. The approach followed one of my corporate responsibility principles: Get involved in areas where the private sector has special expertise. But the project languished. We spent too much time on lengthy meetings and too little on hard work. Developing a computer model was not a glamour project, so we could not satisfy the Urban Coalition urge for visible bricks-and-mortar results. Probably most important, we were out of touch with reality. Computer analysis of real estate was in its infancy. We simply had no market for our product. Community groups, government agencies, even experienced real estate developers did not know what to do with the new analytical tool. And the Urban Coalition didn't have enough staying power for a project whose time had not yet arrived. Today, of course, cash-flow and internal-rate-of-return analysis are packaged in computer programs, accessible to the public and private sectors alike. And today the Urban Coalition still exists, although much scaled down in its objectives and public posture.

In those early days of social responsibility, many companies felt uncomfortable breaking away from their long-established mode of corporate philanthropy. Corporations had long been giving away 1 percent to 2 percent of their shareholders' annual profits through separate foundations or through internal corporate philanthropy committees. Money typically would go to the directors' pet charities and to organizations, such as the United Way, serving communities where the company had a physical presence. Now companies were asked to become actively involved in the design and support of social projects. Initially, companies chose highly visible projects with a large public relations content—sponsoring a street clean-up campaign, the branch manager photographed for the local newspapers wielding a broom alongside a black teenager. Corporations hesitated before taking on projects that carried the risk of bringing under fire their mode of running their own business—a not unreasonable fear. Once I was sent to Fisk (a university in Nashville, Tennessee, founded in 1866 to train black leaders) to sing the praises of the Chase urban affairs program in hopes that we might recruit black officer candidates. In those days of dissent on college campuses, students did not want to hear about Chase's social responsibility programs; all they wanted to know was why Chase lent money to South Africa, a country that supports apartheid. And as much as I tried to give the party line—economic growth is the best way to reduce discrimination—I was nearly chased off the stage. The head office didn't send me on such front-line missions again.

However, areas related to corporate markets and corporate operations are exactly where corporations can be effective if—and only if—they undertake the same kind of hard-nosed analysis that they would before investing in a new corporate profit venture, and then, once they approve the undertaking, they devote sufficient resources to the effort. Chase *did* identify targets for corporate responsibility programs that were related to its own operations as a bank. But the early experiments were short-lived because we didn't fully understand the dimensions of the problems and we weren't prepared to stay with projects that had "iffy" long-term payoffs, when our short-term profit position was eroding.

Job training for youth—what better area for a corporation to get involved in? It meets the twin criteria of corporate self-interest and corporate expertise. Corporations need employees who can read and come to work on time; corporations bring the pragmatic experience of having trained their own employees in the past. We could see the emerging mismatch between job content and the youthful labor force in the changing urban environment of the late 1960s. Chase began an in-house program for out-of-school unemployed, sixteen to twenty-one years old, dubbing the effort with the appropriate acronym JOBS, Job Opportunities in Business. In effect, we ran a small school at headquarters, teaching basic reading, writing, and arithmetic skills and exposing young people, mostly school drop-outs, to the world of work. Every once in a while, I was asked to talk to the students about New York City's economy. Urban economics seemed a strange curriculum choice for high school drop-outs struggling with business arithmetic. But the school day was long, and I was a "filler," a diversion to break the tedium of rote learning. I faced a silent, catnapping audience until I tried to translate the principles of economics to the world of welfare and numbers running. Then street-smart youngsters displayed an extraordinary capacity for reasoning along economic lines.

Chase conducted the program as a well-designed experiment and earned "Brownie points" as an innovator in the new field of social responsibility. However, the program lapsed after four years. It was not that high school drop-outs were unteachable—far from it. But Chase was trying to compensate for the shortcomings of the school system as well as the attitudes of young people brought up in an unstable urban environment. Even if we were successful in educating twenty students at a time, 120 in a year, the program was too costly for Chase to mount on a scale large enough to make a dent in the unemployment problem. It would be another story if we innovated and then others replicated the Chase model. But we never reached that stage because bank profits deteriorated and Chase imposed a hiring freeze. How can a company justify a costly education program for drop-outs at the same time that it is turning away qualified applicants for a shrinking pool of jobs? By the time Chase started hiring again, enthusiasm for the experiment had faded. Fully funded by Chase initially, JOBS in its final two years accepted federal money, and along with government dollars came a morass of paperwork, which soured management on the program. Now, fifteen years after that early experiment, the public and private sectors have again "discovered" job training for the unemployed as one of the nation's top economic priorities. Did we learn anything at all? In a sentence, the private sector possesses the skills for training youngsters illprepared for the world of work, but companies can't be expected to bear the brunt of subsidy costs or to create jobs for the unemployed where no jobs exist.

Did Chase develop other models of corporate involvement that worked? Yes, but always with limitations. The concept of training school principals came out of a Chase pilot program developed in the early 1970s. We were convinced that improving education in New York City schools was essential for raising the quality of the City's labor force. By then, we had learned that we could not take on all of the failures of the school system. David Rockefeller called upon Anthony Terraciano, a young Chase personnel executive, now chief financial officer of the bank, to develop a proposal. Tony looked at the task—reading and talking with educators inside and outside the school system so that he could understand the production process of urban education—as if he had been assigned responsibility for designing a new product. Then he developed a set of guidelines.

Chase should concentrate on training principals. A strong principal can make the difference between a good school and a bad school, even in low-income, deteriorating neighborhoods. The key to being a good principal is more than having a record as an experienced teacher. A principal is an administrator, a manager. And few teachers possess management skills. Transferring management skills to principals would be highly cost effective. "An investment in a good principal will spill over to dozens of teachers and ultimately to thousands of students," Tony reasoned. To be effective, the program should be mounted with the cooperation of the educational establishment. The objectives: First, demonstrate that principal-training works, then incorporate training as an integral part of the system. We were not looking for a one-time experiment by "do-gooders," preordained to be ignored by the bureaucracy. Chase accepted the concept and funded a two-year program at the Bank Street College of Education.

Was the Bank Street project a success? Yes, in the sense that corporate funds and expertise focused on an area that the public sector was incapable of addressing at the time. Yes, in the sense that the educational world agreed that the management-training program worked. Yes, in the sense that the program was replicated in many school districts across the nation. Gordon Klopf, dean at Bank Street, evaluates his "baby" this way: "In a third of the schools, we see drastic change for the better; in another third, we see a bit of improvement; and among a third, not much of anything happens." That's a pretty good record of success. Unfortunately, the Board of Education implemented the program only sporadically in New York City. If all had followed according to "blueprint," Chase's original investment would have seeded continuing local public support.

In 1982, Chase announced a new two-year, $435,000 grant for leadership training of principals in New York City's high schools. The grant, which was given to the Board of Education and the Alliance for Public Schools (a consortium of university, public school, and business representatives), was dressed up in language that makes it look like a precedent-shattering innovation. In reality, the new leadership program is an enlarged refinement of the principal-training effort Chase had funded a decade earlier. Change takes time and money as well as a good idea!

Improvement of education is an "acceptable" target for corporate involvement. Corporate dollars and management expertise help the public sector do a more effective job; in return, corporations receive a better public-sector product —an educated labor force. What about corporations focusing on their own products? Can and should corporations modify their goods and services as part of their corporate responsibility agenda? It may be difficult to see how, if you are a manufacturer of buttons or nuts and bolts. But theoretically there are lots of ways a developer of housing or even a producer of movies can alter a product for the benefit of minorities or low-income groups. If you are a bank and your product is money, the prescriptions for reallocating your resources are almost limitless. John D. Rockefeller gave dimes away to the man on the street. Banks can do the same thing, giving away money masked as loans that they know they will never get back. Even in my most naive days, I never went that far, but I did think we could develop untapped markets that would be profitable over the longer term. Admittedly, we might have to utilize government subsidy programs, but, I urged the bankers, success models are out there to emulate. Low down payments and thirty-year home mortgages were never heard of until the federal government introduced FHA-insured and VA-guaranteed loans. Today, millions of middle-income families own their own homes, financed with fully private, low down payments and long-term mortgages, the interest payments a deduction on their income taxes. Credit cards were once restricted to the wealthy who could prove their net worth. Combine aggressive marketing with the tax deductibility of interest and today the credit card is the accepted mode of spending for middle-income households. Why couldn't financial institutions lead the way with the same kinds of innovative approaches for the problem areas in their marketplace?

The theory sounds reasonable. It proved difficult to implement. In my enthusiasm as advocate for innovative financing, I'd ignored an obvious difference between the earlier success models for lending to the middle class and the proposed responsibility programs: By definition, the poor do not have as much money as the middle class. Therefore, the problems of lending money to benefit the poor are inherently intractable. Chase started an Economic Development loan program with the objective of expanding loan activity with minority-owned businesses. The program lasted for only a few years. But it did not die because of its loan losses. In fact, several black-owned businesses, such as Earl Graves Publishing (*Black Enterprise* magazine) and

Vanguard Oil (home heating oil distributors), received financing under the program and developed into successful enterprises. Rather, the program died because we didn't understand the new marketplace and what resources were required to make it work.

First, it turned out to be difficult to generate business— blacks and Hispanics didn't stream into Chase's posh downtown headquarters to apply for loans. And branch managers were too preoccupied with the pressures of producing profits on their everyday business to pay attention to head office memos urging them to send clients to that fuzzy-brained experiment going on downtown. Besides, "bankable" situations were then few and far between. Bankers— whether overly conservative or simply acting in their fiduciary responsibility to depositors—find that they can play only a limited role in lending to undercapitalized small business ventures that are just beginning, and if this is true for small business generally, it applies even more to minorities, who do not bring the experience of entrepreneurship to their proposals. Administrative costs were high. "It takes as much paperwork," said Larry Toal, the first director, "to process a $50,000 economic development loan as it does to complete a $50-million loan to a Fortune 500 company. And once a loan is extended, bankers spend hundreds of hours with the borrower, helping with bookkeeping and marketing and tax advice if they want to get their money back." Young lending officers, fresh out of business school, gave unstintingly of their own time. Sometimes they were too green themselves to give sound advice, or, just as bad, they could not communicate with blacks and Hispanics, who spoke a "different language" and resented outside "meddling in their affairs."

As the program matured, we couldn't agree on what to do next. It is one thing to conduct a pilot program, confined to a few black and Hispanic entrepreneurs. It is another to decide how to incorporate the effort into the larger branch system. How do you avoid mixed signals—urging managers to book minority loans at the same time that you base their performance rating on bottom-line profits? If blacks and Hispanics receive special treatment, how do you deal with women, Orientals, Jews, or Italians? Should loans be targeted to certain neighborhoods or to certain types of businesses? Should a commercial bank participate in government subsidy programs to lower the cost to the borrower and reduce the risk to the lender? Chase rejected Small Business Administration loan guarantees. As George Champion, former Chase chairman, drove home to the troops, "A bankable loan does not require a guarantee. Working with government only adds time, paperwork, and costs to the process."

We debated issues endlessly, not satisfactorily resolving the thorny questions. Larry Toal moved on to bigger and better things—this is typical when talent is spotted in large corporations. Replacements, not fired by the enthusiasm that goes with a new venture, failed in their advocacy role. And as the bank cut costs under the pressure to make profits, the Economic Development loan program was quietly buried. Not that the loan losses amounted to a hill of beans! (In retrospect, if the major banks had spent as much time monitoring their Fortune 500 clients, big real estate developers, and Latin American borrowers as they did overseeing their small minority entrepreneurs, U.S. banks would have avoided some of the major financial debacles of the 1970s and early 1980s.) Some commercial banks—Chemical, in particular—kept with their programs and carved out a niche for themselves in the marketplace as specialists in packaging economic development loans, combining private money with city, state, and federal programs. But the notion that there is a magic way that banks can responsibly infuse large sums of money into the minority community on goodwill alone turned out to be wrong.

Chase and other financial institutions went through several false starts in the housing area, too. Then the major New York City banks developed a model of acknowledged, if limited, success. Commercial banks were under fire to provide financing for low- and moderate-income housing. The New York Clearinghouse, the trade association of the major New York City commercial banks, conscious of the poor public image of banks, put together a task force to develop a housing proposal. Nat Bloom, my counterpart at Citibank, and I were asked to do the underlying economic analysis. We wanted to present a concept that made economic sense and that could be sold to a group of conservative bankers. This was not an easy order to fill, given New York City's vast housing market with its web of rent controls and its rapidly deteriorating housing stock. About 30,000 units of housing were abandoned each year—two to three times as many units as were replaced by new construction. If we could reduce the rate of abandonment, we could make a significant contribution toward ameliorating New York City's housing problems. There was no point in focusing on the worst neighborhoods, where the downward momentum looked unstoppable. Rather, we recommended, the banks should concentrate on moderate rehabilitation of multifamily housing in neighborhoods in transition. We selected two demonstration neighborhoods that were begin-

ning to deteriorate but which contained a large stock of
basically sound multifamily housing—Crown Heights, in
Brooklyn, and Washington Heights, in upper Manhattan.
The costs of moderate rehabilitation—replacing the boiler,
installing new windows, rewiring—were far below those of
new construction or gut rehabilitation, where buildings are
emptied out and stripped. Permitting tenants to stay in place
would add stability to the neighborhood. If the program
worked, sound older buildings would be saved, neighborhood
deterioration would be staved off, and, ultimately, additional
private investment would be encouraged. This approach,
we concluded, "would give banks the biggest bang for the
buck."

The Clearinghouse accepted the concept, a bit gingerly
at first. But research recommending a specific, limited objective was only the first step. Translating theory into
actuality required the pragmatism of bankers. The bankers
said, "No bank is going to do this alone. We'll all contribute to a pool of funds." The establishment banking
community borrowed a page out of the United Jewish Appeal's fund-raising book—make everyone stand up and be
counted so that no one can avoid doing his share. More
substantively, commercial bankers lacked experience in the
rehabilitation loan market. Establishing a separate corporation whose sole mission was to make the program work
increased the chances for developing the necessary skills.
The banks obtained clearance from the Justice Department so that they could pool financial resources without
running the risk of antitrust charges. Then they began to
shape the working rules for the new Community Preservation Corporation (CPC). Warren Lindquist—one of David
Rockefeller's advisors, and "Lindy" to everyone who knew

him—took on the role of chairman. Lindy brought preconditions along with him. The commercial banks were not going to take on this experiment alone. The savings banks held mortgages on older apartment properties and therefore had to be brought in. Then, banks were not going to refinance apartments as a charitable undertaking. The venture need not produce the maximum possible return on capital, but the CPC would not be a private-sector "giveaway." Most important, before the banks would go ahead, the City had to agree to a restructuring of rents. Rents in the buildings could not be held to the irrational patterns of rent controls. After a long, hard fight to convince the City that there was no way to finance rehabilitation without providing more rental income, the City agreed. The program took time to get off the ground. Owners were reluctant to participate. "Put money down a rat hole?" Landlords seemed resigned to a fate of continuing deterioration. After eight years, the results are impressive—10,000 rehabiliated units and $100 million committed in mortgage financing. The CPC has extended the demonstration project to additional neighborhoods. And perhaps most important, the experiment is leveraging additional private-sector investment as other lending institutions find out that the rehabilitation market, with the right ingredients, can work. Is the CPC program an unqualified success? The answer, of course, is no. Finding ways to bring private-sector financing into an area where it ordinarily would not go is only one element in the housing picture. Government, with its regulations, is part of the problem. Landlords, too, with their limited management skills, are part of the problem. And certainly tenants who throw garbage out the window and scrawl graffiti in the halls are part of the problem. But the most severe constraint is the differential between the costs of rehabilitating and maintaining apartments and the rent that low- and moderate-income families can afford. The CPC found that some tenants, particularly the elderly, could remain in place with higher rents only if they obtained Section 8 federal rental housing supplements, and when that source of funding dried up, a hunt for new government subsidies began. The hard realistic lesson of the exercise is that when there is a large shortfall between the costs of a service—whether it is housing or medical care or job training—and what low- or moderate-income families can pay, private companies cannot be expected to make up the deficit. If there is a consensus that these services should be provided, then it is government's role to meet the shortfall.

The need for private-sector initiatives will diminish if the United States succeeds in sustaining economic growth, but it will not disappear. What can the new private-public partnerships learn from the corporate responsibility trials and errors of the past? Here are ten maxims for minimizing failures and building on successes:

1. Avoid knee-jerk responses to each day's crisis—today's headlines fast turn into tomorrow's shredded news clips.

2. Give clear guidelines to staff—the middle manager who must both maximize bottom-line earnings and please senior executives who preach corporate responsibility is doomed to ulcers and the demise of his corporate responsibility endeavors.

3. Concentrate on areas that build on business skills and self-interest, and the chances of doing something that works will be greater.

4. Research the undertaking as if it were a new product.

Business needs a realistic appraisal of probable costs and benefits.

5. Set limited, defined objectives. Don't promise more than an organization can deliver in money, expertise, or personnel.

6. Work with the institutions and individuals who are the intended beneficiaries—the private sector doesn't know all the answers.

7. Leverage investment by drawing in private-sector partners.

8. Make sure government programs are in place if subsidies are needed to fill the cost-income gap. It's not the private sector's role to redistribute income.

9. Expect a long learning curve and a certain number of failures.

10. Replicate success! True successes can be incorporated into the private sector's modus operandi or can be delivered to the public as tested models, which means the job of the private sector as innovator has been completed.

PART THREE

People

Who are the survivors?
Ultimately, the people, of course.

—The survivors are the men and women of the postwar "baby boom" who are reaching middle age. They flooded the labor force in their twenties and influenced the rest of us with their high-consumption and liberated life-styles. They are turning more conservative as they approach the magic age of forty, but they are not discarding all the trappings of their past.

—They are the new immigrants, survivors of economic and political hardship in other countries. Arriving legally and illegally in record numbers, they are making their way in an economic environment that has been hostile to many Americans, their presence affecting—in controversial ways—those working and living around them.

—They are the outsiders who persist in a life of crime past the age when sociologists tell us they should have outgrown their youthful habits.

—They are the women taking on new roles—the "new poor" on the urban scene, unmarried, tenuously tied to the invisible poor, the fathers of their children, and, at the other end of the spectrum, the new achievers gaining economic independence as they pursue their careers.

In this altered world, a question mark hangs over one long-time survivor—the family.

14
The Post-World War II
Babies Are Reaching
Middle Age: What Does
This Mean for the Economy?

The first group of post–World War II babies is passing through its thirties and heading toward forty, that much-feared age signaling actuarily that more than half of your life is behind you. The postwar babies are reaching middle age! The 75 million boys and girls born between 1946 and 1964 are no longer bursting onto the scene, flooding first the elementary schools, later the colleges, and then the labor force. Rather, with the bulk of them in their late twenties and early thirties, they are entrenched as seasoned members of the work force.

What does the aging of the baby boom generation mean for the economy? The postwar generation is trying to move up the career ladder into the narrower executive ranks— and there clearly isn't room at the top for all of them. As consumers, most are in the prime of their house-buying years, torn between carrying forward the unfettered life-styles of their youth and settling into middle-class respectability. No doubt, they will be more conservative in their social and political habits than they once were, but they *are* unique and therefore will not be a mirror image of the generation that preceded them. By the sheer weight of numbers, the aging baby boom generation will shape our economic, political, and social climate. Mellowed by age, their influence will be more subtle than in the past as youth worship fades and gray hair becomes respectable once more.

Each generation is influenced by the times in which it is born. My father used to tell me that he considered himself to be a hero. Too young to participate in World War I, too old to be drafted in World War II, he claimed that he was as brave as any soldier when he (and I assume my mother, too) went ahead with plans for a second child in the depths of the Great Depression. I was born in 1932, at a time close to the low point for births in the twentieth century. Shaped by growing up in the Great Depression, my generation expected to struggle for jobs when we entered the work force. Instead, as the post–World War II economy prospered, we proved to be a scarce commodity—there just weren't many of us. Employers began paying relatively high salaries to inexperienced workers and promoted employees at a younger and younger age in order to fill the expanding ranks of middle management. In our new affluence, we married young and produced the postwar surge in babies even though, with our Depression heritage, we were not entirely secure in our economic status. As an historic event, that oversize crop of babies that we gave birth to in the 1950s and early 1960s represents a sharp break in the long-term decline in the U.S. birth rate.

I view those postwar babies from several personal perspectives—as a parent raising two children born in the peak birth years, as a working person watching the influx come up through the employment ranks, and as an economist trying to attach numerical values to the income and output generated as this mass of humanity moves through the population age stream. There are those who blame the postwar generation for a good portion of our society's recent ills—high unemployment, crime, drugs, low voter participation are all closely correlated with the growing up of the post-war babies. That conclusion, of course, is not 100 percent correct. The postwar babies are both products of the values of earlier times and shapers of the environment. The post-war babies passed through adolescence and came of age with great expectations that their middle-class security was an inherited right at the same time that they questioned their middle-class values under the tutelage of the non-conformers of the 1950s and early 1960s—Kerouac's "Beat Generation" and the Beatles. The conflict between their middle-class values and their desire to rebel accompanies them as they age, but in a far less strident form.

Brought up in the comfort of suburban America (in single-family homes, driving their own cars in their teens), the postwar babies did not feel the same economic pressures to earn a living as did those raised in the 1930s and the World War II years. Some postponed entry into the labor force by extending their college education. Men avoiding the Vietnam draft bloated college enrollments. Young men and women rejected traditional entry-level jobs and pursued alternative life-styles—weaving woolens, farming organically, playing electric guitar in a rock group. Insecure parents, who feared worse alternatives for their children, subsidized their "drop-outs" from society rather than sever the financial umbilical cord. Of course, the majority of postwar babies did enter the labor force, and as they started the search for work, they encountered a more hostile environment than they expected initially. As teenagers, they competed with each other for part-time jobs. By 1970, teenage unemployment had passed the one million mark, for an increase of 55 percent in a decade. A parallel rise in crime among youth impressed itself on the national consciousness as one of "the" social issues of the 1960s.

Then the population bulge entered its twenties, and large numbers of young men and women started working full-time, only to find their competitive position eroding. They finally poured out of colleges in record numbers, to discover that the value of their college degrees had been debased by oversupply. The college graduate waiting on tables or driving a taxicab became a common sight in the early 1970s. The massive increase in new entrants provided business and other employers with an almost inexhaustible supply of "cheap" labor. The gap between the earnings of young men and women in their early twenties and the higher income earned by that scarce commodity, their parents, widened. Then, as the 1970s progressed, the twin drags of rapid labor force expansion and slow economic growth reduced their leverage in the competition for jobs even more.

Now, the young, green employees of the 1970s are the older, experienced workers of the 1980s. They've reached their prime working age, when they should become firmly established in their careers and start catching up to their elders in earnings. They are not dropping out of the scene permanently, in large numbers, as their parents feared they might. Sobered by the need to support themselves when their parents became too old or no longer willing to subsidize them, some of the mavericks converted their alternative life-styles into marginally profitable economic endeavors. Our cousin, at age thirty-eight, continues to farm organically in Maine, but today he sells his produce commercially to nearby restaurants, and just about breaks even. The vast majority of the postwar children are, as adults, members of the conventionally tabulated labor force. Today, 95 percent of all men in their late twenties and early thirties are in the labor force, either working or looking for a job. That's only two fewer percentage points than about twenty years ago. And more than two out of three women in the same age group are in the labor force, a much higher proportion than in earlier years.

No, entry into the labor force is not the issue. It is what you do and how well you are paid once you are there. And young men and women are finding that the drag of excess supply on their earnings is moving in tandem with them. True, their income is increasing as they leave their twenties and enter their thirties, but they are not catching up with their elders as fast as past experience says they should. In the early 1980s, a man aged thirty earned only $8 for every $10 earned by a forty-year-old. In 1970, he would have received $9 for every $10 earned by his senior. (The pattern is similar for women, but not as striking because increased participation in the labor force has swelled the ranks of older working women, too.)

The postwar generation looks to be headed for an employment bottleneck. The weight of large numbers will follow them as they age and will continue to depress their earnings relative to those of other workers. As mature adults, they are firmly ensconced in the labor force. This bodes well for raising productivity in the nation, since business will no longer have to contend with a huge influx of young, inexperienced workers. But those of the postwar generation who have already passed through the entry-level gates will find that too many of them are reaching middle age at the same time to squeeze into the ranks of upper management. The most capable and lucky ones will forge ahead, filling management gaps left by the undersize Depression generation. Still, many postwar babies are beginning to have a gnawing feeling that they're stuck in a rut, watching the anointed few among their peers pass them by. Two thousand Chase vice presidents compete for 100 senior vice president spots. A lawyer marks time after a half-dozen years in the District Attorney's office; he's hardworking and capable, but there is little chance to move up in the bureaucracy, and the skills he developed as a prosecutor of muggers and auto thieves leave him poorly prepared for competing with younger law school graduates in the private sector. An American couple spends ten years abroad in Italy, living comfortably by giving piano lessons and translating from and into Italian. Now they want to come home. What kind of jobs will pay enough so that they can buy a modest $200,000 Manhattan apartment? Maybe Mom and Dad will help out, subsidizing the apartment purchase of their thirty-five-year-old children—but maybe their parents cannot afford to, now that they've reached retirement age.

Coming from backgrounds where higher education is taken for granted, many of those who find their careers are at a standstill will look to additional schooling to sharpen their management skills or to provide them with the training for our rapidly changing technology. Adult continuing education will be encouraged by colleges and universities left with empty seats after the postwar baby boom has moved on. Employers, overloaded with middle management, will search for ways to utilize their experienced staff more efficiently, and, almost acting in loco parentis, they will send an increasing number of mid-career employees back to the books. Corporate sabbaticals will not become the norm, but I wouldn't be surprised to see paid leave used more extensively as an alternative form of fringe benefit (employees trading retirement time for short-term mid-career leaves). This innovation would complement the continuing trend for women to pursue careers, rather than to work sporadically at "jobs." And I don't think there is any doubt about it: Economic pressures to maintain two-career households, with both men and women working for wages, will be great. This is how couples sustained their high-consumption lifestyles when they were in their twenties, and this is what they will do in their thirties and early forties, years when most households carry the additional financial burden of raising children.

The life-styles this generation chooses to follow as it reaches middle age will have a pervasive influence on the economy. And, as any economist knows, each age group follows distinctive buying and saving patterns. The consumption patterns of a group as large as the postwar babies are so pronounced (and overdrawn by the advertising and news media) that they influence how the rest of us spend our money: Whether we look upon their life-styles with disparagement or approval, the values of the postwar generation have rubbed off on the rest of us. Rock music, drug use, long hair, travel with backpacks, physical fitness, health food, eating out, coed dorms, box stereos, political marches—few of us, whether younger or older, are not conditioned in some ways by the life-style changes that pervaded the 1960s and early 1970s. Who hasn't seen the older version of "liberated" children in their middle-aged friends—shirt unbuttoned to waist, chain dangling from neck, designer jeans? Our tennis club, predominantly thirties and older in its clientele, abolished family memberships several years ago—there were too many unmarried couples (with frequently changing partners) and too few children for the traditional family membership to work. The owner finally gave up when two young women flight attendants sharing an apartment demanded a family discount.

The question now is: What will happen to their youthful habits as the postwar generation ages? What "baggage" will the matured baby boom take along with them? How will the values of youth be modified when the consumption patterns of middle age gain in importance? Marketing specialists make fortunes for their clients by accurately predicting these shifts. Astute entrepreneurs figure out how to cash in on the changes. When aggressive soft drink companies see their vast teenage market disappearing, they don't fold up and die. They diversify, moving into newly expanding fields. Or they modify their product so that it appeals to adults. Combine the health consciousness of the 1970s and early 1980s with an expanding group of older consumers, and the result is low-calorie soft drinks, "light" beer, and caffeine-free cola. Of course, successful marketing is complicated. The very same consumers in their twenties and early thirties who drink diet colas acquired expensive tastes at an early age. Our children entertain their friends. The next day the house is filled with empty beer bottles, bearing labels in a half-dozen foreign languages. Each guest brings his or her favorite brand of imported beer, bought at roughly twice the price of the ordinary mass-produced American product drunk by their elders.

No, predicting precisely when habits will change and what new form they will take is not easy. And assuming that everyone in the massive postwar population group fits into the same highly advertised mold can be a major mistake. Many of the very first children of the postwar baby boom grew up nearly as "old-fashioned" in their attitudes as the Depression generation did. One friend, in her late thirties, tells me a bit ruefully that she missed out on it all—she didn't know what marijuana was until her senior year in college, when she noticed all those freshmen smoking strange-smelling "joints." Those born at the tail end of the baby boom entered college when the Vietnam War was a memory, inflation was running rampant, and unemployment was pushing to record highs. The harsh reality hit home that jobs would not be easy to find, even with an advanced university degree. These late postwar babies began to turn their backs on some—certainly not all—of the values of the 1960s. And the shift in attitudes came quickly, within two or three years. Our daughter graduated from high school in 1975. She and her classmates refused to wear caps and gowns at graduation—a form of minirebellion that typified the 1960s. Three years later, our son graduated from the same school. Caps and gowns were back in favor. Daniel asked for a three-piece suit as a graduation gift and announced that he wanted his long hair styled by my haircutter. The unisex barber had arrived on the scene a few years earlier. Older men, influenced by the symbolic freedom of the younger generation's long hair, discarded their own closely clipped haircuts. And women, admiring the natural manner of their daughters' hairstyles, rejected the rigid look of hair stiffly set in curlers and sprayed into place. The $2 haircut turned into the $20 styling, and the unisex barber was born. It was the older generation's turn to influence younger men and women, who looked at their modishly groomed parents and decided that "style" wasn't such a bad thing after all, particularly if you had to compete for a job.

The flow of values back and forth between generations is unpredictable both in its timing and in its dimensions. Still, in many respects, the future is shaped by the past, so we can limn the outlines of the postwar generation's social and economic behavior. As mature adults, these people will be saddled with the financial trappings of middle age; as postwar babies grown up, they will carry along their propensity for instant gratification, which they can satisfy because both husband and wife work for pay and do not carry the burden of large families. The postwar babies did *not* produce their own crop of children as they reached their early twenties. That's documented history. However, women who postponed decisions about child-bearing began to confront the time clock of their decreasing fertility, and births gradually started to rise in the mid-1970s. According to demographers, births will increase until the closing years of the 1980s. But the number of births will not match the 4.3 million annual record of the early 1960s. Even if couples should make a massive decision to go back to larger families (which I doubt) or to have their children at a younger age (which I think could happen), it is difficult to see how recent trends could reverse themselves quickly enough to produce more than 4 million babies a year during the 1980s.

What is happening can be called a "baby boomlet." You don't need to go to the statistical records to know that more babies are being born. It just takes looking around. A children's high-fashion clothing boutique opens on Columbus Avenue, close by the gourmet food store that caters to "gentrified" New Yorkers. Toddlers crawl around close by their parents at tennis courts where no children have been seen for years. We, of an older generation, watch with mixed feelings. We rarely brought our children with us on those rare occasions when we went out. But this is a different generation. The parents are older, with one child, two at most, and they dote on their offspring. They are used to a lifestyle that they are not about to sacrifice—eating out, traveling, playing tennis. As two-income families, they can afford to continue that life-style, and they include their child as part of it.

Still, even with two incomes, choices must be made, and the key one for couples in their late twenties and early thirties is housing. The average age for a first-time house buyer is twenty-eight; for a repeat buyer, trading up, the average is thirty-five. If age alone were the trigger for home-buying, we would have been in the midst of a great housing boom in the early 1980s. Instead, interest rates on mortgages soared and the housing market collapsed as housing costs rose faster than personal income. Young couples remained in cramped quarters or moved in with parents. But pent-up demand for housing increased as more of those couples who had postponed child-bearing finally went ahead and produced children. The underlying demographics point to a high level of housing purchases until the late 1980s. Then the population bulge will move into its late thirties and early forties, years when more expensive, but fewer, homes are bought, and the "baby bust"—the small cohort growing up behind—will begin to depress the total size of the market.

Whether or not the potential demand for housing will be met will depend in large part on how successful we are in containing inflation and sustaining economic growth.

And that's the catch-22: The postwar babies have reached the stage of their life cycle when they tend to incur both consumer (installment) and mortgage debt. Their needs (wants?) are larger than their incomes, but they do have the earnings record on which to borrow and they have grown up in a society that encourages them to consume now and pay later. They will be competing for credit in the marketplace with government, which will be financing its huge deficits, and private industry, which will be borrowing funds for expansion and modernization. My guess is that we will see adult couples with young children in the market for housing, but the costs of that housing will be high. Since their families are small, they will scale back on housing size before sacrificing quality. The financial burden of carrying that housing will consume a large proportion of their income, eating into their capability to save, and keeping economic pressures on women to work. More women (and some men) will step off the career path for short periods to care for their children, but they won't stay off for long.

As this massive group inexorably moves toward middle age, their patterns of consumption of a wide range of goods and services will resemble those of the people who preceded them. They will buy furniture and appliances for their homes. They will buy shoes and braces for their children, but they will postpone worries about financing their college education because children came to them so late in life. Their romance with travel will stay strong, but they will stay in hotels not in hostels. Their usage of medical services with shift dramatically, solely as a function of age. The demand for emergency services at hospitals will drop off, since injuries from auto accidents decline when young men cross the twenty-five-year threshold. But medical services for long-term illnesses will increase, since the incidence of maladies like cancer and heart disease rises at middle age, even though great progress is being made against both these diseases. But their patterns of consumption will not be an exact replay of the patterns their parents followed. The changes in life-styles and values that emerged from those who passed through their teens and their college years in the 1960s and 1970s are traveling with them as they approach middle age in the 1980s. Rock music turned out to be enduring, not an ephemeral teenage fad. The Beatles, the Grateful Dead, the Rolling Stones—they remain a powerful influence on music, performing live or through their records nearly a quarter of a century later. Now most of the early rock stars are truly middle-aged, well into their forties. The survivors modified their product over time; they reached down to new, younger audiences and eventually acclimatized older generations to their sound.

Drugs, sexual freedom, the high propensity for crime among youth—the common wisdom of the sages was: "Be patient; they'll outgrow these habits." The reality is that most of the postwar babies outgrew extreme forms of drug abuse and sexual experimentation and ceased their dabbling in crime, but the process of maturation did not bring social mores back to what they once were. Crime rates of the postwar babies are dropping as their generation ages, but their crime rates have not come down to the level previously associated with men and women their age. Tolerance for drugs and nonmarital relationships has spread upward to their elders as well as filtering downward to the younger generation that is coming up behind them. For the most part, these activities are carried on with greater knowledge of the risks and less as a symbol of rebellion. They're accepted by both the middle-aged *and* the middle class. EST is no longer the province of those "California crazies" lolling in hot tubs. It's big business, with secretaries and salesmen enrolling their friends at sessions in downtown business convention hotels as if they were selling Tupperware on commission. Couples in their late forties and fifties who would have gone to great lengths to hide their nonmarital relationships in an earlier age openly flaunt their living arrangements. Couples in their early thirties who had lived together for years decide at last on conventional marriage, propelled to the decision, perhaps, by the mutual desire to have a child. Weddings amidst the daisies in open fields are on the way out, but personalized vows composed by bride and groom are very much in. Some say the pendulum has swung: "Traditional weddings with brides in their twenties wearing white gowns and grooms decked out in black ties are back." Yes, I can see that, but . . . it's not quite the same when Uncle slips out from the reception, champagne glass in hand, for a bit of "coke." And marriage, even when the vows are exchanged in a traditional setting, is certainly not forever—divorce rates, although no longer rising, remain at historically high levels. And although many observers believe that later marriages make for more enduring and more stable relationships, I think strong countervailing pressures—small families and the greater financial independence of working women—pull the other way. It is wishful thinking to believe that we will slip back into the "ideal" mode of earlier times, when marriages were legally maintained until one of the partners died (even though these unions were all too often marriages in name only).

The postwar baby generation marked the 1960s and

1970s with its political discontent. That same group of men and women is becoming more settled in its political habits as it ages, but it has by no means completely abandoned its past. The political marches of the 1960s are mostly memories, revived on special occasions for special causes. As they get older, those who once marched and shut down their college campuses are expressing themselves through traditional channels by registering in political parties and voting. The postwar generation is becoming an increasingly powerful force in influencing elections and government policies. When they were younger, they were highly visible and vocal, but few of them voted. Now they are at an age when more than half of them vote, and by the 1988 election, masses of them will be up in their late thirties, an age when at least six out of ten men and women will vote. It is possible that they will vote in lower proportions than their parents once did. Even so, there are so many of them—those born between 1946 and 1964 comprise 45 percent of the voting age population—that they'll add up to a lot of voters.

Clearly, the postwar generation is not bringing the radical antiestablishment extremes of the 1960s with them. They *are* bringing a pronounced tendency to participate in the political process as independents, ready to swing their votes between the two major parties and to become actively involved with special interests close to their hearts. They seem likely to remain liberal on social and environmental issues. But given their own difficulties in the job market, they will be more conservative on economic issues than they were in the past. Wanting to protect their own economic security, they will not be automatic allies of those at the bottom of the income ladder—blacks, Hispanics, or women heading households with children. The result is that, neither definitely conservative nor liberal, their political behavior will be highly unpredictable. And the demand for the services of political pollsters (like the demand for economists) will be strong, even though their record of predictions is weak. The need to read the pulse of a volatile electorate will ensure that pollsters remain fully employed.

Perhaps the most subtle of the many changes that are occurring with the aging of the baby boom is the ebbing of youth worship. Just because of its undue size, youth dominated attitudes toward age as the postwar generation moved through its teens and twenties. Movies, television, journalism, and advertising all inflated the advantages of youth by the relentless repetition of the youth image. Middle-aged women wore jeans or short skirts and colored their hair in a determined effort to look young. "Does she or doesn't she?" The celebrated Clairol advertisement of the 1960s made changing one's hair color socially acceptable, and anyone, young or old, could do it. Men in their forties and fifties, facing increased competition from younger colleagues breathing down their necks in the race for career advancement, pursued a parallel effort to look young, wearing contact lenses, dyeing *their* hair without apology, worrying about their weight less out of fear of heart attacks than out of dread that a protruding stomach would label them "middle-aged."

Now, almost overnight, the phobia of middle age is lessening. Why? Because the great hordes of postwar youth are much closer to their forties than to their teens, which they've left far behind. Advertisers and the media study the demographics and modify their products to reflect the shift. Television superstars such as Johnny Carson and Phil

Donahue proudly sport gray hair. Evening newsmen in their early forties display their gray locks. Not quite ready to be identified with old age, they style their hair a little fuller than their elders'. The image of the mature adult is "in" and youth worship is "out"—at least among men. The image change comes a little more slowly for women. With few exceptions, youth reigns supreme. Women modeling in advertising brochures and women appearing on television still have the demeanor of little girls. (Perhaps, as Marlene Sanders, a pioneer among women in television news broadcasting, suggests, this is because middle-aged men control the media—and they still like their women to be young.) But I haven't given up hope. Against the advice of my peers, I'm a holdout against coloring my gray hair. I'm convinced that as the postwar generation moves to the forty-year line, gray will become respectable for women as well as for men—stylishly and expensively coiffed, to be sure!

15

Will High Tech Destroy
More Jobs Than It Creates?

Spring 1982: I was watching television in a slightly seedy
hotel room in Chester, England, after a long day of "selling"
New York to potential British investors. The discussion
among the panel participants on the BBC was sober. The
Midlands—the industrial heart of England—was in serious
economic difficulties. The focus of the debate was the poor
preparation of the British labor force for the new era of
high technology. Everyone—the schools, the labor unions,
the national government, corporate management—received
a piece of the blame. One panelist wistfully looked to West
Germany as a model: "If we British only had an apprentice-
ship system like the Germans have, we could train our labor
force for the new technology. Our system is so rigid that
we're teaching industrial skills of the 1920s instead of preparing our youth for the technological world of the 1980s."
The accents and phrases were slightly different, but the
theme was the same. I could be back in New York City

watching national television, reading *Time* magazine, or giving a speech myself on the linkages between education and economic development.

As the United States strives to move through the 1980s on a path of sustained, strong economic growth, diagnoses of the nation's shortcomings fill the academic and popular press. We've all become instant experts on what went wrong in the 1970s and early 1980s, blaming inappropriate monetary and fiscal policies at the macroeconomic level and structural weaknesses—poor management practices, stubborn unions, an oversupply of inadequately trained labor (i.e., blacks, women, youth)—at the microeconomic level. Those looking for instant cures latch onto single-factor explanations. The truth, of course, is that we're part of a complex world economy, and many forces operate simultaneously to affect our economic performance. A common theme that runs through much of the discussion is the economic significance of high technology. We may not all agree on just what "high technology" means, but there is a broad consensus that to compete successfully in the world economy, we must encourage innovation and the growth of high technology. At the same time, we feel ambivalent about high technology. We recognize its potential role as a source of economic growth, but we have an uneasy feeling that high technology will destroy more jobs than it creates. The dehumanized factory without a worker in sight is not science fiction—it's in place today. Two separate, but related, questions loom: First, can we train our labor force for the new technology? And second, even if we can, will there be enough jobs to absorb all the workers? The pessimists paint a picture of an increasingly polarized society, with highly paid "technocrats" at one extreme and a permanently unemployed "underclass" at the other. If this view is accurate, the future will be bleak for older industrial areas and the urban cores, which already suffer from high unemployment. The optimists point out that high technology means more than computer programming and robotics. It spawns industries requiring a full range of skills, from the untrained messenger to the genetic engineer.

Experts who have studied the question for years differ in their assessments of high technology's potential for creating jobs. I think history is on the side of those who view technological change as a plus for the economy. We only have to go back to the 1950s and 1960s and recall the books, the popular articles, and the conferences on automation after the computer was introduced. The fear, then as now, was that automation required new skills and that more jobs would be destroyed than created. I remember the early 1960s at Chase. The bank was under the dual pressure of implementing a computerization program at the same time that its clerical work force was rapidly changing. I was surrounded by secretaries who had been hired in the 1930s. Chase did not fire clerical workers during the Depression. Its clerical work force—white, female—rewarded Chase's "social responsibility" by staying on loyally until retirement. In the early 1960s, long-tenured secretaries, payroll clerks, and key punch operators were retiring en masse. Their replacements were young blacks and Hispanics. The adjustments were not easy. Then, as now, managers complained, "They can't be trained." And at first, it looked as if the managers were correct. Productivity fell; turnover rose to an astounding 45 percent—nearly one out of every two clerical employees left within a year. But then a strange thing happened. As Chase (and other New York City banks) felt the pain of a profit squeeze, managers learned to train their new employees, and, even more important, bank executives discovered how to put their computers to new uses. As we all know, the world of banking has been revolutionized. Banks perform all kinds of new functions—from credit cards to international trading in Eurodollars to econometric forecasting for a fee. Computer technology, although not the only reason for the innovations, is integral to the expansion of diversified financial services. Old-time bank officers nostalgically look back to the good old days and their Katie Gibbs graduates who remained their secretaries as they themselves worked their way up the executive ladder. They forget that many of these "old-time" gems were fixed in their ways and stubbornly resisted change. The fact is that technology changed the world of banking, and with it both employment and economic output expanded. In New York City, banking and the related securities industries have been sectors of employment growth. And the growth that they experienced fed into the rest of the local economy, leading to employment expansion in a wide range of service-sector jobs—from busboys in hotels to million-dollar-a-year Wall Street lawyers.

What, if anything, is different today? If we understand the similarities of the 1960s and 1980s and the differences between them, we will have a better chance of reaping the economic potential of high technology than of suffering the pain of structural unemployment. I believe that it is not so much the nature of the new technology that separates the 1980s from earlier periods as the environment in which innovation is taking place. First, we are much more part of the world economy today. New technologies cross national borders faster than ever before. Even if we strike ahead in one field, there is no assurance that we will maintain a monopoly or even a competitive edge for long. Second, we started the 1980s with a large residue of unemployment. The unemployment rate passed 10 percent in 1982; that is more than twice the average of the 1960s and, with more than 10 million unemployed, the largest number of people without jobs since the Great Depression. The combination of greater international competition and higher national unemployment makes for powerful differences between the environment of the 1960s and that of the 1980s. Adjustments will be painful and take time, but I would argue that the difficulties are not insurmountable.

New technologies affect both manufacturing—*what* is produced and *how* it is made—and the broader service sectors, where the output of high technology manufacturing is put to work in everything from telecommunications to medical diagnoses, from inventory control in department stores to automatic banking at home. New technology means changing skills, but the direction is not all one way. Yes, the number of scientists and engineers needing higher education will increase, but so will the number of data processors and factory assemblers who perform jobs utilizing skills where the formal educational requirements may not, in fact, be greater than in the past. Two distinct groups are most likely to be affected: older industrial workers and youth, particularly minorities.

Displacement of industrial workers is not new. New York City's manufacturing work force shrank from one million employees in the early 1950s to fewer than 500,000 in the early 1980s—one out of two manufacturing jobs disappeared. Jobs first went south, then overseas to Taiwan, the Philippines, and Korea. A large proportion of the vanishing jobs were held by young women and newcomers to the City (principally Hispanics) in the garment and textile industries. Many, but not all, the women moved with relative ease into the expanding clerical and service sectors, where they earned as much as or more than they had before. The shrinkage closed access to entry-level jobs for young black males who had neither the training nor the motivation to enter the female-dominated service sector. New Yorkers felt the loss in their manufacturing base, but no one else paid much attention. Such job displacement was not considered a national issue; experts said it was inevitable, given the almost inexhaustible supply of low-wage labor in developing countries all over the world.

The 1980s industrial job displacement differs. Striking at the heart of our industrial fabric—our basic steel, auto, and machinery industries—displacement hits high-wage men, many of them in their thirties and early forties, the primary earners in their families. This kind of displacement is hard to ignore. Part of the employment dislocation is a direct consequence of the 1980–82 recession, when more than two million manufacturing jobs disappeared. But weakness in manufacturing employment is not purely cyclical— there's been no net expansion in manufacturing employment since the end of the 1960s. As to the future, new jobs will be created in high technology manufacturing industries, but most of these gains may well be offset by losses in other manufacturing sectors. However, we'll be fooling ourselves if we think job losses occur just because the computer is replacing workers in unmanned factories. One analysis of why the Japanese produced small cars for sale in the United States at a $2,000 cost advantage in 1982 concluded that better management systems comprised 64 percent of the cost differential; lower wages and benefits, 25 percent; and union-management relations, 8 percent. Superior technology accounted for a mere 3 percent. Another analysis put one-third of the cost differential on an undervalued yen, one-third on higher U.S. taxes, and the remaining one-third on greater Japanese manufacturing efficiencies. These are vastly different viewpoints, but both suggest that automation is not the prime source of our employment problems.

I understood a bit more about what is happening when I visited the Welbuilt Electronic Die Corporation, in the South Bronx, of all places. The occasion was a celebration. Welbuilt, a company owned by John Mariotta, high-school-trained, of Puerto Rican heritage, had just received a $70-million contract from the U.S. Army for production of multipurpose engines. John Mariotta's story was everything that economic development officials dream of: a Hispanic employing minorities and ex-offenders in skilled factory jobs in the South Bronx. The City had sold Welbuilt a vacant industrial building, and several government agencies were assisting in financing the plant renovation and new equipment. Mr. Mariotta took me on a tour and demonstrated the new computer-controlled equipment that was to be used in the production of his engines. The label on the machines read *Mazak*. "It's a Japanese-owned company controlled by the Yamazaki Machine Works," said Mr. Mariotta. "Why," I asked, "do you buy your equipment from the Japanese?" His answer: "They're the only company that provides adequate service in the boondocks of the South Bronx. Americans—all they're interested in is selling to the big guys; they won't provide service to the little fellow." It turns out that Mazak assembles its product in Tennessee, uses Americans to sell and Japanese to service its equipment. I was struck by the answer. It meant that Japanese manufacturers were competing with the United States not just in the production of high technology equipment but in its servicing as well. The larger implications of my on-site South Bronx tour were clear. The question is not, simply, how do we train thirty-five-year-old machinists to be computer programmers, but how do we organize our manufacturing industries so that we can compete in the full spectrum of skills required by high technology? Only if we tackle the problem this way will employment options for the older industrial worker turn out to be broader than many think is in the cards.

Youth employment presents a different set of challenges. High unemployment among teenagers predates our preoccupation with new technologies. Teenagers typically experience unemployment rates that are two to three times greater than those of the older population. This did not present much of a problem in the 1950s, when teenagers comprised a small part of the labor force and when national unemployment rates were only 3 percent to 4 percent. But the teenage population increased rapidly in the 1960s and 1970s, and unemployment rates generally climbed higher. So teenage unemployment became a larger and larger problem. In 1982, when the national unemployment rate reached 10 percent, teenage unemployment hit 23 percent. Nearly 2 million teenagers were unemployed, three times as many as in 1960.

The youth bulge has peaked. The teenage population is declining and will continue to drop through the 1990s. Shrinking numbers will ease the adjustments to the new technologies. But we will be making these adjustments in an environment where more than one out of five teenagers is unemployed. In the older urban cores, and for blacks in particular, the situation is far worse: One out of two black teenagers living in New York City was reported unemployed in 1982, and if we included all of those not even looking for work, the true unemployment rate would be much higher. How do you prepare unemployed youngsters and those who are already in entry-level jobs for the new technologies, when they can barely read or do elementary arithmetic? The problem is acute in urban areas, but it is not unique to cities. Have you ever watched a teenager try to make change in a gasoline station or found yourself stuck on a check-out line in a suburban supermarket that has not installed electronic price-scanning? The answer lies in simultaneously upgrading education and downgrading requirements for performing the new jobs.

When my secretary at Chase Manhattan Bank married and deserted Brooklyn to raise a family on suburban Long Island, I searched for a replacement among the new entrants to the City's labor force. One of the candidates was a young black woman. I'll call her Martha James. She lived, in census terms, as female head of household, with three small children in the Bronx. Martha barely passed the typing test. Our human resources advisor ("personnel" has long been an obsolete corporate term) warned, "Don't take her. Her skills are poor. She's got too many personal problems. She'll never last." Ruth Clark, a black entrepreneur who runs a personnel agency specializing in placement of blacks, was even tougher. She cautioned me, "You're not doing blacks a favor if you don't hold them to standards." I hired Martha anyway. I'd been advising Chase on urban issues for years. If I wasn't ready to give a young woman on the verge of welfare a chance to work, who would? On a practical level, the naysayers were right: My new secretary's grammar was poor, and the difficulties of handling small children nearly overwhelmed her. My patience wore thin. "Why do you always take the children to the hospital when they come down with the flu?" I complained. "I don't take mine." The difference was that I used a private pediatrician and telephoned her when my children were sick with minor ailments. Dr. Halkin, a female pediatrician with children a few years older than my own, listened to me carefully, had confidence in my judgment, and dispensed advice on the phone. Martha was the beneficiary and the victim of medical assistance programs. She had no one she could call for advice. At the first sign of trouble, she ran to the hospital clinic and arrived late for work at the office.

I stayed with my secretary and she stayed with me. She was intrinsically bright. She learned routine operations on my desk calculator and our office computer. Her transformation came when we introduced word processors into the department. Now preparing copy became an entirely different matter. Editing my work had been a painful process. Martha rarely corrected a grammatical error and sighed deeply when I sent copy back to be redone that I had corrected. However, with the word processor, preparing statistical tables and editing memoranda had become machine operations. As the days went by, she performed those operations with increasing skill. She still relied upon me to correct grammar, but I no longer hesitated to make the changes that should be made because she could incorporate them into my copy so quickly.

I carried the example of Martha with me when I left Chase and joined the City government. (After I left Chase, Martha James enrolled in a business course at a community college and then became an administrative assistant in a hospital.) In designing our programs we were concerned with how we could effectively train our labor force on a much broader scale. I felt there were more "positives" in the picture than many people realized once we understood our "client" and the nature of the skills that are needed for the new technologies. First, training means more than formal educational skills. It means learning to function according to the rules of business—rules as fundamental as getting to work on time and a clear-cut standard office procedure, but not easy to meet when you're a single parent of three small children. (In retrospect, I probably went further than was good for either my secretary or my employer in being flexible rather than firm on standards.) Second, training will not solve all the problems of youth unemployment. The motivations to undergo the training necessary to get and keep a job may not be great for a young man or woman who sees opportunities to obtain higher monetary rewards from other sources, whether it's public assistance or "street" income from illegal activities. My own experience and recent studies of the Manpower Demonstration Research Corporation indicate that many youngsters, including black teenagers, will stay in school when they have jobs, even minimum-wage jobs, but a substantial core will not rise to the lure of employment that goes with appropriate training. Third, training must be shaped for a clientele that lacks basic reading and arithmetic competency. Still, in some ways, it is easier to train youngsters to function in the computer age than it was to prepare them for a world where secretaries were expected to type sixty words a minute, correct grammatical mistakes, balance the boss's checkbook, serve coffee, and buy a birthday present for his wife.

Once we recognize that the modern data-processing facility is more like a factory than an office, we will see that training is a matter of breaking jobs down into repetitive machine skills. The youngster who has sharpened his eye-hand coordination by playing arcade video games can transfer those skills to the word processor and computer. Manual dexterity is instantly rewarded with images on a screen. The drawback is this: The new specialization will result in well-paid "production" workers (analogous to blue-collar factory assemblers), but their upward mobility will be limited by the narrow base of their technical skills. The line between electronic "production" workers and the professional and managerial elite will become even more sharply defined than the stratification between jobs today.

When I describe this scenario to educators, many are horrified at the prospect of a new electronic "factory" era. But I believe a realistic assessment of what the future work place will be like raises our chances for success, particularly after the many failures of the 1960s and 1970s. And there are "success" models in place. As Deputy Mayor, I attended a graduation at Murry Bergtraum High School, a high school in Manhattan specializing in business education. The audience was a sea of 600 black, Hispanic, and Oriental faces. The youngsters listened to me politely. When their principal, Barbara Christen, rose to speak, there was no doubt she was their leader. A feeling of mutual respect for and enthusiasm about their accomplishments filled the auditorium. This school had met its goals. (Perhaps too well—according to local news reports, some students got to the computer and altered their grades!) Most of the seniors were going on either to community colleges or to office jobs in the nearby financial district. Why does Murry Bergtraum work?

A strong principal set firm standards of social behavior and educational performance and established links with the nearby financial community. Many of the youngsters work part-time in "co-op" educational arrangements with banks, insurance companies, or securities firms. Employers hold a vested interest in the functioning of the school. Co-op education is an old concept that nearly died in the Great Society days of the 1960s, when we thought that every child should be directed to a four-year college. It's a mode that is being rediscovered and repackaged in a variety of computer age forms. It is not so much that the training obstacles are overwhelming, given the youngsters in the system, or that new technologies require skills that can't be taught. It is that we don't recognize formulas that work and therefore can't implement them on a continuing, large-scale basis. New York City, with its 300,000 high school students, had only one Murry Bergtraum in 1983. And New York youngsters know a good product when they see one—four to five teenagers compete for each vacancy.

But will there be jobs after all the training? That's the gnawing question. Executives surround themselves with personal computers in their functionally decorated offices. Isn't the need for secretaries, file clerks, and even administrative assistants negated when an executive can effortlessly prepare memoranda and retrieve statistical reports at the touch of a button on a personal computer? The answer is that the structure of office jobs will change, but I do not doubt our ability to invent new functions when we have the technical capacity to carry them out. My concern is that we'll repeat the management misfortunes of the 1970s—utilizing computers for costly "make-work" (reams of printout that nobody reads) rather than for functions that increase productivity.

Sometimes we become overly consumed with the drama of high technology and concentrate on the breaks with the past rather than with the continuity with it. A rather down-to-earth innovation provides useful parallels. Supermarkets were a true retail innovation in the early postwar period. "Mom-and-pop" grocery stores appeared doomed to extinction. And many of them, indeed, died a lingering death. But Americans, especially those living in urban centers, soon tired of the homogeneity of large-scale, efficient supermarkets. Specialty stores sprouted all over, catering to neighborhood tastes—pizza, chili, falafel, chocolate-chip cookies, health food—and breeding a new type of small business, owned by a new kind of young, often college-educated, entrepreneur. Now we're in a third stage. The giant supermarkets are fighting back, renovating their space to include specialty trappings. Freshly baked bagels are now as American as apple pie (and as poorly baked!). The specialty stores are becoming so large and varied in their merchandise that they are turning into high-priced supermarkets. What's the next phase? I don't know, but further changes and adjustments that mean pain for someone will surely occur.

The conclusion: High technology is the latest form of innovation. It is spreading through the U.S. economy in an environment where unemployment has been high and inter national competition is an ever-growing force. The adjustments will not be easy for older industrial workers, whether they opt for retraining in new fields or for restructuring of their jobs in their present industry. The obstacles facing young men and women who lack adequate social and educational preparation for work are great, particularly in older urban cores, where unemployment is at epidemic levels. However, if we go about training with a realistic assessment of the technical requirements of the new technologies, we will find the obstacles are not insurmountable. More of our young men and women can be brought into productive jobs; the downside is that lines separating jobs of varying skills will be even sharper than they are today. The doomsayers should stop shaking their heads in despair and start looking around for models that work.

16

What Will All the
Lawyers and MBAs Do
for a Living?

- **35,647 law degrees and 30,186 MBAs conferred**—*Statistical Abstract of the United States, 1982–83.*
- **One lawyer for every 390 Americans, twenty times as many per capita as Japan**—*New York Times,* June 1, 1983.
- **MBA salaries down 9 percent**—*Time,* June 6, 1983.

I had just received my master's degree in economics from Columbia University in the mid-1950s. After weeks of searching for a job, I accepted a position as a researcher at the Bank of Manhattan Company (which merged shortly thereafter with Chase National Bank to become the Chase Manhattan Bank). My salary was $60 a week, $3,120 a year —probably a bit below market because of sex discrimination and less than the pay of a factory worker. When I married a few months later, my husband, a recent Harvard Law School graduate, was earning about twice as much as I at a small, well-established law firm. Nearly thirty years later, starting salaries have climbed many times: $25,000–$30,000 for economists in New York financial institutions, $30,000–$40,000 for MBAs, and $40,000 and higher for lawyers at top New York City law firms. During this period, the number of economists graduating with an M.A. has doubled, the number of law degrees conferred has more than tripled, and the number of MBAs, that newly discovered holy of holies, has multiplied roughly tenfold.

How could salaries climb so high—up two to three times the cost of living—when supply had increased so much? On the surface, it seems as if we've abrogated the law of economics: Supply increases rapidly, and prices (salaries) do not go down, as expected; instead they go up faster than in most other sectors of the economy. The answer, of course, is that demand grew even more rapidly. But what about the future? With more than 35,000 degrees in law and more than 30,000 master's degrees in business administration conferred annually, what will all the lawyers and MBAs do for a living? As we moved into the 1980s, the unbroken chain of higher incomes for more and more lawyers and MBAs was finally dented. The marketplace was questioning whether so many MBAs and lawyers represent a misallocation of our economic resources. The demand for lawyers and MBAs is not going to collapse, but there'll be difficult adjustments for law schools and business schools and their graduates during the 1980s.

It almost seems as if the American economy faces a paradox. We blame our schools for the lack of trained and properly educated workers at the same time that we are concerned about an oversupply of "overeducated Americans," symbolized by the ubiquitous MBA and lawyer. The issue is not entirely new. The phrase "overeducated American" surfaced during the mid-1970s. College graduates flooded the labor market, in a combination of the maturing of the postwar baby boom generation and growing proportions of college-age youngsters pursuing higher education. Stories of newly graduated B.A.s taking jobs as taxicab drivers, receptionists, and bartenders filled the press. The earnings advantage of college graduates over high school graduates actually narrowed. The "oversupply" began to correct itself by the end of the decade, as growth in the pool of eighteen-to-twenty-four-year-olds slowed and the proportion of young adults attending college edged down. With the end of the Vietnam War, young men no longer enrolled in college solely as a means of avoiding military service, and with the financial value of a college education becoming slightly tarnished, many young men had second thoughts about spending additional years in school. The total number of new college and university graduates expanded only slightly from 1975 on. But in spite of the near-leveling in total degrees conferred, law schools and business schools spewed out graduates in even larger numbers. The marketplace said, "This is where the action is," and law schools and business schools expanded to meet what looked like unlimited demand.

What produced this extraordinary growth in business and law school enrollments? Women, for one thing. When I was at Radcliffe College, in the 1950s, the first women Harvard Law School students were just graduating, and women had not yet been admitted to Harvard Business School, across the Charles River. As the barriers broke down and women looked to the professions for careers, a law degree or a MBA became viewed as a "union card" for entry into man's world. By the early 1980s, four out of ten law students and three out of ten "B School" students at Harvard were women. The proportion at other schools is even higher. Nearly half the business school students at New York University are women. Universities expanded to accommodate women rather than cut male enrollment. Why not, when the demand for their product appeared to be rising inexorably?

I watched the explosion in college-educated corporate "talent" during my years at Chase. Shortly after I started in the economics group, William F. Butler, the man to whom I reported, was promoted to vice president. It was a big event. Bill was just under forty years old—the youngest vice president at Chase. A protégé of David Rockefeller, Bill entered the ranks of senior management as one of about 125 male vice presidents in a sea of roughly 10,000 employees. (Of course, there were no women vice presidents at the end of the 1950s, since women were not allowed into officer-training programs.) By 1982, Chase counted 2,000 vice presidents (200 of them women) out of 35,000 employees worldwide. Receive an appointment at the age of forty? That's almost tantamount to failure. New vice presidents, most of them with advanced degrees, are appointed in their late twenties. The real achievers, the elite of banking—senior vice presidents who receive salaries of $100,000 and more—not infrequently receive their promotions in their mid-thirties. How the corporate world has changed in twenty-five years!

What brought about these changes? First, the currency was devalued. "Everyone," that is, virtually all college graduates, received a title. I started out with my M.A. in economics on the clerical payroll. At that time, it took five years for a young man who entered one of the bank's officer-training programs to receive his title. We reached our mid-thirties during the 1960s with enough working experience to move into middle management ranks, but there were too few of us Depression "babies" to fill the growing number of slots. Companies began competing intensely to draw the new, young college graduates into their ranks, sweetening the package of "perks" and compensation. Today, few

M.A.s or MBAs would work for a financial institution such as Chase without the immediate "perks" of official status and the lure of official appointment within six months to a year and a half. By 1983, about 7,000 men and women were officers at Chase—nearly one out of every five employees, compared with only one out of ten from a much smaller pool in 1960. The bloating of official ranks was so outsize that the Chase headquarters, built at the end of the 1950s to accommodate growth, was not big enough to provide window space and the appropriate square footage, according to rank, for all Chase officers. No, executive titles and "perks" were not enough. Competitive salaries were needed to draw and to keep competent people. Banks transformed themselves from institutions that gave out titles instead of pay to corporations that combined competitive salaries with the trappings of the good working life. Those titles and salaries were distributed with largesse not out of charity but because the banking arena, along with the rest of the corporate world, was changing rapidly.

The corporate merger movement of the late 1950s and 1960s spawned conglomerates that had an insatiable appetite for in-house specialists and external consultants. Companies reorganized their personnel structure on a crash basis and learned to manage their often dissimilar newly acquired businesses. Bankers turned into retailers; retailers became insurance salesmen; insurance companies delved into real estate; chemical companies became restaurateurs. Lawyers prepared the legal documents, and investment bankers negotiated the deals. Systems analysts churned out cash-flow and internal-rate-of-return printouts at the press of a button. An army of bright young men and women interpreted the statistics so that financial decisions could be made on a "factual" basis. The economist moved from little-noticed research in an austere cubicle to formal advisory sessions in the corporate boardroom. As corporations enlarged their markets worldwide in an era of inflation and rapidly changing interest rates, new elements of uncertainty clouded the corporate profit picture. The economist became the corporate "guru," consulted frequently, rarely credited if things went right, but invariably blamed when forecasts were wrong. Corporate boardrooms were equipped with the latest technology so that we economists could give our presentations with elaborate visual aids that were executed by an expanding group of sophisticated graphic technicians. The late 1970s and early 1980s brought additional specialists onto the scene—the bankruptcy lawyers and takeover "artists" who tried to patch up the mistakes of the previous experts.

As companies began to enter new lines of business, committees became so large and meetings of task forces lasted so long that it looked as if we would never get through the printouts of reports and presentations and actually arrive at a decision. Matrix management became the new tool to rationalize the process. I couldn't fathom the meaning of a matrix with columns headed by departments and rows listing functions to be performed (or maybe the other way around) and officers' names written in the boxes. What matrix management meant, in reality, was that the corporate structure had become so complex that it was virtually impossible to define clearly decision-making authority in overlapping areas. A crew of MBAs would be assigned responsibility for diagnosing an issue and recommending whose names should be inserted into the little boxes in order that everyone theoretically would know what he or she was to do and with whom he or she was to work. The meetings and reports, of course, continued to multiply.

The expanding role of government and the increasingly vocal posture of special interest groups buttressed demand for specialists with advanced degrees. Complex tax codes, environmental protection, consumerism, affirmative action —the intertwined world of government, business, and community relations produced a new world of specialists, with lawyers at the center of the action. Lawyers draft legislation and regulations, advise clients on their plaintiff's or defendant's role, and carry litigation through the courts. Corporations, government, and community groups rely on the services of lawyers on their own staff or outside counsel to protect their interests. And the lawyers work with other specialists—economists, engineers, scientists, at consulting fees that run to $2,000 a day—to carry out their tasks.

Large law firms in major cities employ 200 to 400 lawyers. A cadre of associates and paralegals using advanced computer technology supports a pyramid topped by partners. The fiction of an old-fashioned fraternal partnership is maintained, but large law firms are more akin to medium-sized corporations with many of the same management and capital investment decisions that a company faces. Major corporations build up huge in-house legal staffs with the capacity to handle a wide range of legal responsibilities. Outside counsel may be retained only for specialized tasks. AT&T, before divestiture, employed more than 900 lawyers on its legal staff; General Electric employs more than 400 lawyers. New York City's Corporation Counsel's office provides jobs for more than 300 lawyers, and this doesn't include the hundreds of lawyers spread throughout the City's separate agencies. New York City's Legal Aid Society employs nearly 700 full-time attorneys who provide legal assistance to the poor through private funds and government support.

Not everyone with a law degree works as a practicing lawyer. Legal training can be an asset in both government and business even if you don't function as a lawyer in your job. Mayor Edward Koch started his career as an attorney, as many politicians do. A commissioner facing the Mayor's "cross-examination" of a budget request for his agency can be painfully aware of the Mayor's skill in delving to the heart of an issue. When the police commissioner or the schools' chancellor presents his case, the Mayor's office is so crowded that aides sit on the windowsills. It looks disordered, but when the Mayor starts his questions, the atmosphere changes to that of a courtroom with the prosecuting attorney conducting cross-examination. When I worked for the City, I needed a person with legal training close at hand, not to prepare legal papers (there were lawyers to do that), but to advise me on the legal documents, negotiations, and regulations that other people presented to me. So I hired a young attorney from a private law firm for "protection." Jim Rouen helped me ask the right questions—and it was just as important to pose the right questions to those who worked for the City as it was to challenge my opposites on the other side of a negotiation. For example, the City's Public Development Corporation wanted the flexibility to negotiate independently with private developers. I supported their goal, but how did I make sure that the Mayor wouldn't be embarrassed by their actions? The City Corporation Counsel's office, protective of the Mayor's powers, wanted the contract with our own development corporation to be as tight as possible; the development corporation wanted looser oversight. Jim Rouen sits somewhat uncomfortably in between, trying to unravel the contractual language so that I can understand what is at stake.

Today, government regulations are so complex that sometimes only a lawyer who has been part of government can lead private-sector clients through the maze. John Zucotti, onetime Deputy Mayor and chairman of the City Planning Department, says, perhaps a bit self-effacingly, that he's one of the most successful development lawyers in New York City because he arrived on the scene at the right time. "A developer can't think of undertaking a project in New York City without hiring a lawyer who knows the ropes. It is not so much the attorney's political connections as it is his expertise in knowing how the system works." And in New York City this means zoning laws, air rights, tax abatements, historic preservation, environmental air quality regulations, building codes, government grants and loans—each of which has its separate body of law and regulations, administered by essentially separate government units. A developer negotiates with a dozen city agencies, several state and federal governmental units, as well as local community organizations and special interest groups. After years of shepherding a developer through the process, the attorney's role is not over. As often as not, one of the parties litigates to halt the development or change its terms.

Attorneys carve out specialties within the development field. I'd see the same faces over and over again seeking partial real estate tax exemptions for their clients at the monthly meetings of the Industrial and Commercial Incentive Board (ICIB). A young lawyer "cornered" the ICIB market on Staten Island. His clients were small-time developers and business owners whose investments might make them eligible for tax exemptions of perhaps $5,000 to $10,000. The exemptions did not amount to big dollars; but to small businesses, the tax relief could be significant. This lawyer knew how the complicated ICIB program worked. Perhaps more important, he knew that the program existed, which gave him a competitive edge over many of his colleagues. Successful presentation of a case for a huge Manhattan office project could result in millions of dollars in real estate tax savings. A handful of attorneys who knew the intricacies of the system were hired by developers to "win" tax abatements and, I am sure, were paid handsomely for their efforts. They brought a legion of experts with them when they made their presentations—architects, bankers, financial analysts, real estate brokers, office space specialists, all of whom would testify for hours about why a tax abatement was essential. Armed with charts, architectural drawings, and computer cash-flow analyses, they would make their case. I became convinced that we had no way of predicting whether they were right. We were tied up in a cumbersome process costing both time and money—and causing political controversy! We moved away from case-by-case decision-making to a system whereby tax abatements are determined under broad city guidelines—a small dent in the City's overreliance on lawyers with their supporting cast of experts.

As we entered the 1980s, a consensus was developing that we had become a nation overloaded with lawyers and their bedfellows, the management experts. The marketplace itself sent out signals that showed a weakening in salaries and difficulties in placement. The prestige law firms continued to cast their webs around the brightest law students, paying them $700 to $800 a week for summer jobs, with the added attractions of country club privileges and an apartment in Manhattan. And the $40,000 or more salary for newly hired associates stayed intact. But many of these same law firms found it difficult to pass on their costs to corporations that were feeling the pressure of reduced profits. The bloom was off unfettered growth. Major law firms had become used to acting like oligopolists. This small, select group of perhaps ten to fifteen firms in New York City, and thirty to forty in the nation, had convinced their clients that they provided "unique" legal services. Higher costs for premium salaries? Just pass the costs along to the corporate client, who has no choice but to retain the firm for its "unique" qualifications. That "oligopoly" status no longer looked quite so secure in the early 1980s. Partnership income declined, squeezed by increases in operating costs and a decline in the volume of business. A few old-time law firms disbanded; several reduced their staffs.

Cracks appeared earlier in the markets where the vast majority of lawyers compete for jobs that pay far less than the premium salaries paid for new lawyers by large New York City law firms. The large corporations are deluged with résumés from attorneys who fail to become partners in large law firms and from attorneys who have been struggling to eke out a living in small firms. Young lawyers from big firms may take a salary cut of several thousand dollars when they move to a corporate setting. The trauma of a wage cut is not easy on the ego of a young man or woman who has become accustomed to personal and financial success. The lawyer from the small firm sacrifices the entrepreneurial freedom of private practice for the security of a corporation job—and that, too, is not easy on the ego.

Lawyers working for government also find their options

are narrowing. Many young lawyers start their careers by working for government—some because of a sincere desire for public service, others because they do not have the credentials for a job in a good law firm. The typical pattern is to stay three to four years and then move on to the private sector. A young lawyer in the right spot in the City's Corporation Counsel's office or the District Attorney's office is exposed to wider experience and carries more independent responsibility than most junior lawyers in private law firms. But it has become difficult to make a transition to the private sector or to move up the ranks in government, where budgets are tight. Attorneys are turning into long-term career government lawyers because they have no place to go. My cousin went to work for Legal Aid, defending the poor in criminal cases. Now, in his late thirties, he has been there for ten years. It's time to move on, but as he sees it, "there's no place to go" for a specialist in defending alleged small-time drug dealers and muggers.

MBAs, too, wonder whether the unchecked growth in demand for them is finally coming to an end. Many companies now reject raw MBAs. They turn directly to B.A.s, who can be brought on board for $10,000 a year less than can MBAs. Then they put them through their own corporate training programs or send them selectively, after a few years' experience, to business school. With the economy pulling out of recession in the spring of 1983, new MBAs from all but the best schools discovered a job market where placement officers reported "salaries are down 9 percent from the year before." Recession had forced corporations to cut back on middle management. For many companies, this was simply one of those oft-instituted "tightening the belt" moves that loosened as soon as profits turned up. But I think a reevaluation of the economic worth of MBAs is taking place that goes beyond the short-term adjustments related to a recession. We're beginning to ask more fundamental questions, such as: Does the extensive use of lawyers and MBAs (and, heaven forbid, economists!) represent a sound allocation of our resources? And the questioning springs from several perspectives. Derek Bok, president of Harvard University and former dean of the Harvard Law School, takes a social scientist's long look and observes that "most people find their legal rights severely compromised by the cost of legal services, the baffling complications of existing rules and procedures, and the long, frustrating delays involved in bringing legal proceedings to a conclusion." In other words, for all of our lawyers, we provide inadequate legal services.

Economists are asking whether economic growth lags because we devote too many of our resources to activities that do not result in increased productivity. Their question is phrased in a variety of ways: Is business obsessed with a financial numbers game that emphasizes the paper profits of takeovers and mergers at the expense of "real profits" from producing more and better goods and services? Is business lulled into false security by the pseudoprecision of strategic planning or matrix management? Does our emphasis on short-term profits suppress high-risk innovation and blind corporations to the productivity gains that spring from skilled management of a company's human resources? Is our litigious nature and our desire to protect our special interests foisting an army of lawyers on us to write legislation and regulations and then to litigate against their rules in court? Worst of all, does our economy suffer from a "conspiracy of participants"—the lawyers and managers who create make-work jobs for themselves by selling their clients a bill of goods on the value of their services?

I think we have to take a hard look at the bottom line, and if we do, we will conclude that the answer is, at the very least, a partial yes to each of those questions. Won't demographics and students smart enough to pick "winners" take care of the glut of "overeducated" Americans? Only partially. It is true that the population in its twenties is shrinking, easing adjustments of new entrants to the work place. Students who filled seats at business and law schools because they did not know what else to do with themselves in the face of a hostile job market will reevaluate the time and high costs of attending school against the uncertain financial returns from entering the legal and business administration fields. The top students in the top schools won't have to worry, but those considering entry to the "diploma mills" will.

But supply shifts will not correct the deeper imbalances in our allocation of resources that rise from an excess of *demand*. Here's an analogy. Protective services—security guards, electronic alarms, "unpickable" locks—are a growth industry, particularly in big cities such as New York. Outlays, which can run into the millions of dollars for a large corporation, add substantially to costs but only minimally to economic output. We can tackle the problem in two ways: We can provide security services more *efficiently* (with more sophisticated protection devices, better-trained guards, and deployment of ferocious dogs!) or we can *reduce the demand* for security services by dealing with the underlying motivations to commit crime. The analogy may not be to everyone's taste, but it is pertinent. Improve the delivery of services? Whether it is because they fear drops in enrollment or are sensitive to the tide of criticism, business and law schools are reexamining their product. "How do you promote entrepreneurship, the risk-taking that is essential to innovation, in large corporations?" That was the subject of a spring 1983 Board of Overseers meeting at New York University's Graduate School of Business Administration. How do you teach business administrators to function in a high technology environment? Elizabeth Bailey, dean of the School of Industrial Administration at Carnegie Mellon University, announced plans to train business and engineering students in a new, combined MBA program. Law schools question whether they are stressing training in adversarial skills and ignoring training in mediation and negotiation, the arena many lawyers actually operate in once they enter the real world. Lawyers trying to eke out a living challenge the legal ban on advertising, and we find that increased competition leads to streamlined, lower-cost ways of executing divorces and closings on house sales.

We can improve the "product"—what we teach our lawyers and MBAs and how they perform their tasks. Then maybe we will need only one room instead of two rooms to spread out all the documents to be signed in a complex merger. But that's not enough. We must force ourselves to reexamine our demand for services. What is it that we want our lawyers and MBAs to do? And that is a tall order that can't be left just to the lawyers and MBAs alone. Unless we are prepared to ask those hard questions, we will find that jobs may be out there for a new crop of lawyers and MBAs but oversupply—in the sense of misallocation of our resources—will remain a deep-seated problem.

17
The New Immigrants:
A Bane or a Blessing?

- 34 languages spoken in P.S. 89—New York City, 1983.
- One million illegal aliens seized along Mexican–U.S. Border—September 1982–83.
- Taxes aliens pay to Texas found to top benefits—*The New York Times*, November 15, 1983.

We are a nation of immigrants. Every schoolchild learns that, except for the American Indians, we all are descended from immigrants or are immigrants ourselves. The mode of transportation has changed from the cramped sailing ships of the Pilgrims to giant jets of the 1980s, but nearly all of us can tell stories of our immigrant origins. My grandmother regaled us with tales of how the Dreyfus family emigrated from Alsace, France, in the early 1870s to New York City's Lower East Side. She'd point to the faded photograph in the family album, showing Grandpa in the driver's seat of a wooden wagon, the sign "Heinz and Dreyfus—Pickles" painted on its side. Grandpa Dreyfus didn't think there was a future in pickles, so he stayed on the Lower East Side, while Heinz went off to Pennsylvania to join the H. J. Heinz Company, founded by his relatives in 1869. (Grandpa later became a successful businessman and moved his family "uptown," to Riverside Drive.) If many of us have similar histories, why has immigration become one of the issues that create controversy today?

Today's immigrants come for the same reasons that have always attracted people to the United States—economic opportunity, political and religious refuge, and reunion with a family that is already here. But the immigrants of the 1970s and early 1980s differ from earlier waves—they are largely Asians and Hispanics, rather than Europeans, and many of them arrive illegally. They flocked to the United States in increasing numbers in the 1970s and 1980s, even though these were years of slow economic growth and rising unemployment in this country. Typically, immigration declines during a period of U.S. economic recession, but as bad as the economy appeared to us, it looked like a preferable option to those who left their home countries.

And this, I believe, is the crux of the matter. As we looked for cures for our economic difficulties, more and more people asked, "Is the growing number of aliens (legal and illegal) adding to unemployment and increasing the demand for government services—for education, medical care, public assistance—at a time when economic growth is failing to improve the standard of living of the average American?" Controversy swirls around these questions; the answers are not at all clear-cut. But I think before we succumb to the media image that all newcomers are Mexicans illegally sneaking across southern U.S. borders, we should look at who the new immigrants are, why they come, and what they do once they are here.

My perspective, of course, is colored by my upbringing. Living in a city where immigrants have long been part of the fabric of life, I probably view the recent influx with more sympathy than those who are witnessing a brand-new alien presence with large overtones of illegality. Even in a city such as New York, there is little doubt that a new wave of immigration is changing the economic and social environment. Nearly one out of four New Yorkers is foreign-born. According to the 1980 census, more than 1.6 million foreign-born residents, the largest and most heterogeneous concentration in the nation, live in New York City—and this figure excludes the vast majority of illegal aliens who won't let themselves be counted by the census-taker. The numbers of foreign-born rose by nearly a quarter of a million in the decade 1970–1980, even though New York City's population declined, according to the census takers, by 800,000. In a neighborhood such as Elmhurst, Queens, 30,000 immigrants from 110 countries live side by side. The Board of Education reports that thirty-four languages, from Spanish to Pakistani, are spoken in P.S. 89, Elmhurst's elementary school. Recent Russian émigrés produce young chess masters in the local public schools serving the Brighton Beach section of Brooklyn. Colombian residents crowd Washington Heights, once the enclave of Jewish refugees and the neighborhood where Henry Kissinger spent his teenage years.

New York City is not alone in experiencing a rising tide of immigrants. More than one in four residents is foreign-born in San Francisco and in Los Angeles, ports of entry on the West Coast. And more than half of the residents of Miami, principal landing point for the massive Cuban immigration, are foreign-born. Increases reported by the census in the foreign populations of major cities and their suburban rings largely reflect the rise in legal immigration that has occurred since the end of World War II. The Immigration Act of 1965 eased up on the restrictive quota system enacted in the 1920s and permitted Asians, who had been effectively barred since the "Yellow Peril" scare of the late nineteenth century, to enter legally. And we opened our doors to more than a million political refugees, including large numbers of Indochinese and Cubans, perhaps partly out of belated guilt for our refusal to admit significant numbers of Jewish refugees during the Hitler years. The traditional motivations for immigration—economic and social pressures—"pushed" millions of people from their homelands, while inexpensive air fares provided a new pull, drawing immigrants to the United States from all over the world. The sum of these trends adds up to more than 10 million newcomers who immigrated legally to the United States between 1950 and 1980.

What are the new immigrants like? Myriam Otero, a Ph.D. candidate in economics who worked for me at Chase, represents an early phase of the Cuban immigration. Myriam emigrated as a child from Cuba with her mother and her father, a solid civil servant. By the time I met Myriam in the 1970s, her mother owned a dress shop on Manhattan's West Side and her father had invested his savings in several apartment houses in a New Jersey suburb. Myriam kept all the books and handled financial matters for her father. To my amazement, Myriam, at the age of twenty-seven, had no checking account of her own. She put all of her salary into savings, and Papa gave her an allowance. Strange practice to my American "feminist" thinking, but Myriam's strong sense of kinship typifies family and work attitudes that enable many Cuban immigrants to move almost directly into middle-income status.

These days I buy my bagels, cheese, and beer at the corner Parisian Deli. The Parisian Deli is one of several stores in the Shin family "empire." Father Shin, a South

Korean, arrived in the United States in the early 1970s. After a few years of working in a bakery, he had saved enough to send for his wife, three sons, and two daughters, and it was not long before the family started its first entrepreneurial effort, a fruit and vegetable store in Washington Heights, a deteriorating neighborhood in transition between its older Jewish refugee population and the new Hispanic immigrants. Shin soon looked for a more prosperous neighborhood, sold the Washington Heights store, and set up business first on Manhattan's West Side and then later in a second store, on the East Side. The Chin family was part of a larger group of South Korean immigrants who were finding their niche in the produce business. Grandmothers, children, wives—all worked endless hours in the 900 Korean-owned fruit and vegetable stores that operated in the New York area in 1984.

The Parisian Deli represents diversification for the Shin family. Brother Shin, now in his mid-thirties, went to high school in Korea and served in the South Korean Army. He tells me he "knew absolutely nothing about the retail business" when he came to the United States. The Parisian Deli replaces a green grocery owned by the Zingone brothers, Italian immigrants from an earlier period. The store is open seven days a week, from early morning to late at night. Two Hispanics stand behind the counter serving hero sandwiches to Shin's key clientele—black and Hispanic teenagers who attend the nearby high school. Cousin Shin rings up my strawberries and asparagus at the produce store a few steps away. "Is my English improving?" she shyly asks. A health food store becomes the latest addition to the Shin "empire." The young Korean managing the store looks disgruntled. No, he is not a nephew. He works for the Shins and is trying to save enough money so that he can attend engineering school. But he is not happy. The hours are too long; the pay is too low. The Shins have run out of family. The health food store fails, victim of a problem that has plagued generations of small business entrepreneurs—how do you manage an expanding enterprise when you run out of loyal family members to share the burden of long hours and low wages?

These profiles are typical of many of the new immigrants who flocked to the United States in the postwar period. First, the vast majority of the new immigrants are *not* Europeans. Eight out of ten are Asians and Latin Americans. In the good old days, virtually all immigrants were Europeans. The new immigrants look different from their predecessors and this is one reason, I'm convinced, why many Americans assume that they are all illegal. European immigration dried up both because of limitations imposed by law and because economic prosperity in Europe for most of the postwar period reduced incentives to migrate to the United States. In the less-developed countries, political and economic upheavals acted as powerful forces propelling out-migration. Asians, permitted entry into the United States for the first time in this century, arrived in large numbers. Hispanics filled their immigration allowances—and then an overflow entered the United States illegally.

Second, a substantial proportion of new immigrants arrive from urban backgrounds and with strong educational credentials. Many of the first wave of immigrants forced out of Cuba and South Korea by political repression had engaged in professional and managerial occupations in their home countries. Once in the United States, they could not pursue their former occupations, largely because of their inability to speak English and because of the legal barriers of licensing requirements. Instead, they used their training and experience to start their own businesses, forming a whole new class of entrepreneurs in cities where the experts had written off small business as dead.

Third, many of the new wave of immigrants bring a culture of strong family ties with them. This culture of family loyalty is buttressed by the immigration legislation of 1965, which gives immigration preference to relatives of U.S. residents. When a tradition of family support is combined with an emphasis on educational achievement, a new group of immigrants can make rapid strides in an inhospitable environment. Orientals barely able to speak English make their way quickly into the stratospheric realms of higher education. New York traditionally wins a large proportion of the Westinghouse Science scholarships awarded to high school seniors each year. The typical winner used to be the son of Jewish immigrants, attending the Bronx High School of Science. New York ran true to form in 1983, winning eight out of the ten top prizes in the nation. But something had changed—three of New York's winners were Asians. I've interviewed high school seniors applying for admission to Harvard. As recent arrivals to the United States, Asian youngsters scored as low as 400 on their verbal aptitude tests, but they would score close to a perfect 800 on their mathematics SATs. The admissions office had little doubt that once at Harvard they would quickly overcome their English-language deficiency.

Of course, not all new-wave immigrants fit the "ideal" of rapid, painless adjustment. Most men and women arriving from the less-developed countries, where the transition from an agricultural to an industrial society is producing economic and social upheaval, do not bring advanced labor skills. They are employed in industries long associated with immigrants—garment and textile manufacturing; service jobs in hotels, hospitals, and restaurants; or migrant labor on farms. And more than half the new immigrants are young women; many of whom arrive without the support of an intact family structure. They'll be found in low-wage service and manufacturing jobs, often working side by side with, and indistinguishable from, illegal immigrants in the sweatshops of New York and other urban centers.

This profile of legal aliens is reasonably accurate. But when we come to illegal immigrants, it is hard to know where truth ends and fantasy begins. The Immigration and Naturalization Service (INS) estimated that between 4 million and 12 million illegal aliens lived in the United States in the mid-1970s. The U.S. Census narrowed the range to 3 million to 5 million "undocumented aliens" at the end of the 1970s. If that is a reasonable base, how much higher is the figure today? We really do not know. We do know that the INS arrests 1 million illegal aliens crossing the U.S.–Mexican border each year, but nobody knows how many arrests involve the same people going back and forth.

Partly because our knowledge is so inaccurate, critics tend to polarize—those who cry that we are being "inundated by a flood of illegal immigrants" and those who close their eyes, labeling illegal immigration a "nonproblem." In my view, the presence of illegal aliens must be viewed as a problem, if only because of the inequities that arise when millions of people (whether the correct number is 5 million or 10 million doesn't really matter) live in an illegal status. A fundamental rule of a democracy—equal treatment for all—is violated when large numbers of people do not abide by the rules of the game, whether it is the aliens themselves or the employers who hire them. But having said that, we should look at the recent inflow of illegal immigrants in economic and historical contexts.

Has the situation changed in any important respects? First, the "push" sending Mexicans across the border has intensified. For years, the Mexican economy could not fully absorb low-income agricultural workers into its urban industrial sector. Under the "bracero" program, more than 400,000 Mexicans used to be admitted each year as temporary agricultural labor. When the program was terminated in 1964, onetime braceros simply crossed the border as illegal aliens. When the demand for oil weakened in the early 1980s, Mexico's hopes for rapid economic development evaporated, and the pressure for poor workers to migrate became even heavier. Second, growing numbers of Mexican aliens are moving to urban areas of the Southwest—Los Angeles, San Diego, El Paso—and to urban areas farther north. They are working in low-wage manufacturing and service-sector jobs rather than as seasonal labor on farms. These aliens are more likely to stay long periods of time, even permanently, and to begin to raise families, make use of government services, and become a political force. Third, Mexicans no longer have a monopoly on illegal immigration. It is thought that Mexicans make up only 60 percent of illegal aliens. Illegal immigrants from other Latin American countries arrive with visas as short-term visitors or they come in via San Juan, passing as Puerto Ricans, and then stay on illegally. Their port of entry is typically southern Florida or New York.

Thus illegal aliens are a bona fide issue, not just because more of them rush the border, but because they are becoming a permanent part of the fabric of urban life. How many illegal aliens live in our largest metropolis—New York City? The range of estimates is wide. When the 10 million plus estimate for illegal aliens nationwide was taken as gospel, analysts of the local New York scene scaled the national total down to a figure of more than 1 million for New York. After the census developed more conservative national estimates, the INS reduced their New York figure to 650,000 illegal aliens. Emanuel Tobier, an economics professor at New York University, examined Health Department records of births to non–Puerto Rican Hispanics. He compared recorded births with the number of births that would be expected on the basis of census enumeration of non–Puerto Rican Hispanics. More babies had been born than could be accounted for by legal residents. The number of "excess" births implied an illegal alien population of between 400,000 and 500,000. Illegal aliens do not want to be counted by the census-taker, but they do go to hospitals and give birth to babies!

Does the true number make any difference? It sure does! The higher the number of illegal aliens, the greater the demand for municipal services, but if aliens are excluded in the census (and for the most part, they are), the City loses out in legislative representation and in hard dollars of aid tied by formulas to population and measures of poverty.

If it were just a question of accurate counting, immigration would not be an interesting economic issue. More substantive matters are involved. Unemployment in the United States passed the 10-million mark in 1982. Family income, after adjusting for inflation, declined during the late 1970s and early 1980s. It is natural to ask: Are the new immigrants (particularly illegal aliens) taking jobs from resident Americans and depressing wages of those who are employed? Assuming that more than 5 million illegal aliens work in the United States, could unemployment of legal residents be cut in half if all illegal aliens disappeared? Few analysts seriously argue that each illegal alien means one more unemployed American. And at the other extreme, only a few observers, wearing blinders, maintain that aliens do not take any employment away from anyone. Most analysts recognize that some job displacement and downward pressure on wages take place, but they can't agree on the size or seriousness of the problem.

A neighbor of ours, a Harvard Law School graduate, resumed her law practice. She hired a Colombian illegal alien to care for her young child. During her first day back in the office, she telephoned her apartment and asked her young daughter how Maria, the new housekeeper, was getting on. (She couldn't ask Maria directly because Maria didn't speak English.) "Oh," said the two-year-old, "Maria's working so hard. She's cleaning out all of the closets." Yes, Maria was cleaning out the closets. When my friend came home, Maria was gone—and so were the clothes and the silverware, too. How could this young woman attorney hire a non-English-speaking illegal alien to take care of her two-year-old? Her explanation was that no American resident would take a job as a domestic worker at the wages she was willing to pay. If Maria had not been available, would the young attorney have paid higher wages and found a "native" (perhaps a welfare recipient) willing to take the job, or would she simply have given up her own position as a lawyer and stayed at home? Presumably, in the real world, with many players in the marketplace, some people will pay higher wages, thus providing a job to a legal resident, whereas

286

others will not because the economics do not work out for them.

The garment manufacturer argues that hiring aliens—legal or illegal—causes no job displacement or depressing of wages. He maintains, and most observers agree, that if a supply of low-wage labor were not available, he would simply close up shop. Apparel manufacturers have traditionally relied upon low-wage immigrant labor—Jews in the early 1900s, Puerto Ricans in the 1950s and 1960s. The new immigrants, Latin Americans and Asians, are the latest sources of low-wage female labor in the garment industry. Thousands of Chinese women sew garments in the century-old lofts of Chinatown that resemble the sweatshops where the Triangle Fire took 154 lives nearly seventy-five years ago. Thousands of South Koreans and Colombians labor in small contracting shops in Queens and Brooklyn, just as their Mexican counterparts do in Los Angeles. And it is just about impossible to separate the legal alien from the illegal variety. Wages are at the bottom of the union scale, sometimes even below the minimum wage. Rents in old buildings are low. Productivity of the immigrant worker is high. The air is hot; safety and health regulations are violated—"the shame of the 1980s," says Jay Mazur, secretary-treasurer of the garment workers' union.

The union looks to government to limit the entry of aliens, to enforce wage and working standards, *and* to restrict imports so that higher-cost, locally produced garments can be sold in U.S. stores. Manufacturers accuse unions of failing to aggressively organize immigrant labor and of looking for a scapegoat by blaming industry and government. But manufacturers admit that if union pressure and government regulations should increase their costs, they will either go out of business or manufacture their product overseas—on Taiwan, in the Philippines, or in whatever nation emerges as the next developing country. We have a policy dilemma: Sweatshop labor adds to economic activity, increasing the volume of locally produced clothing—but at the price of illegal working conditions and pay scales that often fall below the minimum wage.

The situation for other kinds of labor is not all one-sided, either. Thousands of aliens work at unskilled, low-wage jobs as dishwashers in restaurants, as porters in commercial buildings, or as loaders in warehouses. Is substitute labor available to take those jobs, at comparable pay and under the same working conditions? We know that men and women will take "unpleasant" jobs if the pay is high—thousands apply every time New York City administers civil service tests for sanitation workers—a tough job, but one that pays more than $20,000 a year plus generous benefits. But when the pay is low *and* the working conditions are difficult, I'm not sure who the takers will be. Presumably, the potential pool would be drawn from those who experience high unemployment rates—blacks, Puerto Ricans, and teenagers.

However, labor markets are complex, and it is not a simple matter of direct substitution. In New York City, for example, the restaurant market is segmented into many specialties. Minority teenagers work at minimum-wage jobs in fast-food outlets like McDonald's and Denny's. Middle-class college students and unemployed actors serve health food and high-priced hamburgers in the exposed-brick, hanging-fern restaurants of "gentrified" neighborhoods. Family members, the wives and children of legal aliens, labor long hours for low wages in ethnic-food restaurants. In a city with the variety of New York, this means Thais in

Thai restaurants, Indians in Indian restaurants, Cubans or Haitians or Hondurans in specialty Hispanic restaurants. Illegal aliens from many countries work in the back kitchens of hotels, gourmet eating establishments, and ordinary "greasy spoon" restaurants. Who is competing with whom? You're forced to the conclusion that some job displacement and wage depression occurs through circuitous routes, but these effects cannot be quantified with precision. Professor Tobier concludes that "job competition is largely between immigrants and minority teenagers and operates indirectly through adjustments in the structure of the industry." In other words, without low-cost immigrant labor, New York would probably have more McDonald's and fewer ethnic and gourmet restaurants.

On the positive side, immigrant labor means more competition, greater variety in goods and services, and lower prices. On the negative side, employers engage in unfair competition when they do not pay their fair share of fringe benefits and taxes and when they avoid costly regulations— all of which go hand in hand with employing illegal aliens. And illegal aliens themselves do not pay their full quota of taxes. It is not that they fail to pay any taxes. Surveys conducted during the 1970s indicated that about 70 percent of illegal aliens paid Social Security and income taxes. Fearful of deportation if they got caught, most illegal aliens obtained fraudulent identification. A Honduran husband-and-wife team ran a lucrative printing business in our neighborhood, selling forged Puerto Rican birth certificates and mock Social Security cards to illegal aliens. Employers asked no questions. But even if only one out of three illegal aliens does not have taxes withheld, the tax loss could be as high as $3 billion nationwide.

There are those who say, "Why bother to track down the cash?" After all, illegal aliens pump taxes into government every time they buy gasoline for their cars and furniture for their homes, although they do not utilize government services to the same extent as legal residents. As transients, they do not need certain services such as schools; as illegal residents, they are not eligible for services such as food stamps and medical care—and they may just be afraid of being found out. According to this view, failure to pay full taxes balances out with below-average use of government services. I have trouble with this reasoning on both theoretical and pragmatic grounds. I've never accepted the notion that tax liabilities should be directly linked to usage of services. If I did, I might decide to withhold tax payments because my children are not in public schools—and I wouldn't and shouldn't get away with that.

But beyond the "equity" question, I'm not sure we fully understand the flow of taxes and spending that stems from illegal immigration. To the extent that illegal immigration leads to job displacement or wage reductions for legal residents, government spending will increase for unemployment benefits, public assistance, and other social costs incurred when legal residents are not fully employed. Individual cities where aliens concentrate can experience a drain on services that is not fully compensated by an equal inflow of local taxes—that's called "municipal overburden." Illegal aliens, according to a study in Texas, paid more into the state treasury during 1982 than they took out in government services. However, for individual cities such as El Paso, where large numbers of illegal aliens live, the cost of providing services to the illegal population exceeded the local taxes they paid. The findings should not have been unexpected. The thrust of recent immigration is to urban areas—to cities and their inner suburbs. The new aliens do not shuttle back and forth between the United States and their home countries. More and more of them stay. And when they stay, they marry, have children, and assume the characteristics of their neighboring, legal residents. This means, in turn, that they begin to use health and medical services, they send their children to schools, and a few of them, not too many, find their way onto public assistance rolls. In New York City, we have found that illegal aliens do get sick, give birth, and die. And when they do, they use municipal hospitals at local taxpayer cost—they are not eligible for federally funded medical assistance. More than 80,000 New York City schoolchildren have "limited English proficiency"—this is governmentese for eligibility for bilingual education instruction. Three-quarters of the students with "limited English proficiency" speak Spanish. But pick any language, from Arabic to Hebrew to Russian, and you will find it taught in New York City public schools. And teaching in a second language costs taxpayer money. New York City spent $27 million in 1983 and devoted 2,500 teachers to fulfilling its bilingual-education mandate. Although most of the pupils are children of Puerto Ricans and legal immigrants, some unknown fraction are offspring of illegal aliens.

When I try to fit the pieces of the immigration puzzle together, whether for New York City or in the larger context of the nation, I am frustrated by my inability to delineate precisely all of the costs and all of the benefits. I am sure, from the narrow perspective of a New Yorker, that the new wave of immigrants is a powerful plus, infusing vitality into the economic and social life of the City. I am also sure that the American economy can neither absorb all of the "tired and hungry" pushed out by adverse conditions elsewhere nor provide international aid in enough volume or with enough skill so that the motivation for migrating to the United States will disappear. Finally, I am sure that illegal immigration produces inequities that go beyond the unquantifiable economic and fiscal consequences—and for that reason alone it should not go unchecked. So I have sympathy with the need for legislation aimed at correcting abuses, although I have grave doubts that the legislation struggled over in Congress for eight years would produce the results that its advocates expect. Amnesty for "permanent" residents, stricter enforcement at the borders, and penalties for employers hiring illegal aliens—these are the three legs of the legislative triangle that have been debated for years. But I doubt that stricter enforcement can successfully stem the flow across the southern border unless we develop and intelligently administer a temporary-worker program—a modern-day version of the "bracero" program —that provides flexibility in entry to reflect current economic conditions. Someday, we will face up to the reality that between Medicare, Social Security, and federal income tax withholding, we are 99 percent of the way toward universal identification. The next step, universal identification, means crossing a big psychological barrier, but it is not far different from where we are today. And applied uniformly to all U.S. residents, it would not bear the taint of discrimination.

As we move through the 1980s, the U.S. labor force will expand more gradually than it did in the 1970s. If we can deal with our economic problems in a manner that produces strong, steady growth, we will find that the issues surrounding immigration will not be argued over with such passion. I recall Grandpa Dreyfus and his pickle story with nostalgia. When I see the Shin family building their Korean-American retail food "empire" under the tough competitive rules of New York City in the 1980s, I know they are following a well-trodden path.

18

What Do We Really
Know about Crime?

One of the evidences of the degeneracy of
our morals and of the inefficiency of our
police is to be seen in the frequent instances
of murder by stabbing.—Philip Hone, Mayor
of New York City, 1825.

I used to think that crime was an issue that had been invented by the media. I know better now after a few personal
confrontations as a victim and after two years in city government, sitting in on heated discussions in the Mayor's
office. But I still think that the sensational attention devoted
to crime by the newspapers, filmmakers, and television increases people's perceptions of crime and raises their fear
of crime out of proportion to the dangers they face. Rational
decision-making in an area that has baffled the experts for
years becomes even more difficult when perceptions over-
take realities.

One of my early duties as Deputy Mayor involved paying
a courtesy call on Ko-Rec-Type, a New York City manufacturing company that had recently expanded its facilities.
The founder, a self-made millionaire and a sixth-grade drop-
out, proudly took me around the plant. I was impressed to
see a high technology manufacturing firm operating profit-

ably in one of Brooklyn's older industrial districts. "Any trouble getting a skilled labor force?" I asked Victor Barouh, the owner. "No problem," he answered. "The local young people are capable and I train them." "What about crime?" I asked. "No problem," Mr. Barouh answered. "I know this neighborhood, and the people know we're good for them; they don't bother us." What a terrific success story! I wanted to publicize it, but no one was interested. A few months later, Mr. Barouh was mugged and robbed near his plant. Almost overnight, he veered from a staunch supporter of the City to a vociferous detractor. On February 7, 1982, *The New York Times* ran a front-page story featuring a photograph of Victor Barouh in his office, with a huge guard dog at his side and a pistol, a .38 Colt detective special, in a holster strapped to his ankle. He was organizing a vigilante movement to protect his turf.

That story was read around the world. Dozens of people called me about the article, saying, in short, "Forget about economic development programs. That's what it's like doing business in the Big Apple." Victor Barouh's earlier confidence that he was shielded from crime was naive. His 180-degree shift in attitude was, in turn, an exaggerated reaction, perhaps natural for someone whose illusions had been shattered. But Victor Barouh's experience and the public's identification with his emotions reflected the twin problems we face: the reality of crime and the fear it engenders.

I began to add up my personal experiences and I realized that the world had changed around me. I have been the victim of two muggings, one assault by a woman demanding a handout, one apartment burglary, and one country-house break-in, all in the span of five years. I recently served as a juror in criminal court in Manhattan. All fourteen prospective members of one panel had been victims of a crime. Not all were serious or recent or big-city crimes (in one case, a bicycle had been stolen twenty years earlier, in Shaker Heights). Some crimes may have been imaginary (jurors learn quickly how to avoid being selected). Five out of the fourteen potential jurors had personally known someone who had been murdered! This group may not be what statisticians call a representative sample, but the group matches the perception of a society pervaded by crime.

What is perception and what is reality? Our perceptions are clouded by statistics that tell different, sometimes conflicting, stories. Few of us are smart enough to understand what they mean. A typical banner headline in 1983: "Crisis in Crime: Prison Population Tops 400,000." That's an increase of nearly 50 percent in only five years. The prison statistic is a reality based on head counts. What does the rapid rise mean? Arrests are up only 10 percent—that's a reality, too. The answer, in this case, is not too difficult to arrive at: Juries are convicting more criminals, and judges are sentencing these criminals to prison. Crimes reported to the police soared by two-thirds in the 1970s, then backed off their peak in the opening years of the 1980s. Did the increase and subsequent decline in reported crime reflect a massive crime wave, followed by progress in battling crime? Robert McGuire, former New York City Police Commissioner, said the drop in the crime rate in New York City was no "'statistical glitch—it's the result of more resources and better deployment." But maybe the huge increase in crimes reported in the 1970s is not as real as the numbers imply. Maybe police departments became more diligent in filing their reports to the FBI—that's one sure way to increase the police budget. Or maybe victims of crime started to tell police about the crimes they experienced—they learned you can't take an income tax deduction or collect insurance or get a new credit card unless you file a crime report. And some sophisticates in a modern-day, reverse twist on crime learned that they can make themselves a few (or more) dollars in tax deductions or insurance claims by reporting theft losses that never occurred. (The Feds decided that the virtually unrestricted tax deduction had turned into a "loophole," so starting with the 1983 income tax returns, theft losses had to exceed 10 percent of income before they could be deducted.)

Whether or not a victim reports a crime may depend on his or her perception of the police. When I was mugged in Central Park, I called 911, the emergency number, to report the crime. The call-taker said, "Stay where you are. We'll send a cop." "How long will it take?" "About a half hour," came the answer. "Can't I phone in the complaint?" "No, you have to go to the precinct." The mugger had long since disappeared, out of the park, onto Fifth Avenue. The police response was enough to discourage anyone from filing a report. But I am stubborn, so I telephoned the precinct. The officer advised, "Go home and rest, and when you feel relaxed, call, and we'll take the report." Now, there was an officer with common sense and understanding, and my report entered the crime statistics.

Since accurate reporting depends on the attitude of victims and the competency of police, it is easy to see why there is little correlation between crime victimization and crimes reported. The census periodically conducts surveys asking people whether they have been a victim of a crime. Only one person reports a crime to the police for every three people who say that they have been a victim. If the victimization surveys are accurate, that represents a lot of un-reported crime—25 million crimes a year! The strange thing is that the victimization rate has barely changed over the past decade. Does this mean that the whole crime wave is a chimera—that we have always had a lot of crime, but that we have just got around to reporting crime and arrest-ing criminals—and that after a delayed response, we are finally "getting tough on crime" and putting the convicted away in prison? We *are* getting tougher on crime, but my sense is that there is something unreal about the victimiza-tion surveys, too. My own "anecdotal" research belies the notion that the increase is *all* a figment of overzealous re-porting. The increase is probably not on the scale por-trayed by those with an interest in promoting crime as a growth industry, but my sense is that more crime strikes at the bodies and purses of the middle class, who talk and write about such things, and that is why the perception of crime has escalated beyond the reality.

It is not easy for elected officials and administrators to separate the strands of reality from false perceptions. We live in a world of instant reporting that blows ordinary events into bigger-than-life crises, and in a complex society, where self-appointed experts all have their own pet theo-ries to peddle. The mayor and his advisors may have their convictions about what crime prevention measures are effective, but if their approaches do not mesh with public perceptions, their preferred policies will be difficult to im-plement. New York City's financial situation had improved sufficiently by 1981 so that the City could consider several options in making up for some of the cuts imposed during the fiscal crisis. The Koch administration decided to allo-cate additional resources to police. How should the funds be used? For uniformed police? For patrol strength (the police officer the citizen sees on the street)? For civilian employees (who carry out routine clerical jobs at relatively low wages, thereby freeing additional police for nondesk duty)? The administration's choice, based on cost-effectiveness, was for extra civilians to complement additional police. The police weren't too happy with that approach. The count of uniform officers is a source of pride; besides, some of those desk jobs are a cushy form of semi-retirement for patrolmen too old to go out in the cold. The City Council's desire was for more police. More cops on the beat add to a feeling of security. The City is confronted with two goals: increasing the perception of security and actually reducing crime. Councilmen up for reelection in their districts opted for the perception of security and added 1,000 uniformed police to the Mayor's budget.

Crime on the subways is cited as a reason for the drop-off in subway ridership during the 1980s. Business executives add fear of subway crime to the litany of reasons they give for why they are relocating their operations out of the City. The police commissioner rattles off statistics proving "riders are safer on the subways than are pedestrians walking on the streets." But that is not how the public feels. The City responds and adds police resources to the subways. Question: What is the most effective deployment? Undercover police, disguised as vagrants or streetwalkers, chalk up impressive arrest records, but subway riders feel more secure when they see police in uniform in the subway cars. Which is the City's goal: to reduce crime or to reduce the perception of crime so that the public will ride the subways?

Those responsible for the economic and social well-being

of their city find themselves walking a tightrope. On the one side, a mayor faces the danger of hurting the image of a city perceived as a hotbed of crime, so city officials will downplay the issue of crime. On the other side, the mayor faces a political constituency, the individuals and businesses who are victims of crime. City officials need to show by their actions that they recognize the seriousness of crime. And because both victims and perpetrators are disproportionately black or Hispanic in most cities, these conflicts can take on racial and ethnic overtones, as Mayor Koch discovered in his long-drawn-out differences with New York City's black and Hispanic communities.

New York City suffers the costs as well as the benefits of its position as media capital of the world. A small town can shelter crime as a family secret. Everyone in town will know of the disgrace—but that is as far as the bad news travels. A major crime story in New York is instantly replayed all over the world. No matter how many times the Mayor reports the correct figures, New York is portrayed as the crime capital of the nation. Actually, in 1981, New York City ranked seventh out of the twenty largest cities in crime reported per 100,000 residents, and eighth in its murder rate. However, New York City is consistently near the top of the list of large cities in its robbery rate. I think its high robbery rate is one of the reasons why the perception of New York as the center of crime is so widespread. Robbery is an act of *violence* that the victim remembers. Even if the victim escapes bodily injury, he or she views robbery as a personal assault. And long after the stolen money is forgotten, the woman recalls her fear of rape; the man carries the "guilt" of inadequately defending his manhood. *Time* magazine devoted four columns on February 21, 1983, to a personal essay headlined: "In New York: Be Kind to Your Mugger." The writer describes how he had the urge to kill the teenage muggers who robbed him of $17 late one evening on a New York City street. "He knew, *knew*, he would have fired" if he had carried a gun, and he knew, too, that his wife would never understand or condone his impulse to kill. That essay was read by hundreds of thousands of people across the United States and abroad.

When I worked for the City, I made a trip to England and Germany to market New York to international businesses. Our host cities greeted our party with cordiality. But the press had a field day, featuring special investigative stories on violent crime in New York—in perfect timing with our arrival. Coincidence? Maybe, but in Liverpool, England, and Frankfurt, West Germany, I found myself answering as many questions about whether it is safe to walk New York City streets as about taxes and the costs of doing business in New York.

The honest official faces a dilemma, wanting to be a booster for his community but unable to gloss over the fact that crime rates are higher in big cities than in small cities, and higher in suburbs than in rural areas. Every generalization, of course, has exceptions. Chicago reports a crime rate about one-half that of New York City, but that statistic says more about Chicago's police department than about the security of living in the Windy City, since Chicago's murder rate (on occasion, bodies are hidden, but almost all homicides show up eventually and are counted) and victimization rate are both high. Officials in the nation's larger cities are fond of pointing out that crime rates are rising more rapidly in suburbs and small cities than in large urban centers. We listen with thinly disguised glee as suburban families nostalgically recall how they used to leave their front doors unlocked. Now their bolted homes are linked to the local police station by the modern umbilical cord, an electronic alarm system. Our disgrace in the semi-rural town of Sherman, Connecticut, was to have an item appear "On the Police Blotter" in the town paper: "Gerard house broken into last week. Nothing was reported taken." As "weekenders," we had nothing of value for the teen-agers who were looking for cash or assets that could easily be converted into cash (it is still more difficult to fence a television set in the country than in a large city).

When the middle class moves out of cities to suburbs, crime follows in its path. Even so, the core of trading in illegal merchandise remains centered in large cities. "Cat thieves" may burglarize suburban houses for their jewelry and silver—and the chances are they'll "commute" to the Big Apple to fence the goods for ten cents on the dollar. The reality is that crime is concentrated in large urban centers because crime needs a marketplace, and the large urban scene provides a ready-made market—for drugs, jewelry, Mercedes automobile engines, stereos, and cameras. When I described the antique jewelry stolen from our apartment several years ago, the police officer patiently took down the details. "Have to, for the insurance," he noted, "but Ma'am, the gold's already been fenced on 47th Street [the jewelry district of New York] and it's all melted down by now. Dealers in hot merchandise don't like antiques— they're too easy to identify."

We outlaw "sinful" goods and services that many people apparently crave. The result is a market for sex, gambling, alcohol (during Prohibition), and drugs that is supplied by people engaged in crime. And it is far easier to mass-market those goods and services in areas with large population concentrations than in the backwoods of Maine or even the suburbs of San Francisco. Oh, there are ways of meeting demand in the boondocks. Forty years ago, Grandpa, enfeebled by a weak heart, walked slowly every day to the corner grocery store in our suburban town and placed his $2 bet with Murray, the bookie behind the dairy counter. I'm sure the suburbs have their modern-day versions of Murray, who take $100 bets on pro-football games and dispense small packets of white powder. But most likely the nerve center for these activities is located in an urban core, with distribution networks fanning out to reach the markets.

But why did crime suddenly increase in the 1960s? After all, "sin" has been around for a long time. And for those of us not old enough to remember, we have plenty of late-show movies to remind us of the extent and violence of prohibition crime during the 1920s. Isn't the 1983 movie *Scarface*, depicting violence in drug dealing by immigrant Cubans, only an update of the 1932 movie *Scarface*, based on the career of the prohibition gangster Al Capone? Aren't Cubans and Colombians trafficking in cocaine the 1980s version of earlier waves of newcomers, immigrants to cities, who clawed their way up the economic ladder through crime— blacks and Puerto Ricans in the 1960s and 1970s; Italians, Jews, and Irish in the late nineteenth and early twentieth centuries? Are we unable to distinguish between the perceptions of a new form of crime and the reality that violent crime has been around the United States for a long time?

The past and the present share common elements, to be sure, but the differences since the end of World War II are not entirely fancy. First, the economic growth of the post–

World War II economy produced a new cornucopia of goods and services to whet the appetite of consumers—automobiles, television sets, stereos, $60 sneakers. Television and advertising cater to our impulses for instant gratification. But not everyone, particularly the poor and the young, earns the income to pay the full market price for the goods dangled before them. Society and the life-style set by many parents say, "Get it all now!" If he is lucky, the new-era criminal can "earn" the money in five minutes on a crowded city street or in a subway train. My Central Park mugger, dressed in gray flannel slacks, a pale-blue wool sweater, and Adidas running shoes, had clearly set his consumption standards at a high-priced fashion-plate level. That made me angrier than giving up my money!

Second, the demand for "sinful services," especially drugs, reaches out to new, expanding markets—the large numbers of middle-income consumers with the funds to purchase their "highs," and the poor, who rob and engage in violent crime to obtain the financial wherewithal to satisfy their habits. And the poor, particularly the black poor, concentrate in cities. Third, the post–World War II baby boom flooded the marketplace with young people who entered their teens in the 1960s. And young people notoriously account for the bulk of all crime—at least, of all arrests. In the good old days, teenagers stole cars for a joyride and abandoned them a few miles down the road, where the cars were discovered the next morning. "Just a teenage prank," understanding parents said, and often declined to press charges. These days, teenagers steal cars, strip the parts, and sell the engines, the doors, the radios, the hubcaps to auto-part specialists. Or they mug a man or a woman on a city street, ripping off a gold chain, snatching bills from a wallet, and running up hundreds of dollars in stolen credit card purchases before the dazed victim has a chance to file a crime report. The crimes can entail big money, and the potential for violence emotionally scars the victim.

But since youth plays a key role in the upsurge in crime, won't the whole bad dream fade away as the postwar babies reach middle age? Economists observing the vast numbers of young people flooding the labor force in the 1960s and 1970s conclude that there just weren't enough legitimate jobs to go around, particularly with rigid minimum wages that remained high in spite of the glut of unskilled labor. Those lacking education and job skills—disproportionately, inner-city, minority youth—turned instead to a life of street crime. The economic equation makes sense—an hour or two allocated to robbery or to burglarizing a store or to peddling drugs yields far higher returns than a week's work at an entry-level job paying the minimum wage. (The minimum wage gets attacked from two directions: It's *too high* to provide work for everyone who wants a legal job, and *too low* to attract those who find nonlegal activities more rewarding!)

In theory, as the young mature, they marry, raise children, seek steady employment, and put their criminal past behind them. According to this view, the decline in crime in the early 1980s is a function of the aging of the postwar babies, and the further we move out into the 1980s, the steeper the decline will be. Maybe—but I'm not so sure. If crime were just a matter of a shrinking pool of teenagers, the falloff would be more pronounced than it is to date. And if youth alone equals crime, we could not have such large-scale trading in drugs and stolen goods, for youth is only the bottom of a pyramid topped by elders who control organized crime. True, young people under the age of twenty-five accounted for more than one-half of all arrests in 1981. But even that hard statistic does not tell us who is responsible for most crime. Maybe as "amateurs" more young people get caught. We know, as a fact, that only one person is arrested for every six crimes reported, but we do not know with any precision the ages of those who are never caught.

I am suspicious about the accuracy of the perception "youth equals crime," since I see signs that the postwar generation demonstrates a greater proclivity for crime as it ages. Yes, the crime rate of the baby boom children dropped sharply—it was cut almost in half—between their teens and their late twenties. Still, as adults in their late twenties and early thirties, the postwar generation comprises more than one-quarter of all arrests. Not only has the baby boom moved with its bulging numbers into the twenty-five-to-thirty-four-year age group, but the proportion of young adults getting arrested is higher than in earlier years. In 1981, arrests of young adults equaled nearly 7 percent of the twenty-five-to-thirty-four-year age group, compared with only 4 percent a decade earlier. The increase adds up to nearly 1 million more arrests. The aging of those onetime youthful offenders makes them candidates for trial, conviction, and sentencing to prison as adults. Young men who have spent more than half of their life in crime—particularly when they have been involved with organized crime—do not drop the habit just because they reach the magic age of twenty-five if they have not somewhere along the way acquired the education and the work habits for employment in the conventional labor force. A significant proportion of the urban poor seems to be locked in a circle of unemployment, drugs, and crime that will not be broken as a function of age.

So I do not think we can take comfort in the commonly held perception: Youth equals crime. Youth is shrinking in numbers; therefore, serious crime will inevitably decline. What does the reality suggest are our options? If I am correct in concluding that crime will not disappear just because masses of young people are growing up, then we need to focus simultaneously on two factors: on the shrinking universe of youngsters who could become tomorrow's hardened criminals and on the growing numbers of "mature" criminals who have already crossed the age barrier to persistent, continuing patterns of crime. Nipping crime in the bud logically becomes a high priority once we understand that crime does not disappear with age. If we zero in on young repeat offenders, the long-term payoff should be large because these are the youngsters most likely to carry their habit forward with them as they age. The task should become easier as time goes on because the youth pool is indeed shrinking, and, perhaps equally important, because crime rates among the new crop of teenagers are no longer rising. A less permissive approach to child-rearing during the difficult economic years of the late 1970s and early 1980s may have had something to do with changing attitudes. This should give us hope that the problem is manageable.

The bad news is that with the aging of the children of the baby boom, a larger proportion of those arrested will be candidates for prison terms. And that means we will face the prospect of courtroom backlogs and increasing prison populations for many years after the crime wave, as measured by reported arrests, continues to decline.

We'll have to work much harder to make the arrest, trial, and sentencing process both predictable and equitable. And the dollar costs will be high—New York City's newest jail is coming in at a cost of $140,000 a cell!

That *Time* magazine reporter describing his innermost feelings after a mugging wrote: "When enough muggers get shot up, word will get around that the work is a losing proposition." As dramatic journalism, raising perceptions about our failure to punish criminals, that sentence is superb. But it is a simplistic, illegal non-solution, since our society frowns on private citizens who take the law into their own hands and exact violent retribution. The "if-we-could-only-shoot-them" prescription is no more constructive than is the sentimental idealism that absolves individuals of responsibility for crime, blaming instead the ills of society —poverty, discrimination, too many young people, too much ostentatious wealth—and paralyzing us into inaction. Young people need the "lure" of access to training and real jobs and the reinforcement of a supportive family. But young people also need strong reminders that crime is a "losing proposition." The expectation that criminals will receive punishment for their crimes is a reasonable goal for a society tired of facing actual and perceived threats of crime.

19

Is Poverty Still an Issue
in the 1980s?

In December 1983, Geraldine Ferraro, congressional representative from Queens, New York, spoke before the Executive Committee of the Association for a Better New York,
a civic organization of business executives founded in the
days of New York City's fiscal crisis. Representative Ferraro's topic at the early morning session was "The Feminization of Poverty." Geraldine Ferraro is looked upon as a
no-nonsense, level-headed political figure, admired by men
and women alike. Was the time really ripe for a new social
issue?

The New York audience listened attentively in the comfort of the St. Regis Hotel and were impressed by Representative Ferraro's presentation. I have thought about the
concept, the feminization of poverty, and decided the phrase
provides an apt description for the poverty situation in the
1980s. In 1982, more than 16 million poor people—just
about half of all persons below the "officially designated"

poverty level—lived in households headed by women. That raw statistic, in essence, is what we mean by the feminization of poverty. But that number, no matter how startling, tells only part of the story. We need to understand a few facts about this phenomenon.

First, female dominance in the poverty picture did not burst upon the scene overnight. Women began to assume a larger presence in the poverty picture during the 1960s, years when we were making rapid strides in reducing the total size of the poverty population. No one seemed to notice that households headed by women were accounting for an ever-larger proportion of the shrinking poverty pie, moving from barely one-quarter to nearly one-half of the total in the span of a decade.

Second, the feminization of poverty is closely tied up with the situation for blacks—about three out of ten persons in poverty are black. And nearly one out of two black families is headed by a woman. Senator Daniel Patrick Moynihan warned as early as 1965 that "matriarchy" was contributing to poverty among blacks, but no one wanted to hear. Liberals chastised Moynihan for views that were "demeaning to black culture."

Third, although poverty is not exclusively an inner-city problem, a disproportionate share of the poor live in cities. When I began research for a group of women's organizations on a study, *The Impact of Women on the Economy of New York City*, I expected to find New York City women following the pattern of American women in general, with more women working in the paid labor force. Instead, we discovered that New York City's participation rate—the proportion of women working or looking for paid work— had fallen, and not risen, as in the nation as a whole, and that by 1976 the proportion was below, rather than above, that of the rest of the United States. New York had reversed its historic position as the mecca for the working woman. What had happened? New York still provided an attractive environment for career women, but with the shrinkage of the City's economy during the 1970s, feminization of poverty arrived on the scene. Black women reduced their participation in the labor force, and Puerto Rican women, who traditionally stay at home when they have young children, turned to welfare and became a growing part of the City's poverty population.

Finally, and most important of all, the feminization of poverty is *not* a "female" problem alone. The rules of the biological game have not changed—males as well as females are required to make babies. All of those mothers heading households with no husband present (in census jargon) are, or have at some time been, involved with men. The question is not just why do young unmarried women, many of them teenagers, get pregnant and give birth to babies, but why do young men *not* marry the mothers of their children, and what are they doing out there—loafing, stealing, working at gainful employment? Some of these men are invisible—at least in official statistics. Although slightly more black boys are born than are black girls, by the time blacks reach their twenties, the census counts only 90 black men for every 100 black women—and higher male mortality does not make up the difference. Most of the missing men are alive, but we do not know what, if anything, they do for a living. Of those we do keep track of statistically, far fewer are employed than their counterparts in the general population. Fewer than one in four black male teenagers is employed (compared with one in two for the white teenage population), and only one out of two black men in his early twenties is employed (against three out of four young white men). Unless we understand what is happening with the young black male population, we won't get very far in undoing the feminization of poverty.

Isn't the existence of poverty vastly overdrawn by our failure to add up the numbers properly? Dr. Blanche Bernstein, who has followed the welfare situation for years, pointed out in the early 1970s that the income of a welfare family in New York, including noncash benefits, exceeded that of the working, poor family. But it's only recently that government officials began to estimate systematically the value of in-kind benefits such as food, housing, and medical care. Depending on the technique used to evaluate these benefits, the numbers of people living in poverty are reduced by anywhere from 15 percent to 40 percent.

Without question, including benefits in kind reduces the *size* of the poverty population. However, the *shape* of the poverty curve remains essentially the same, with a sharp drop in poverty during the 1960s and 1970s, when economic growth was strong, followed by an increase in the poverty population, starting in the late 1970s. The lag in economic growth of the late 1970s and early 1980s squeezed middle-income families and caused declines in their real income. It should not be surprising that the poverty population felt the pain even more.

During this broad sweep of more than twenty years, women became increasingly important segments of the poverty picture. At first, increases in teenage births and in families headed by women were obscured by the overriding thrust of strong economic growth during the 1960s and early 1970s. The incidence of poverty declined at the same time that welfare rolls exploded under a system of benefits that fed upon a weakening family structure. Welfare became perceived of as a right in the heady Great Society days. Social activists tried to force-feed the system, beating the bushes to find welfare clients, anticipating that a welfare "overload" would lead to the collapse of the entire structure. There were suspicions that a few committed Communists infiltrated New York City's welfare department, pulled the wool over the eyes of the liberals with their "good intentions" of promoting national welfare reform, and papered the welfare rolls with mothers and their children living in the Waldorf-Astoria Hotel, driving Cadillacs, and collecting welfare checks in three different states.

I achieved uneasy notoriety in the Chase Bank boardroom in the late 1960s with a slide presentation plotting two lines showing New York City's total population and New York City's welfare population. The City's total population grew only slightly during the 1960s; welfare rolls were doubling every five years. I extended the two lines out into the future. It didn't take long before the welfare line overtook the City's entire population. If public assistance, then totaling roughly 800,000 recipients, continued to expand at its current rate, everybody in New York City—all 8 million people—would be on welfare by the 1990s. I plotted the graph to dramatize what was happening; it was not meant to be taken literally as a forecast. No matter! George Champion, then Chase chairman, loved that chart and repeated my "profound conclusion" each time he gave a talk on New York City's problems.

The chart made a point. We had created a monster that was out of control. And we began to question whether the system itself was adding to, rather than ameliorating, the poverty problem. The objective of an income support program should be to minimize the chances of economic harm and to maximize the prospects for overcoming market deficiencies—no easy task. The closer we look at the welfare apparatus, the more it falls short on both counts. In the near term, it may provide a safety net under poverty; over the longer run, and that longer run does not take long to arrive, the system encourages dependency and a further weakening of the already fragile family structure.

Take the situation of the unmarried mother. In earlier days, as Victor Fuchs, an economist, points out, a shotgun wedding followed the first signs of pregnancy for an unmarried woman. Today, a woman has two other choices— abortion, which terminates two out of three pregnancies of unmarried women, or going to term as an unmarried mother. Frequently, a teenager who decides to keep her baby lives at first with her own parents, who provide financial support. Then, because she wants independence or because her parents throw her out, she'll look to government and become a welfare mother. Our system of government assistance— welfare allowances, food stamps, Medicaid—provides a backbone of financial support that can make the decision to have and keep a baby, without the sanction of marriage, a rational economic choice. If the welfare mother works for pay, her marginal tax rate (that is, the reduction in her benefits) will be 80 percent or more. If the father contributes aboveboard financial support, benefits will be reduced or eliminated. This does not mean that welfare mothers never work (apparently quite a few do, but they obviously do not report their earnings to government agencies) or that unmarried fathers never contribute to their children's financial support. It does mean, however, that the economic rewards and penalties of the system discourage working to achieve financial self-sufficiency.

Still, it is naive, and not supported by the evidence, to conclude that girls get pregnant so that they can solve their economic and personal problems through government financial support. Births to unmarried women began to increase before welfare rolls took off and, even more relevant to the current situation, births to unmarried women continued to rise after welfare caseloads peaked. Government tightened the reins on welfare eligibility and declined to increase benefits in pace with inflation during the mid-1970s (years before the Reagan administration "got tough" on welfare). Welfare rolls dropped, but births to unmarried women rose. Today, mothers are unmarried in more than half of all births to teenagers and in more than half of all births to black women.

The growth in teenage pregnancy seems to be part of a larger cultural revolution in which traditional marriage does not hold the same economic pull or social imprimatur that it once did. Greater economic independence of the educated, middle-class woman raises the "costs" (from forgone income) of child-rearing and reduces the benefits of maintaining a marital relationship. For the less educated woman who does not see economic opportunities for herself in the work place, the "costs" of children do not loom large, but neither do the benefits of marriage if the father of her children does not have steady employment. We can look at this phenomenon as our "inheritance" of the 1960s—the "anything goes" mentality, promulgated, as Blanche Bernstein suggests, by the comfortable white middle class. But I believe that the roots for the spread of unmarried motherhood lie deeper than the 1960s in segments of our poverty population. Many Puerto Ricans, for example, carry what anthropologist Oscar Lewis called a "culture of poverty" from the slums of Puerto Rico to mainland cities such as New York. In his classic 1965 study of an extended Puerto Rican family, Oscar Lewis portrayed a culture characterized by despair and apathy, early initiation into sex, common-law marriages, a high rate of illegitimacy, limited aspirations for children—a culture of poverty that is passed down from generation to generation. The five major characters in the Rios family, the subjects of Lewis's intensive case study, had experienced twenty marriages—seventeen consensual unions and only three legal marriages. Once in New York, observed Lewis, the number of separations, consensual unions, and matrifocal families increased, in large part, he concluded, because of the greater backup of government support. We estimated when we did our 1977 study of women in New York City's economy that more than one in five Puerto Rican women headed a family on welfare and fewer than one in three Puerto Rican women worked or actively looked for work in the labor force.

Blacks confronted the social environment of the 1960s with their family structure already fragile. We can go back to the history of slavery and persistent racism and to the more recent breakup of tenant farming in the South for reasons. When agriculture became mechanized, black women headed North in the 1950s and found a modicum of economic security as domestic servants. Young black men faced a harder time, either left behind in a South that had not yet taken off economically or seeking employment as unskilled labor in the declining manufacturing sector of northern cities. As early as 1960, women headed more than one out of five black households. Then in the 1960s and

1970s the postwar baby boom reached working age, pushing a flood of new entrants into the nation's labor force. Blacks with little education and poor work skills and lacking the backup of a strong nuclear family fell farther behind in the competition for jobs. The black community seemed to split apart at the seams, dividing itself between those attaining middle-income status, the college-educated huband-and-wife families with both partners working, and those on the outside, unmarried women with children, and young men not employed in the conventional labor force.

The picture of polarization between those blacks who have made it economically and those left trailing behind is too sharply drawn. We visualize the media picture of successful blacks—basketball stars, and bankers in three-piece suits, attending civic functions, eating in the best restaurants, sending their children to private schools. But there's also an unheralded group of families who arrived at their middle-income position following a time-worn path for economic improvement. Ann Rhymer, our housekeeper for twenty-five years, is one of them. A product of the Deep South, Ann moved North as a young girl during the Great Depression. Her husband has worked, often under trying circumstances, for all of the years we have known him. Injured in a construction accident, Jack Rhymer invested his disability settlement in a service station, only to find the property condemned a few years later for urban renewal; the next station was virtually swallowed up by the encroaching drug traffic in central Harlem. Jack and Ann Rhymer share a home with their son, an X-ray technician, and their daughter-in-law, who works in a day-care center and is studying for her teaching certificate. The family bought their brownstone in Harlem at a foreclosure sale, hoping that eventually the neighborhood will improve. Grand-daughter Shanie is enrolled in a parochial school. Ann travels all over the world with her Baptist church group. She's an old-timer. "God's good to me," she says, but she also announced firmly when she first started work with us in 1958, "I won't use the servants' entrance—the doorman lets the white maids through the front door." She was right! And that ended the practice of black maids' using the back entrance in our West Side apartment building.

But the reality is—and Ann Rhymer would be the first to acknowledge it—that there is another group of blacks that *is* set apart, objects of study and discussion, viewed, if at all personally, as a threat because of the disproportionate participation of young blacks in urban crime. Journalist Ken Auletta, writing a series of articles that appeared in the *New Yorker* in 1982, suggested that a large segment of our poor population (perhaps more than one-third) is turning into an underclass—those who are alienated, living outside the economic mainstream, women dependent on welfare, and men "dropping out" through drug addiction or a life of street crime. Richard P. Nathan, professor of public and international affairs at Princeton University, told the National Urban Coalition in 1983 that the "concept of an underclass should be taken as an opportunity to put the social issue [of poverty] back on the domestic policy agenda."

When I thought about this chapter, I mulled over focusing on the underclass—the term is a shocker; the concept of an underclass is anathema to Americans. I looked through some of my old papers and discovered that I was thinking along those lines in 1977, after the massive electric power failure in New York City one hot summer evening. Looting and arson followed throughout the night and into the next day, much of it carried out by young blacks and Hispanics in their own neighborhoods. Asked to "explain" the event, I wrote, "What may be developing is a split that is along *class lines* rather than purely a racial phenomenon. A large group, predominantly black and Hispanic, is cut off, or has cut itself off, from the values of society as we generally perceive them." Today, we are even closer to developing an underclass than we were in 1977. But I decided not to dwell on that theme because an underclass has a permanence about it that I am not yet prepared to accept.

Diagnosing the current situation is one matter; prescribing for change is another. I've learned by now that there are no easy solutions for issues we have been debating for nearly twenty-five years. During the Nixon days, we spent weeks calculating alternative formulas for a standardized national welfare system, earnestly discussing which formulas would work most to New York's advantage. We argued about whether the federal government should assume the full costs of the existing welfare system, setting a uniform standard for all of the states, or whether we should move to a full-fledged guaranteed minimum income that would operate, with minimal bureaucracy, through a negative income tax. The subject quietly disappeared due to the inability to agree on a formula, a potential for escalating costs, and a shift in political philosophy moving away from federal to state responsibilities. I can still make strong arguments for a single, simplified system of income support, but it would be like whistling in the wind. If consensus could not be reached a decade ago, it would be even harder to reach it today, with the extensive overlay of in-kind benefits that now count for more than one out of every four federal dollars spent on income security.

Besides, I'm convinced now, as I probably was not some

years ago, that transference of income (whether as cash or as in-kind benefits) will not take care of our poverty problems unless we achieve strong enough economic growth to provide jobs and develop a labor force with the skills and motivation to engage in paid employment. So we come back to some fairly simple, straightforward generalizations. Strong, sustained economic growth is the sine qua non for reducing poverty. Strong growth helped the nation to reduce the poverty count by over 40 percent between 1960 and 1973. Weak, sporadic growth contributed to the increase in poverty that occurred in the next decade. If we can maintain vigorous economic growth for much of the 1980s, poverty will again decline. However, experience over those years also suggests that the problems associated with the feminization of poverty will not disappear through the workings of the economic growth engine alone. And that is a tough nut to crack, for we are talking of social attitudes and family structures as well as the cold economic play of supply and demand. If we don't concentrate on approaches that work, we will find ourselves in a period where welfare dependency is handed down from mother to child. The experts used to tell us that families do not stay on welfare for extended periods. That may, or may not, have been true in the past. But we are only beginning to see the potential for extensive, long-term intergenerational dependency. Children born during the first surge of welfare expansion are just now in their teens. They form the first real test of whether there is such a thing as passing on a tradition of dependency from welfare mother to child.

Can the cycle be broken? As a first, seemingly elementary step, teenagers need to understand that unmarried parenthood at the age of fifteen does not provide independence; it leads to the opposite, dependency. And the life of a welfare mother is not fun; uneducated and untrained, the young welfare mother can barely manage the mechanics of life, unable to stretch out food stamps for the month or to bring the children to the health clinic on time. She'll squander money on taxis, or maybe do a few "tricks" on the side to earn money for her children's birthday presents, but it's no fun. Education is, of course, one answer—not just sex education to teach youngsters how to avoid pregnancy, but education in a disciplined setting that gives youngsters the self-confidence that they can acquire the skills for employment in paying jobs.

A commitment to work and to acquiring the skills for employment is an appropriate goal for those receiving welfare. Welfare administrators used to shake their heads in dismay when anyone mentioned the possibility of welfare mothers' working. They would recite by rote: "Seven out of ten welfare recipients are children, so who can go to work?" They failed to turn the equation around: If one welfare mother works at a steady job, three to four recipients will leave the welfare rolls. Our fairly extensive history since the late 1960s with work-welfare experiments indicates that it is difficult, but not impossible, to build models of success. Real jobs, preferably in the private sector, are essential. And so is the training that bolsters self-confidence and emphasizes discipline as well as work skills. My sense is that we may have gone overboard in the past with our concerns about high "marginal tax rates" and underestimated the need to hold out the more abstract "carrot" of the benefits that come over time with self-sufficiency. I also think we sometimes close our eyes to one-step-at-a-time approaches. If welfare mothers are to be encouraged to work or to go back to school, adequate child care facilities are needed. Many people feel that it is neither socially desirable nor cost-effective to encourage work or additional schooling for mothers of young children. I think they make a mistake. The longer young men and women delay entry into the mainstream world, the harder it is to overcome obstacles. Mothers of young children need not work full-time, but part-time work (or study) provides a constructive transition. What would be more positive for welfare mothers than to develop work skills through formal responsibility for taking care of children in a cooperative or family care center? (Middle-class suburban mothers do it so they can continue their schooling or take part-time jobs.) Welfare mothers (and ex-welfare grandmothers) working in a family care center may be several steps away from a regular, full-time, paying job in an office, but they will be on their way.

It's not easy; none of it is easy. And if we are uncertain which "carrot-and-stick" approaches are most effective in dealing with the female side of the poverty equation, the male counterpart is even more difficult—and runs the gamut from education and training to searching for the fathers of unmarried children, requiring financial contribution to their children's support. "Not cost-effective," the program administrators say. "It costs more to catch an errant father than we'll save on welfare payments." They are right—in the short run, but not in the long run. And as in many deterrent efforts, it is not necessary to catch everyone to reduce the practice. You have to raise sufficiently the risks of being caught so that offenders, in this situation, unmarried fathers, have second thoughts about evading their responsibilities.

The "feminization of poverty"—maybe the phrase won't

catch the imagination the way the more shattering "emerging underclass" will. It does not really matter. Either way, a strong economy and a combination of carrot-and-stick approaches is necessary to make lasting inroads on the problem. But neither free-market economics nor legislated programs will undo the feminization of poverty unless we reexamine our attitudes, the personal values we teach, and the role models and mentors we provide to guide young people. Anyone who doubts the power of individuals to "overcome" should look around. I've seen children of welfare families struggle to better themselves in a hostile urban environment, traveling hours by subway to an academic high school—public, private, or parochial—gaining admittance as graduates of these schools to Harvard or Fordham or the City University. As children, they are perched on the edge of dependency; as young men and women, they pull themselves away from poverty.

20

What Is Woman's Proper Place?

Work is *work*—not play. Work is not always
fulfillment; it is 90 percent drudgery and 10
percent illumination—like motherhood.—
Linda Sexton, *Radcliffe Quarterly*, March
1980.

In the late 1950s, women were fired for pregnancy. In the
1960s, we were admitted into official ranks at Chase Manhattan Bank. In the 1970s, those of us in the bank's executive physical fitness program fought for (and won) gym
shorts tailored especially to fit women. In 1981, I left Chase
after twenty-five years to become Deputy Mayor for the
City of New York on practically the same day that Sheila
Bond became Chase's first female senior vice president,
after twenty-five years at IBM. Yes, women have come a
long way in a quarter of a century. As we move through
the 1980s, more and more women are making it to the top
in business and in government, and the path is much easier
to travel than it was for an earlier generation. Most of the
legal and institutional barriers to women's advancement no
longer stand in the way. But on the path of economic advancement, women are confronting new stumbling blocks
and many are wondering, "Is this the only route to take?"

The new questioning comes as women in their thirties, facing the reality of their biology, struggle with the choice of family versus career. And all of a sudden, "What is woman's proper place?" turns out to be a question that continues to have meaning after all.

I'm convinced as a participant in, and observer of, the world of women that there's no retreating to an earlier economic and social scene, with the idealized suburban mother and her 2.7 children greeting Daddy after his hard day's work in the office. Women will continue on the path of participation in the paid labor force for both economic and personal reasons. The persistent gap between the sixty cents earned by women for every dollar earned by men will gradually narrow (but not close) as more women work for longer periods of time at higher-paying jobs. But one issue that will not fade away as long as women compete in the world of work on terms traditionally set by men is the family—whether and when to have children; how to combine work and family. It's an issue that is not just the province of the young MBA graduate. It's faced by the unwed teenage mother and the older divorced female as well. It's one that I've thought long about. I worked part-time for many years (by the male world's standard—less than five days a week in an office). There were trade-offs in lost earnings and pace of career advancement, to be sure, but, on balance, my choice worked out well. I was sure that many women would choose a similar path as they juggled with the world of work and family. I was wrong! Throughout the 1970s and into the 1980s, most women and the organizations they worked for rejected that route. Today, the environment is ripe for change. Women's economic leverage is increasing, and the men they live with and work for are finally beginning to recognize that women need flexibility in the patterns of their working life if the conflicts between family and work are to be reduced. I'm convinced that attitudes as much as economics blocked those choices up to now.

Of course, I didn't choose a part-time career in the same economic and social environment as women live in today. My working part-time was almost an accidental happening in the predawn of the women's movement. At the end of the 1960s, married women were beginning to enter the paid labor force in increasing numbers. As Victor Fuchs, analyst of economic and social trends, points out, barely one out of ten women with children under six years of age worked for pay in 1950. By 1963, the year Betty Friedan's *The Feminine Mystique* was published, the proportion had already doubled. But although more women were working, their attachment to the labor force in those early post–World War II years was not strong. Our class report on my Radcliffe tenth reunion (also in 1963) capsules those attitudes. Nine out of ten of us were married; nearly eight out of ten were mothers. We'd produced 2.4 children per mother by the time we were thirty. Like most of our generation, we married early and had children while we were young. Although one out of seven mothers was working, careers did not preoccupy our thoughts. "Occupation" followed "Our Children's Education," "Religion," and "Politics" as a subject we wrote about in our report. We devoted more space to "Interests and Activities" than to attitudes about the world of work. We were ambivalent about the proper place for a wife with young children. Our class recorder notes, "76 percent of all who expressed an opinion approved the combining of motherhood with a part-time job although half (and no doubt more who didn't say so) stipulate no job until the youngest child is in school." We were aware of work-family choices, but we were hardly committed to the concept of work as a continuing, full-time career.

And that is one of the principal differences between the pre- and post-Friedan eras. The number of married women entering the world of paid work increased during the 1950s, but women were going to *jobs*, not *careers*. Fuchs says pre-feminist women were responding to a change in the economic equation. The U.S. economy was strong; job opportunities were expanding in female-dominated occupations—there were positions for teachers, typists, nurses, and sales personnel. The labor force, on the other hand, drawing new entrants from that small population cohort born in the Depression, was growing slowly. The economic result of the interplay between supply and demand was an increase in real wages sufficient to lure married women with young children into the marketplace of paid work. The economic reasoning rings true, but as a person who is one of those statistics, returning to the work force shortly after the birth of our first child, I know it doesn't tell the whole story. By the time we paid for our housekeeper (federal tax deductions weren't what they are today), my clothes and transportation, and the added income taxes from being lifted into a higher tax bracket, the net monetary gain was little, if any, from a part-time job. Rather, my choice came out of a hazily defined feeling that I belonged in the world of work, not accompanied by any conviction that I knew where my choice would lead. When I was in high school, Daddy said, "Better take shorthand in case something happens to your husband and you have to get a job." Later, he advised, "Why not major in economics—that's a good career for a woman." That ambivalence about the proper place for a woman was echoed in our institutions. College was fine for a middle-class woman, but graduate school, leading to a professional career, was something else. The prestige law schools, medical schools, and business schools were just opening their doors to women in the 1950s. A woman had to be dedicated to pursuing a career almost from the time she left her cradle to vie for one of those coveted places. Most women never entertained the thought. We took jobs upon graduation, marking time, without much thought to the future. And although the work place welcomed us to fill its expanding requirements for low-pay and low-status service jobs, neither government nor business encouraged us to plan for sustained careers.

"Bank policy is that women have to resign at the first sign of pregnancy," I was told, and the law provided no protection under which to challenge the demand. Women were so inured to the dictates of the establishment that they usually did politely resign rather than force their employers to fire them. Bill Butler, my boss, was a maverick. "Just don't get up from your desk when I come into the room," Bill cautioned, and so I stayed on, desk-bound, until a few weeks before Deborah was born. Enforced termination of employment made it easy for women not to plan for their future. There was no need to agonize over what might happen to your career if you stayed away from your office for more than the six weeks' maternity leave automatically granted today. After trying to freelance at home, changing diapers with one hand and punching numbers into a calculator with the other, both on an emergency basis, I did go back to Chase on a part-time basis. The organization wasn't set up to deal with the situation. There were messengers who worked by the hour and per diem bank tellers who came in to carry payday peak loads, but no one on the professional or managerial staff worked part-time. "Don't worry," said my boss. "We'll find a way." For years I was carried on the books as a clerk. Colleagues were appointed bank officers, while I continued to sign a time sheet and be paid on an hourly basis. I was turning into a long-term employee but received none of the fringe benefits—from medical insurance to profit-sharing to pension contributions —extended to permanent employees. David Rockefeller would introduce me to a room full of executives as "our New York City expert." But I could then walk into the street and be hit by a car, but then, as far as Chase was concerned, I was a nonperson. It was not that Chase was behind the times. Far from it! I knew no others in the business world who enjoyed my work-schedule flexibility. Chase employed only one "quasi-official" part-timer, but other comparable companies employed zero. That made my bargaining position terribly weak—there was no place else to go.

The institution bent its rules step by step—first an engraved business card that said "Economic Consultant," implying but not conferring official status. Then, executive dining room privileges. ("Why," I asked the medical director, "is there no scale in the ladies' executive washroom when I have it on good authority you've just put one in the men's room? Don't you care about the health of your women officers?" Dr. Walker quickly rectified the oversight.) Far more substantive, fringe benefits coverage and compensation for forgone profit-sharing came next, after months of difficult negotiations on what could have turned into a legal issue. Finally, after twenty years, appointment as a four-day-a-week vice president. Today, when I look back, I feel good about those "achievements." What I feel bad about is that the part-time route for women in professional careers remains a rare exception rather than an accepted mode of work. The legal barriers have been lowered—in 1974, federal legislation was passed that requires companies to offer certain financial benefits to employees who work the equivalent of a twenty-one-hour week. Still, business considers part-time employment to be temporary work, sporadic, a sign of lack of commitment to a company. And most women join in attaching that stigma.

The victories of the women's movement have been bought at a price. Today, few women would approach their careers in the unplanned way that I did and then stubbornly stick to their "right" to work part-time. ("What do you *do* on Fridays now that the children are grown?" was a constantly repeated question. The idea of valuing "free time" is out of keeping for a professional career woman.) No, most women reject this route as an unrealistic option. To work part-time or to take a summer off or to leave the paid labor force for several years is considered disastrous to one's career and a betrayal of the gains women fought for. The women's movement sparked the desire to seek fulfillment outside the confines of home, to put education to use in the world of paid work. The legal and institutional setting loosened the constraints against women's full participation—graduate schools welcome women, executive-training programs recruit women candidates, affirmative-action legislation encourages women to seek a place in careers once reserved for men. And the economic environment of the 1970s and early 1980s buttressed their decision to enter and stay in the work force. For the wife whose husband—whether a laid-off automobile assembler or manager of a shut-down steel plant—lost his job because of the national recession, work became not only a choice but an economic necessity. For men and women, married or simply living together, two incomes became essential, in the world of low economic growth and high inflation, to maintain the high-consumption life-style to which young professionals had become accustomed.

As more flesh and blood examples of women's success appear on the scene, young women see their aspirations confirmed—if they just stay with it, they can make it to the top too. The decade-old Women's Forum, one of the early organizations for women achievers (Betty Furness, Bess Myerson, and Muriel Siebert are among its founders), sprouts affiliates in seven cities across the nation and sets its eyes next on London. The Committee of 200, formed in early 1983, brings together successful businesswomen who either own a business with a volume of at least $5 million a year or who run a corporation or division with more than $20 million in sales. Its stars are women like Patricia Cloherty, president of an investment banking firm in New York; Jane Tobin, president of a venture capital company in Washington; and Diane Johnson, executive of a field-pipe distribution company in Houston. *Fortune* magazine features "Women: The New Stars in Banking," a photo study of ten women in banks throughout the nation—well-groomed, good-looking senior officers in their thirties and forties. The days are long gone when women were barred from handling clients like U.S. Steel or forbidden to go on assignment in Mexico City or Cairo. *Fortune* follows the careers of Harvard's female MBAs in the class of 1973.

Ten years after graduating from business school, five out of thirty-three women are earning more than $100,000 a year (only one woman was working part-time). In politics, Diane Feinstein, mayor of San Francisco, Katherine Whitmire, mayor of Houston, and Geraldine Ferraro, representative to Congress from New York, provide images of women of an age, appearance, and professional bearing to whom young women relate and say, "Why not me?" The media flash the new-woman ideal across the television screen, along with the Diane Sawyers and Jane Pauleys of the television news world. The woman who makes it today is neither the dried-out, middle-aged spinster of the 1930s nor the destructive, hard-driving, Joan Crawford–like executive of the 1950s. She is the 1970s and 1980s counterpart of suburban housewife Doris Day, successful in her career, yet personally likable, the role model for young, ambitious women.

But for all the successes, even the most ardent I-did-it-all-on-my-own career woman recognizes that outstanding issues from the trivial to the substantive confront women in the world of work. Many women enter the corporate race on the same footing as men, but few move ahead as far or as fast as men. Those Harvard women MBAs *are* making good money, but after ten years their salaries are lagging behind men's by a large margin: Two men earn more than $100,000 a year for every woman who makes the grade, and far fewer women than men corporate successes are married and have children. Women form their own networking organizations, in part because they are not welcomed on an equal footing in many of the old-line private organizations that serve as the formal and informal meeting grounds of decision-makers. And perhaps most unsettling of all, women face wrenching conflicts in their lives as they attempt to maintain healthy personal relationships and still meet the demanding requirements of the work place. When one member of a working couple transfers to another location, someone has to sacrifice, and it is usually the woman. When two executives find themselves involved in a love relationship, one of them leaves the company and, again, it is usually the woman. "Managers and Lovers," a fall 1983 article in the *Harvard Business Review*, poses the question: "What should a CEO do when two of his executives develop a love relationship?" The answer: "A love affair threatens an organization's stability. Whoever is less valuable to the company should be asked to leave." By today's standards, this will usually be the woman.

These small life dramas may look to be merely fodder for television soap operas, but they are symptomatic of larger conflicts surrounding the role of family in a world where women and men both work. Does a woman choose to have children, and if so, how does she rear them? This was a nonissue in an earlier time, when "nature" and society's cultural values dictated the answers. Today, these choices are made consciously by women, and they seem to polarize at two extremes. Young, poor teenagers (mostly blacks) choose to bear children, stay at home, unmarried, supported by public assistance, unprepared for and often unwilling to enter the world of paid work. College-educated, middle-class women, with the bait of economic opportunities held out before them, plan their lives with career advancement as their primary goal. They defer marriage and postpone or reject child-bearing and pursue their career with determination and pride in their accomplishments. Then one morning they wake up and discover that they are nearing the end of their child-bearing years. Nine months later they give birth to a "rice-paddy" baby—the 1980s version of the Chinese mother squatting in the rice field, delivering her baby, and then, without pause, resuming her work in the fields. Today's career woman pauses—for a total of six weeks. Then it's back to the office, 8:00 A.M. to 7:00 P.M. —you can't stay away from the desk for too long, or when you return someone may be sitting in your seat, in possession of your key to the executive washroom. The idea of taking time off for an extended period or returning to work on a limited schedule is a choice that women have spurned, in large part, out of fear that they will fall behind in the career competition. And it is a choice that the system reinforces. Personnel people say, "Our firm sinks a large investment into the training of young managers and executives. We can't afford the disruption to the organization and the resulting loss from encouraging flexibility in career paths." So the career woman working outside the establishment continues to be a rarity—an oddball who negotiates a special arrangement with her boss in much the same way I did twenty-five years ago.

But is there really only one legitimate route for working women to follow? I sense that more and more women who are traveling on the path of work are not prepared to retreat, but they are looking for choices in the directions they can take. Women are beginning to express openly dissatisfaction about being forced to make an all-or-nothing choice between full-time continuous work that leaves little room for family life and staying at home with no paid work at all, the latter branded as failure in our value system today. Linda Sexton, Radcliffe '75 (daughter of poet Anne Sexton, and an author in her own right), brings the perspective of a younger generation. Interviewing women in their late twenties and early thirties a few years ago, she concluded that women are "overwhelmingly confused." "Led to believe that they would be happy and fulfilled if they work, women are finally beginning to wake up to an intrinsic truth, a truth men have taken for granted and accepted for generations: work is *work*—not play. Work is not always fulfillment: it is 90 percent drudgery and 10 percent illumination—like motherhood." (I'm not sure her ratio is accurate, but her conclusion is valid.) Linda Sexton challenged women to recognize reality and "dare" to make choices rather than to feel pressured to excel at it all—as wife and as mother and in her career. I first began to sense this questioning among women a few years ago. The new breed of women, earning their vice presidential stars at Chase in five years, thought of my work arrangement as a curiosity, a relic of a bygone era. For them, less than full commitment to the world of work was a cop-out, a psychological wish to fail. Then more and more young women started to drop by to talk, confused about their surfacing desires to raise a family. They'd reached their early thirties, advanced in the company, and didn't see how within the framework of their career they could have the child (rarely, children) that they and their mate now wanted.

Women students taking a course on women in the economy at New York University's Graduate School of Business Administration display the same confusion. Sooner or later, the question arises: "How can we combine career and family?" My answer is framed a little differently from Linda Sexton's, but the point is much the same: "Twenty years ago, there'd be two or three women in a business (or law) school class of hundreds of men. The women who entered those classes were extraordinary in their determination and those who reached the top in business or government were truly 'superwomen.' Even so, only a small minority of this rare kind of woman managed to raise children, keep a marriage intact, and live the life of a high-powered executive with fifteen-hour workdays, out-of-town travel, and paperwork carried home. Today, there is nearly one woman for every man in your class. You are going to resemble any normal distribution curve. Some of you will turn into blatant failures. A few will become top-ranking executives, and fewer still will combine it all—one husband, two houses, three children, a beautiful woman entertaining twenty for dinner at home, and, of course, a lover on the side. No, most of you are going to be slightly above average. Like your male peers, you'll end up as middle managers. When you look at your prospects in this light, are the economic trade-offs really so great if you choose to place more emphasis on family and less on the demands of your career?" The profile is sobering.

A tiny proportion, a minuscule percentage of working women, can take time away from the full-paid work force and still reach the pinnacles of success. Supreme Court Justice Sandra Day O'Connor stopped working full-time for five years when her children were young. She feels that "women can reenter the professions and make up for lost ground." Perhaps some can. But shorter work weeks or breaks in service will mean less income for most women. The male-female earnings gap will take longer to narrow if women do not follow career paths that exactly parallel those of men. The financial sacrifices are real, but they will not be as large as most people assume. Full-time work carries costs that go with added income. For example, child-care expenses (even considering tax deductions) come directly out of a woman's earnings. And there are additional costs to the general tax-payer as child-care income tax deductions grow in volume and requirements for subsidized child-care arrangements expand. (Most working mothers earn salaries too small to cover the full costs.) Flexible work patterns—whether part-time schedules or longer vacations to coincide with the school year or extended leaves—are said to hamper the efficiency of an organization and add to costs. But I have a feeling that the income penalty attached to such arrange-' ments far outweighs the incremental costs. The penalty is in good part a legacy of bureaucratic traditions combined with the weak bargaining position of women. (I never—well, hardly ever—left my desk for lunch on a six-hour-a-day, three-day-a-week schedule; on an eight-hour-a-day, four-day-a-week schedule, I began to resemble the full-time species and joined in two-hour lunches with only a twinge of conscience.)

The bargaining position of women *will* improve with the demographic slowdown in labor force growth during the remainder of the 1980s. Today's women in their late twenties and thirties will form a cadre of trained, experienced labor that employers won't want to risk losing when there is no longer a massive inflow of younger entrants to take their place. But women must feel that it is worth using that new leverage to change long-standing traditions. Some people say institutional change will occur only when men themselves alter their attitudes about the balance between work and family. And they see signs that this is already happening, as Betty Friedan argues in *The Second Stage*, with men taking time off for paternity leave, attending PTA meetings, and turning down job offers that involve relocation. I don't see it happening on a grand scale if we mean splitting child-rearing responsibilities fifty-fifty down the middle. This approach makes neither biological nor economic sense. Specialization, the division of labor, as Adam Smith pointed out more than two hundred years ago, is the key to an efficient, productive society. Women are downgrading their special role if they don't recognize the reality of their biology as the bearers of children, with a nurturing instinct that appears nearly universal. But change can happen if men, who still largely control institutions, join with women in reducing artificial barriers to flexible arrangements in the work place. And this means more than giving abstract lip service to the concept; it means advocating and implementing changes in the "rules of the game." For example, flexible compensation plans allow employees to trade off one form of compensation for another. A woman with children might choose X dollars of near-term paid maternity leave against Y dollars of deferred retirement benefits. That option will also be attractive to the man or woman who sees value in a break from a straight-line career path by writing a book or attending a university or working in a government agency. The educational world extends these breaks— sabbaticals—as a matter of course and assumes they yield a return to the institution as well as to the individual. The business sector is just starting to take tentative steps in this direction.

Many women *must* work full-time for economic reasons, and many women *want* full-time careers for personal reasons. There is no reason why society should force them to seek anything less than fulfillment of their economic potential on the same terms as men. However, many women see a need for a better balance between their work for pay and

their family life. The economic penalty for making that
choice is heavily weighted by traditions that say it can't or
it shouldn't be done. It's about time men and women altered
the trade-offs.